A NEW AGE OF REASON

A NEW AGE OF REASON

HARNESSING THE POWER OF TECH FOR GOOD

LARRY WEBER

FOREWORD BY DAVID KIRKPATRICK

WILEY

For general information on our other products and services or for technical support, please contact our Customer Care Department within the United States at (800) 762-2974, outside the United States at (317) 572-3993 or fax (317) 572-4002.

Wiley also publishes its books in a variety of electronic formats. Some content that appears in print may not be available in electronic formats. For more information about Wiley products, visit our website at www.wiley.com.

Library of Congress Cataloging-in-Publication Data:

Names: Weber, Larry, author. | John Wiley & Sons, publisher.
Title: A new age of reason : harnessing the power of tech for good / Larry Weber.
Description: Hoboken, New Jersey : Wiley, [2024] | Includes index.
Identifiers: LCCN 2024014710 (print) | LCCN 2024014711 (ebook) | ISBN 9781394216604 (hardback) | ISBN 9781394216628 (adobe pdf) | ISBN 9781394216611 (epub)
Subjects: LCSH: Technological innovations—Social aspects. | Technology—Social aspects.
Classification: LCC T173.8 .W445 2024 (print) | LCC T173.8 (ebook) | DDC 303.48/3—dc23/eng/20240501
LC record available at https://lccn.loc.gov/2024014710
LC ebook record available at https://lccn.loc.gov/2024014711

Cover Design: Wiley
Cover Images: © MarySan/Adobe Stock, © Bubball/Getty Images
Author Photo: © Racepoint Global
SKY10077587_061824

Contents

Foreword

We live in a sea of technology – it surrounds us and affects every aspect of our lives, mostly in ways we could not live without. But it's too easy to take this blessing of capabilities for granted. Most of us have become so habituated to technology's marvels that we barely even notice them. It's easier to get annoyed when our smartphone battery runs out or a wire doesn't work, for example, than to feel grateful for the truly astonishing feats the device enables for us the rest of the time. None of us will leave home without it. But the smartphone is just one of innumerable amazing technologies that grace our lives.

Larry Weber wants us to stop and marvel. But more than that, he sees the gifts of tech as an inspiration. He believes in the almost infinite potential of innovation to improve our companies, our lives, and our societies.

Even as we collectively face the myriad crises of global warming, threats to democracy, ongoing wars, and fears about the potential downside of artificial intelligence, Weber sees amazing new pathways to progress.

Yet, we also all live, today, in a sea of pessimism and fatalism. Everywhere, even well-informed people increasingly feel paralyzed, even hopeless. Considerable numbers of young people are so demoralized they are starting to say they don't even want to bring a child into a world they see as blighted and degrading.

In this book, Weber makes the case that they are simply not seeing what's happening. He is a relentless, committed optimist – or, as he calls himself, a "techno-optimist." Combatting society's endemic fatalism is a big part of Weber's mission. As he enthuses near the end of this bracing book, "We are on the cusp of a new era where technology has finally evolved to deliver amazing benefits to the world."

For Weber, this is no idle claim. He has come to that confidence, as he recounts, through decades of close observation of what actually happens in the tech industry. He's served tech companies for many years as a senior counselor and advisor on communications and strategy. The book sparkles with recollections of time spent with visionaries like Steve Jobs and Tim Berners-Lee, who created the world wide web and the first internet browser. Weber recounts many stories about the vast progress that technological innovation has enabled and can enable in the future.

But alongside his optimism about technology, Weber also is enormously optimistic about the power of business. He's written this book to inspire businesspeople to think differently about their work as business leaders, so that they can leverage the potential of technology to help construct a better world. It's a handbook for how to create value in a world infused with deeply-promising technologies. Weber believes embracing tech can help companies remake themselves for the world's benefit.

This is urgent, because companies and business generally face urgent pressure to demonstrate the social value of their organizations. For alongside that fatalism about the future, many in modern society also hold a deep cynicism about the role of business, or even its culpability in bringing us to what they see as the world's sorry state. People will no longer tolerate inaction in any realm; they are so upset and worried.

Weber gives business leaders a call to arms, not to fight back but to inspire – to methodically find ways to turn companies into engines for social good. It is the mission of our age. But it's not easy. Tech is complicated. Luckily, Weber is good at explaining it.

For over a decade I ran a conference and media company called Techonomy. It was dedicated, among other things, to the notion that every company is a technology company. When we began in 2010, that idea was seen by most business leaders as radical, even nonsensical. Today, it is practically a given. Larry helped me understand that from the beginning. He was a big part of the Techonomy community, which I always deeply appreciated. He knew even then that every company was a tech company. And he believed that every business leader has a critical responsibility to engage with and embrace technology, regardless of their industry.

With this book, he has finally set out to explain just what that responsibility means. He is an advocate of what he calls "the moral corporation." It's all about contributing to a better world. Companies that do so will thrive, he argues. His message is meant for business leaders who are rethinking the direction and ethos of their companies – a process he believes is indispensable and urgent. Business leaders are in a spectacularly good position, he argues, if they take stock of the transformations and possibilities all around them.

Much of the book is devoted to carefully explaining and assessing a range of important technologies that are poised to deliver spectacular value to the world. Artificial intelligence tops the list, unsurprisingly. But Weber also explains the importance of cloud computing, quantum systems, emerging energy technologies, and the potential of biotech. But even more importantly, he explains, they can all increasingly work in concert. The combination of all these now-highly-evolved capabilities bequeaths the world far more potential than could any one alone. Now, he writes, we have "tools to solve problems that seem unsolvable. They can impact our world in ways never before possible, evolving us into this new era: *A New Age of Reason.*"

More than once Weber recounts a famous line spoken by one of his mentors and heroes, MIT's Michael Dertouzos: "Technology should be our slave." Weber wants leaders to learn to willfully and consciously take advantage of technology's power. In his many decades advising tech leaders, he has seen the perils of techno-determinism – the passive deployment of powerful technologies without clear ethical oversight. Several times he mentions the cautionary example of Facebook, a company I wrote an entire book about and now deeply criticize. It moved fast and broke things, to paraphrase its longtime mantra, and the world paid the price. But such heedlessness is neither inevitable nor necessary, he argues.

It all comes down to rethinking business leadership in a time of technological possibility. After charting the six waves of technology that got us here, beginning with mainframe computing, Weber now sees a kind of apotheosis. This new era is one in which tech can be put to service for humanity: "Technology has finally evolved and reached a tipping point in which it can address world problems." With the perspective of someone who has lived this evolution over many decades, his conclusion is deeply gratifying, and empowering.

It won't be easy for businesses to rise to this challenge. It means planning differently, communicating differently, and organizing the corporation differently. Weber advocates, for example, that every company create new positions like a "chief ethics officer" and even a "chief humanitarian officer." Take that, cynics about the role of business!

My own career has been spent writing about big companies, the evolution of technology, and its potential to improve society. Thank you Larry Weber for so clearly and passionately arguing for this essential new shift in business consciousness. I suspect his passion and knowledge will be as inspiring for you as it is for me.

—David Kirkpatrick

Introduction

For the past nearly five decades, I've had the privilege of having a front-row seat to the many waves of technology that have swept across our world, changing everything in their wake from how businesses operate to how we work and live. My focus during these waves was helping companies create new categories for their breakthroughs and market them to the world. However, I've always held a fascination with how technology can solve so many problems across business and our personal lives.

Today, I'm excited to see this next wave of technology break, as it holds the promise to impact an entirely new level of our world: *humanity*. Innovations coming from the digital world, the biotech arena, and the clean energy space hold the promise to address some of our most pressing problems, from feeding an ever-growing population with less land to battling against climate change to delivering better outcomes in healthcare. In many cases, it's the integration of multiple technologies that are fueling these breakthroughs.

This pivotal moment we're in now echoes back to the original Age of Reason, a time when the world shifted to focus on science, technology, reason, and the spark of imagination to find new solutions to the problems of that era. We stand at a similar place today, as technologies have finally evolved to give us tremendous opportunities to better our world. We need to apply those very same concepts to deliver on the promise of this era. Naturally, we also need guardrails for new innovations like generative AI, as we've all seen the damage technology can do when it is weaponized against us.

Along with the immense opportunity this wave of technology presents comes responsibility. Companies must find ways to leverage these evolved technologies to deliver outcomes that positively impact our society. This requires new thinking from the C suite, as the executive team's role will broaden to take on new responsibilities and new levels of problem solving, as well as embracing the ethics and morality required to succeed in this new era.

As companies infuse solving world problems into their business strategies, marketing holds the promise of delivering an entirely new level of transparency by enabling customers to experience the good a company is doing for humanity, ultimately building new levels of engagement and trust. As such, marketing can become a powerful, self-fueled force capable of building an irrefutable reputation that will attract all constituents, from customers to investors to talent.

In this book, you'll hear inspiring stories of organizations doing just that. You'll also hear from experts across many fields who offer insights into the promise today's technologies hold to solve so many problems that seem unsolvable. I hope when you read it, your takeaway will be to find your place on the path of "tech for good," a powerful catalyst that will transform your brand as you contribute to the greater good of humanity.

PART 1

Technology, Humanity, and a New Age of Reason

CHAPTER 1

A New Wave of Technology to Better Humanity

One of the best parts of my career is that I've had the privilege to sit with CEOs of major companies and ask them this: *What do you want your legacy to be?* Most often, I get the expected answers around establishing their company as the biggest, the best, or the first. But, every once in a while, I talk to a CEO who really gets it, who sees the bigger picture and has aspirations around the good their company can contribute to our world.

This was the case with Deere & Company. When I asked this of Sam Allen (former Deere chairman and CEO), his answer summed up the essence of what this book is all about . . . and how I believe every CEO should think. Most people might logically guess his answer would be to dominate the agriculture and construction business by selling more of those green and yellow machines. But his answer showed how Deere thinks and operates on an entirely different level; the company focuses on the impact it can have on humanity. Allen's answer was to help farmers maximize their land to produce more crops so they can feed the world's burgeoning population . . . and to do all of this in a sustainable way. As lofty as it sounds, that's precisely what Deere is doing.

The "how" is accomplished with innovations that are part of an amazing new wave of technology – one that is ushering our world into an entirely new era. The past several decades have been defined by many technology waves, which have impacted business operations and productivity – personal computing, connectivity, access to information via the web, connecting with each other via social media, and the internet of just about everything.

The wave we are in now stands apart from those before it, because technology has finally evolved to impact a much higher purpose: *humanity*.

Current breakthroughs in AI and robotics, along with leapfrog advances in areas like quantum computing, biological systems, data analytics, sensors, chips, the web, and cleantech (renewables, carbon capture, etc.), have been evolving over decades to reach this point in time. These technologies have built the foundation for a plethora of new innovations that address some of today's most pressing problems, from feeding the world to climate change.

- Computer chips that can fight global warming
- Smart beehives that protect bees to ultimately help our food supply
- Blockchain systems that enable electricity sharing
- Computer vision tech that enables farmers to maximize crops to feed our burgeoning population
- AI/robotics that identify and fight wildfires
- Robotic-assisted surgery that expands the capabilities of a doctor's eyes and hands
- Wearable technology for cows so they emit less methane
- Carbon capture tech that has removed more than a million metric tons of carbon
- Affordable medical diagnostic technology that can be used without electricity or an internet connection to help under-served communities
- CRISPR gene editing technologies capable of addressing everything from blood disorders to cardiovascular disease

These are just a few of the advanced innovations available now or just on the horizon. The proliferation of these types of inventions gives us the tools to solve problems that seem unsolvable. They can impact our world in ways never before possible, evolving us into this new era: *A New Age of Reason.*

Science, Reason, and a Passion to Impact Our World

This moment in time echoes back to the original Age of Reason that took place in the seventeenth and eighteenth centuries. This major turning point in history was a time of new thinking, tremendous innovation, and inspired imagination applied to problem solving, as society embraced science and reason to improve humanity. Enlightened thinkers propelled the populariza-tion of science, which revolutionized many aspects of the world, including communications, transportation, medicine, and the textile industry, along with a better understanding of the mechanics of the human body and the natural world. Among the many discoveries of this era are the law of gravity, the telescope, the steam engine, the cotton gin, and the vaccine, along with a breakthrough understanding of blood circulation – all of which had a

profoundly positive impact on society then and are the foundation of many aspects of life today.

Like most innovators, the greats of this era – among them Sir Isaac Newton, William Harvey, Eli Whitney, Edward Jenner – started by asking questions, saw the potential of how science could answer them, applied both reason and the magic of their imagination to "see" what could be, and then set out to create new inventions or theories that changed the world.

This new era presents us with a tremendous opportunity – and responsibility – to follow their lead, applying the combination of today's innovations, reasoning, and the spark of imagination to address today's most critical problems. This is the pressing call for every CEO. Today's business leaders need to think not just about their company's impact on shareholders, but more importantly how their organization can better our world.

Key elements have converged to usher us into this pivotal moment. We are grappling with critical global issues such as the raging battle to save our planet from climate change and the challenge to feed the world. Emerging alongside these problems is this wave of evolved technologies that are enabling our brightest minds to create new, innovative solutions that enhance the well-being of our planet and our population. The last component is a growing financial community focused squarely on investing in these types of breakthroughs to make sure they are brought to market and scaled for impact.

As these components converge, it is creating opportunities for companies like Deere and others you'll read about in this book to heed this clarion call and make a difference in the world. The notion of tech that serves us well, or tech for good, will not only do good for the world, but also create an entirely new value creation for corporations. When companies use technology in profoundly positive ways to benefit our world, their marketing will become a powerful, self-fueled force capable of building an irrefutable reputation that will attract all constituents, from customers to investors to talent.

Looking Ahead

In the next three chapters, we'll explore this wave of technology's impact on three key world issues: the fight to feed our ever-growing planet with less land, the battle against climate change, and the need to evolve healthcare for improved patient outcomes and better working conditions for medical providers. After that, we'll take an essential look at the critical moral responsibility we have to ensure our innovations are used for good and not weaponized against us.

CHAPTER 2

Agtech and Deere: Tech for Good at Its Best

You may be wondering why my lead example on a new wave of technology would focus on one of the oldest occupations on the planet, farming. And you may ask why this is even relevant when farmers represent only 2% of the US population. Well, that 2% shoulders the tremendous responsibility of feeding the other 98% of us. And that 98% is expected to grow from 8 billion to 10 billion people by 2050.[1]

The world's staggering population growth is only part of the issue. The land itself is another critical problem, as US farmland has been declining over the past several decades, in part due to the land being converted into developments to meet the housing demand. According to the US Department of Agriculture, acres of land in farms have continued the downward trend with 879 million acres in 2023, down from 900 million acres in 2017.[2] What's more, farmland is expected to continue to decline, while our population continues to grow.

But farmers face more than just those problems. There are also labor shortages, caused by a number of factors, from less interest in agriculture among younger generations to wages to immigration policies that limit the work pool. Climate change is another major factor, as warming temperatures, floods, and droughts have a direct impact on yield. Farmers face all of these issues and more, making the business of farming . . . and feeding all of us . . . extremely challenging and unpredictable.

In his 2023 CES keynote, Deere Chairman and CEO John May articulately summed up both the challenge *and* solution to today's farming. "In the past farmers would grow more by using more. Bigger machines, more horsepower, more seeds, and more nutrients. This approach alone doesn't work today. There's less arable land, less rural labor, less time to do their jobs due to weather volatility, and rising input costs. Technology is the solution to these challenges. Technology allows farmers to create more with fewer resources."[3]

This exemplifies how today's innovations are providing solutions to the increasing challenges of farming and of feeding the world. And, what might surprise you is that although farming is one of the world's oldest industries, farmers are actually among *the earliest adopters* of today's innovations. The next time you fill your plate consider this: It takes everything from AI, robotics, and computer vision to advanced sensing, cloud computing, data analytics, and more to put that food on your table.

Deere Leading the Agtech Revolution

As mentioned in Chapter 1, Deere has been at the forefront of the agtech revolution and has transformed itself into a technology-powered organization bringing game-changing offerings to farmers. Through this mission, Deere is empowering farmers to do more with less so they can put food on an exponentially growing number of plates across the world, both today and for future generations (see Figure 2.1).

As a company nearly 200 years old, Deere has always had innovation in its DNA, from inventing the first steel plow in 1837, and replacing horses with engines by introducing the first two tractors in 1918, to inventing the first all-hydraulic bulldozer in 1958.[5]

Figure 2.1 An example of Deere's use of advanced innovations that help farmers do more with less is its See & Spray™ technology. The technology enables farmers to only spray herbicides on the weeds, which reduces the amount needed by up to 66%. The technology can "recognize the difference between plants even in conditions that would challenge the human eye. See & Spray has 36 cameras . . . [that] scan more than 2,200 square feet of land and capture 1.2 billion pixels per second. If you tried to match that level of sensing and processing with human eyes, it would take nearly 6,000 people."[4]

Source: Copyright © 2024 Deere & Company

In more recent years, Deere has embraced digital innovations as they came to market, developing applications that have literally changed the face of agriculture. For example, in the late 1990s, Deere saw the tremendous opportunity GPS technology could bring to farming and began investing in this technology. The company later integrated GPS into its tractors so they could drive themselves through a field within an inch of accuracy, and then used GPS technology to collect geospatial data on both the inputs farmers used throughout the year and the crops they harvested at the end of the year. GPS technology is now used by farmers in more than 100 countries.[6]

As Deere continued on its mission to transform farming, it used connectivity and the Internet of Things to offer farmers the benefits of cloud computing, giving them access to valuable, real-time information for faster and better decision-making. And in 2022, Deere introduced the first fully autonomous self-driving tractor, which features advanced digital innovations like sensors and computer vision.

Deere is also leveraging AI and computer vision that integrates precision tech and cloud-based data with robotics, as well as computer vision and machine learning. These technologies have enabled Deere to revolutionize the planting process. Advanced sensors and robots place each seed in the ground at a scale and precision beyond human capacity, helping to optimize growth. Deere's computer vision technology enables farmers to quickly and precisely apply fertilizer so that only the weeds are hit with the pesticide, maximizing crops growing in their land. Today, Deere has more than 500,000 technology-powered connected machines running across more than a third of the earth's land surface.[7] Smarter farming for better yields.

Moreover, the company is doing all of this with sustainability front and center in its mission. Deere's Leap Ambitions effort involves working to reduce carbon emission and resource consumption, recycle machinery and materials, and develop intelligent technology to help customers be more productive and profitable. The company has set goals to reduce its greenhouse gas emissions (direct and indirect) by 50% by the year 2030.[8] Since 2017, the company has reduced operational greenhouse gas emissions by nearly 29%. Deere also surpassed its 2022 renewable electricity goal by achieving nearly 59% renewable electricity.[9] These are just a few examples of the many sustainability efforts underway at Deere.

The result of Deere using tech for good has yielded significant quantifiable impacts. For example, the company's intelligent sprayers have helped farmers reduce herbicide use by approximately two-thirds (depending on crop and field conditions). Another example is Deere's current cloud network, which is comprised of hundreds of thousands of connected machines that provide farmers with critical information at their fingertips for better decision-making.[10]

But this mission has not only been good for farmers and our world. The effort has also had a tremendous impact on Deere's bottom line, with the company's net income growing to more than $10 billion in fiscal year 2023.[11] This is proof that a relentless commitment to use technology to solve a massive problem like helping farmers feed our ever-growing population can marry purpose with profit and make a true difference in our world.

From a marketing perspective, Deere has built an irrefutable reputation and produced stories so strong they have universal appeal to all stakeholders. Deere's long and impressive awards list speaks volumes to this. In 2023 and 2024 alone, Deere was ranked #3 in brand reputation in an Axios/Harris Poll (2023), named among Time's World's Best Companies (2023), received CES Best of Innovation in Robotics (2023), named to Ethisphere Institute's Most Ethical Companies List (2024), ranked #1 in Construction & Farm Machinery by Fortune (2024), and ranked #9 in Newsweek's Excellence 1000 Index (2024).[12]

By transforming farming through today's technology, Deere has also created an entire economy around agtech, paving the way for other innovators to offer solutions. One such company is Indigo. Its Carbon by Indigo produces first-of-its-kind, registry-issued agricultural carbon credits, while supporting farmers in their transition toward more sustainable farming practices. This is one of many great examples of solutions now available that help farmers, the world's population, and the planet.

Deere Q&A

I had the pleasure of speaking with Deere Chairman and CEO John May about the company's impressive transformation from a traditional industrial company to a smart industrial company, leading the agtech revolution and doing so both sustainably and ethically. He shared valuable insights about this journey, including key organizational and behavioral changes, best practices, and lessons learned.

Q: What would you tell other CEOs about Deere's re-positioning and its use of technology to deliver on that vision?

A: We've historically been viewed as a traditional industrial company that develops products people use to make a living. I realized around 10 years ago that we could do more. We needed to transition beyond building the highest quality products to also focus on helping our customers do their jobs better, ultimately helping them become more profitable, more productive, and to do their jobs in an environmentally sustainable way.

To realize that goal, we restructured to evolve from a traditional industrial company to a smart industrial company. There were several fundamental changes we made to realize that goal. One was a shift from operating around a traditional matrix of regions and platforms to aligning our business around our customers and their production systems, meaning the kind of work they do. We focused on providing them with solutions that use automation, autonomy, and digitization to reach our goal of helping make them more profitable, more productive, and more sustainable.

Another key change was to centralize all of our technology investments and vertically integrate Deere technology. We also developed better ways to serve our customers throughout the lifecycle of owning our products and solutions. For example, we completely reorganized our parts and customer support functions and offer advanced technologies like predictive analytics to help our customers solve problems before they happen.

Q: While there's a lot of hype about AI today, Deere is leveraging that technology with tremendous impact for its customers. Tell us a little more about that.

A: Our use of artificial intelligence, machine learning, computer vision, and advanced sensors enable us to automate machines that deliver productivity and efficiency outcomes customers couldn't produce on their own. Farming, for example, is a very unpredictable business with so many variables – humidity, moisture, temperature, wind speed, the type of seed you plant, and how crops grow, just to name a few. Effectively navigating through all of those variables is nearly impossible without technology.

We saw a huge opportunity to automate this process by using advanced sensor technology, helping farmers make better business decisions than they could make on their own, and then automating farming machines to maximize outcomes. A great example of this is See & Spray™, a technology that "sees" the difference between a weed and a healthy plant, and only sprays the weed with herbicides. This technology can significantly reduce herbicide use, which has a tremendous financial benefit to the customer and reduces environmental impact.

I remember talking to government officials a few years ago who were asking how we could help farmers in their stewardship of the environment since agriculture can have such an impact, given the use of herbicides, pesticides, nitrogen, etc. I knew the best way to do that was to develop solutions that both improve their bottom line *and* have a positive impact on the environment. That's the wonderful thing about agriculture: we can do both at the same time.

Q: Is there any wisdom you can share on how a company of Deere's size and scope stays on top of new technologies that deliver both sustainability and better outcomes for your customers?

A: The most important change we made was to fully centralize our tech stack. That involved taking that function away from the individual product lines because those teams don't have the time or resources to continually search for new technologies, experiment with them, and then leverage our R&D budget to scale them quickly across the enterprise.

A great example of the effectiveness and efficiency of this approach is the computer vision we use to autonomously drive a tractor and tillage tool, which uses the same computer and camera we put on the back of a wheel loader, so the driver doesn't accidently run into anything. Centralizing the tech function enables us to more readily identify and leverage this type of efficiency and to fully focus on leveraging technology innovations to deliver some of the best solutions in the industry.

Q: How does Deere's positioning around technology, sustainability, and customer focus impact employee morale?

A: One of the things we realized when we bought the AI company Blue River is the tremendous purpose we have in agriculture and construction. Our mantra is, "We run so life can leap forward." That means empowering our customers to have economically and environmentally sustainable businesses so that they can provide the food, fuel, clothing, shelter, and infrastructure the world needs.

How we solve that is extremely complicated and extremely difficult. For example, developing a fully autonomous tractor that's capable of tilling 24 hours a day, seven days a week, and performing the job better than the customer could by themselves is really challenging, and it excites our employees. Giving them our customers' most difficult problems to solve, and not overly constraining them, truly energizes our employees.

Q: What role do customers play in your innovation or your exploration of new technologies and applications?

A: Our customers are central to everything we do. To that end, we've changed the way we develop products to ensure our solutions fully meet our customers' needs. If you're a traditional industrial company, you don't put anything out globally unless it is 100% hardened, because the risk is high, and failure is really expensive. As a smart industrial company, we've turned that thinking on its head.

Today, the way we develop products is to embed our production systems teams with our customers. We are literally on their farms, working with customers day in and day out to fully understand their biggest problems. Once we develop technology to help solve those issues, we put it in the customer's hands. When it's in the early phases of development, we have customers test it and give us feedback. We use pilot programs in which our customers pay for the technology. This process is done at a small scale, and we find that if a customer pays for the technology, they're invested in it and give us highly valuable feedback that is very specific. Through this process, our customers help us refine products to meet their needs and solve their problems.

That process is a massive shift from how most traditional industrial companies operate. It requires a mindset shift as well. We accept that solutions may not be perfect out of the gate and might require further improvement. But we also know that by working directly with customers to test and refine our products, we develop solutions that offer breakthroughs in how our customers do their jobs.

Q: What efforts are you taking to lower your carbon footprint?

A: A couple of years back, we established what we call our Leap Ambitions. These include not only our business objectives, but also our environmental goals. As we've told shareholders, the government, and other constituents, we are committed to reducing the greenhouse gas impact of our operations and products – Scope 1, 2, and 3. For example, we are actively working a number of programs to address Scope 3, category 11, which is the emissions generated by our products. But what's interesting is that, for agriculture, that represents only a small percentage of the negative environmental impact. Addressing the rest involves changing the way farmers prepare and manage their land.

To help address that, we've committed that by 2030, we're going to help our customers improve their nitrogen use efficiency by 20%. How? By developing tools like ExactShot™, which uses computer vision and robotics to place starter fertilizer precisely onto seeds as they're planted, rather than applying a continuous flow of fertilizer to the entire row of seeds. This can help farmers significantly reduce the use of nitrogen during planting. It's amazing. As our engineers explain, that literally means millions and millions of gallons of nitrogen saved, significantly reducing environmental impact while helping improve our customers' bottom line.

There are so many examples like that one. For instance, we're also working with several large petroleum companies on the development of renewable diesel. We're demonstrating the effectiveness of growing oilseeds as a cover crop that can then be processed directly by refineries to create 100% renewable diesel fuel. This renewable fuel can be used by our customers without requiring any changes to their equipment, creating a circular economy, and reducing their overall environmental footprint.

Q: Do you have any advice around how to use technology ethically?

A: One of the things we're really committed to is maintaining the environment of trust and security that we've established with our customers. For example, we've created a cloud-based ecosystem that contains agronomic data for millions of acres. We've been very consistent from day one with our customers that they control the data they share with us, and we will not sell it to anyone, period.

This can include information like what seed a farmer used, what the soil fertility was, and when they put down nitrogen or herbicide. These different data points can explain why a farmer grew 300 bushels of corn on one field versus the field right next to it that only produced 260 bushels. We process and store that data for our customers, but we don't sell it. Our platform allows customers to direct the sharing of data, if they choose to, as part of running their operation. For example, they may choose to share it with someone who does insect treatments on their field to benefit their business.

We use data to serve our customers, either to support the products they already use or to develop new products that will benefit them in the future. For example, when a customer has multiple combines operating at the same time, the data from those machines can show how the variables are changing in two fields right next to each other. The combines can use that data to adjust settings for higher grain quality and less grain loss. But when that happens, we're not sharing anything specific about the data, we're just using it to maximize the outcome of the machine. And we are clear with our customers on how the data is used.

As we said in one of our recent advertisements, it took us 186 years to build trust with our customers and we're not going to destroy that over one technology or one piece of data. Trust and security are very important to us.

Q: Any mistakes made along the way that others could learn from?

A: I'll tell you about one of the mistakes we made early on that we've learned from. Back in 2012, we started putting a telematics device on every large piece of ag equipment. We knew it was going to be important to communicate with the vehicle, for customers to have access to data that's on-board that machine in an off-board location. But at that point in time, our customers didn't see the value in that capability, and we charged them for that sensor. Very few customers renewed the service and, to be honest, some were angry with us.

What we should have done was to embed that sensor in the machine and then work quickly to create value that was obvious to the customer. One great example is that today, every tractor we produce includes components that make them autonomous-ready. This means we install wire harnesses, sensors, and redundant braking systems that have no value for the customer today, and we don't charge them for those. Eventually, they will deliver value as we release new products. So, my advice would be if you can't create clear value for the customer, don't charge them for it. It means nothing just because it's new technology. It's all about technology that brings value to the customer.

Q: What does John Deere look like in 10, 15 years, and what does your legacy look like?

A: I'll use one of the former CEOs, Bob Lane, as an example here. The three living CEOs were together in a room, and Bob said, "Every CEO gets dealt a hand of cards. Some hands are better than others, and it's all about how you play that hand." Two weeks later, the COVID pandemic hit. Bob called me and said, "I'm sorry you just got a really bad hand. I wish you luck." The reality is, there have been multiple periods when our company has gone through a massive disruption and every time, we somehow figured out how to lead through it.

I'm leading the company through this technology disruption, transitioning from a traditional industrial to smart industrial company, and my goal is to do that as successfully as possible. The only way I'll be able to say it was successful is if it was good for our customers – if they are more profitable, more productive, and operating more sustainably.

This also creates an opportunity that is extremely valuable for our employees. They benefit from the opportunity to develop leap-forward solutions and from working with innovative technologies like AI. We never could have offered the opportunity for them to make this significant a difference in the past.

Finally, we offer our shareholders the chance to get a better return from Deere than they can get from many other companies. Delivering on these objectives is how I define success.

Tech for Good Takeaways

The Deere story is a shining example of tech for good. Here are some key threads that offer a great framework for other companies to follow:

◆ Deere brings to life the essence of this book, which is how today's innovations give us the power to address massive world issues. As a smart industrial company, Deere focuses on delivering technology-powered solutions that improve how its customers do their jobs, delivering on the marriage of profitability, productivity, and sustainability. The outcome of this has had a positive impact on Deere's bottom line, brand reputation, and engagement across all constituents, from employees to investors.

◆ Deere's culture is anchored in problem solving. The company embraces its customers' biggest and most complex challenges and answers them with innovations that literally change how farming is done. This approach not only delivers breakthroughs that answer customers' most important needs, but also establishes a culture that engages and motivates employees, and attracts new talent. The bigger the challenge, the more the organization is inspired to solve it.

◆ Deere's laser focus on sustainability demonstrates how companies can deliver both breakthrough solutions that solve real problems *and* do so in a manner that is good for the planet. Battery-electric backhoes, an intelligent sprayer that significantly reduces herbicide use, and reducing greenhouse gases (GHGs) by shifting to 50%+ renewable energy are some examples of the company's push toward sustainable farming.[13] Delivering solutions that both positively impact a farmer's bottom line and deliver sustainability is a win, win . . . an approach our world needs more of.

◆ Deere also illustrates the power of being a true customer-centered company, particularly in terms of product development. By forming close working partnerships with its customers, Deere is able to more fully understand their needs and develop real solutions that address real challenges. Central to this is Deere's process of embedding production teams with customers, enabling farmers to pilot test new offerings and provide critical feedback, from which Deere refines its solutions. As May pointed out, the company understands that early versions of a product may not be perfect and require improvements, but that feedback is precisely what enables Deere to deliver highly effective new innovative solutions.

◆ Deere has established a powerful ecosystem with its customers based on trust and security. One of the many ways it delivers on this is through its approach to customer data, a lesson many companies today could learn from. While Deere stores vast amounts of data (500,000 machines connected and millions of messages processed daily), that data is owned and controlled by the farmers themselves and never used by Deere without their permission.

CHAPTER 3

Technology and the Planet

In this chapter, we'll look at how technology can address one of the most pressing and complex problems of our time: climate change. The year 2023 had the dubious distinction of record-shattering temperatures and was recorded as the world's hottest year by a huge margin, a fact that unnerved scientists around the globe. This issue, as described by the United Nations, is "the single biggest health threat facing humanity."[1]

Global warming impacts our entire eco-system, from rising sea levels and severe droughts to catastrophic storms, wildfires, health issues, food/water insecurities, and loss of species. Averting climate catastrophe mandates we achieve the global mission of cutting greenhouse gas emissions by nearly half by 2030 and ensuring temperatures are kept to 1.5 degrees Celsius above pre-industrial levels. Although scores of efforts are underway to fight this issue, there remains a dire need for the pace to step up. As UN Secretary-General Antonio Guterres declared, "Everything, everywhere, all at once," imploring the urgency with which we must act to meet these goals.[2]

According to the most recent Intergovernmental Panel on Climate Change (IPCC) report, there are four key efforts we must move on as they have the lowest cost and highest potential to tackle climate change this decade. The recommended approach involves the following: moving away from fossil fuels and deploying as much renewable energies like wind and solar as possible, cutting methane emissions from major sources like fossil fuel production and food waste, protecting natural carbon trapping ecosystems like tropical rainforests, and conserving energy and using it more efficiently across everything we do – vehicles, homes, industry.[3]

A Wave of Climate Change Solutions

This path forward will be fueled by a cocktail of innovations available in this current wave of technology, as no one silver bullet can address this complex problem. In short, there is no Amazon of climate change. According to UN Environment Programme Executive Director Inger Andersen, while time is running short, "We already have the technology and know how to get the job done."[3]

Experts I've spoken with, along with research conducted, all point to the fact that we have at our disposal right now the very technologies we need to help address this issue and move our world to cleaner energy. For example, the shift toward renewables like wind and solar is massive right now, and those energy sources will help with the necessary move away from fossil fuels. The International Energy Agency reports that we are planning to build as much wind and solar capacity between 2022 and 2027 as we did in the past two decades.[3] The electrification of our transportation and power grids, along with advancements in lithium-ion batteries, are underway and will aid in the climate change battle.

Beyond those, there are many promising and exciting energy innovations on the horizon, including fusion as a potential new clean energy source, along with direct air capture (DAC), which is the concept that CO_2 can be sucked out of the atmosphere anywhere in the world. Hydrogen is another, which can be used as an alternative fuel to gas in, for example, a power plant's turbines.

Digital innovations have also emerged that aid in the climate change fight. Among the solutions in this realm are blockchain systems that enable electricity sharing. AI can be used in a variety of ways, such as controlling energy use and reduction during peak hours, detecting equipment failures before they occur, measuring and monitoring emissions, as well as forecasting climate change hazards. Cloud computing can drastically reduce carbon dioxide emissions by shifting workloads to locations around the globe to allow the use of renewable energy sources like solar and wind power. There are many IoT energy efficiency applications that can help create smart cities and smart citizens.

This array of innovations combines to provide the tools we need to tackle the problem from a host of angles, helping to minimize burning fossil fuels, reduce CO_2 and methane emissions, as well as maximize the efficiency of energy use.

This surge of innovations is creating an entirely new economy focused on climate change. David Kirkpatrick, journalist, author of *The Facebook Effect* and founder of Techonomy, is among those who see and champion the emergence of this new climate tech industry.

"A lot of us are adamant that there is going to be an economic boom and company creation, a fiesta we might say, around climate tech that is analogous to the internet era," said David. He added that climate tech and climate-conscious companies will become a major force in business that will be "the next giant value-creation opportunity for businesses, investors, and the general public."

That sentiment reverberates in the investment landscape. "Climate is like the internet in that it's going to disrupt every corner of the global economy," said Andrew Beebe, managing director of Obvious Ventures, which has more than $1 billion in assets under management.[4] Obvious Ventures is one of many investment firms with a focus on climate tech and/or sustainable brands. Lowercarbon Capital is another, which invests in companies that slash CO_2, suck up carbon, and offer new ways to cool the planet. There are scores of venture firms across the US and the globe specialized in this burgeoning space.

Among the many hot start-ups is a Seattle-based company called Lithos Carbon, which invented a process that uses volcanic rock dust (basalt dust) to capture carbon on farms. Working with farmers, the company captured more than 2000 tons of carbon in 2022. It also captured the attention of the investment community, securing $6.3 million in seed funding led by Union Square Ventures and Greylock, among other investors.[5] Living Carbon, a biotech company based in San Francisco, genetically engineers plants for accelerated growth and CO_2 removal and storage.[6] These examples show how our brightest minds are finding novel solutions to help slay the climate change dragon.

Chapter 10 features an in-depth look at technologies and companies that are innovating to speed our transition to a more sustainable energy future and lower our carbon world. From exploring EVs and electrifying our grids to innovations in the field of batteries and other technologies like fusion that are on the horizon, this chapter will give you a sense of where we are now and the promise our future holds for this critical energy transition. You'll learn about many innovators from across the globe, like Iberdrola, which is experimenting with water batteries, Commonwealth Fusion Systems, which is paving the way for future fusion solutions, as well as Octopus Energy, which is at the vanguard of building the decentralized grid of the future.

A New Collaboration Among the Public and Private Sectors

Climate change is forging entirely new collaborative efforts between business and government. According to David Kirkpatrick, "We are in a new phase societally for the intersection of government and business. Business absolutely will be the primary engine that addresses the climate crisis, but we need guidance from the government, in the form of tax policies, regulatory requirements and, incentives. The Inflation Reduction Act is a great example; it's a historic shift and a game changing epoch. They're using a carrot instead of a stick to incent businesses."

That carrot includes investing $370 billion in tax credits to the renewable energy industry in an effort to reach the goal of reducing greenhouse gases to 40% below 2005 levels by 2030. As of April 2023, multiple projects valued at a $150 billion investment in clean energy (i.e., wind, solar, and electric vehicles) were in motion. By 2030, the White House estimates the IRA will "lead to the installation of 950 million solar panels, 120,000 wind turbines, and 2,300 battery facilities."[7] The SEC also now requires every company to report their emissions, creating demand for tools that help organizations deliver on this new requirement.

Another example of a recent collaboration between government and business is the First Movers Coalition. This effort involves US Special Presidential Envoy for Climate John Kerry, The World Economic Forum and, 96 members who have made 121 commitments. By 2030, "these commitments will represent an annual demand of $16 billion for emerging climate technologies and 31 million tonnes (Mt) CO2e in annual emissions reduction." The goal is to ensure new technologies are available for scale-up by 2030 and contribute to achieve the goal of net-zero emissions by 2050.[8]

This group is also championing negative emissions through advanced carbon dioxide removal technologies. Borge Brende, president of World Economic Forum, said of this effort, "The coalition's members are truly the 'First Movers' who are focused on scaling disruptive innovations that pave the way for long-term transformation rather than the lower-hanging fruit of short-term process efficiency gains."[8]

This new alignment between business and government around world issues (including and beyond climate change) is also illustrated in the recent move by the leading venture firm Andreessen Horowitz, which is investing $500 million in early-stage companies that support national interest. The firm established its American Dynamism practice with a goal of funding "mission-driven, civic-minded founders" that are building for America to solve "our country's most vexing challenges with an entrepreneurial and technology-first approach." The efforts include reliable and cleaner energy, public safety, global defense, housing, and shoring US manufacturing, among others.[9]

Every Company Will Become a Climate Company

While government plays the critical role of establishing policies, taxes, and incentives that either mandate or incentivize companies to move to net zero, it will be up to the private sector to move the global warming needle. Across the world, many big brands have made big commitments to do their part. Companies like Microsoft, US Steel, Ericsson, IBM, Unilever, Alphabet, Apple, and Tesla are among them.

Here are a few examples:

◆ Microsoft, for example, has one of the most aggressive efforts in the business community. Its promises include being carbon negative by 2030 and by 2050 to "remove from the environment all of the carbon the company has emitted either directly or by electrical consumption since its founding in 1975."[10]

◆ The steel industry is a big contributor to global warming (up to a full 7% of global emissions), and US Steel has stepped up its goals to achieve net zero by 2050 and reduce GHG by 20% by 2030.[11] The company also announced a joint effort with Carbon Free to capture carbon dioxide emissions at one of the largest integrated steels mills in North America, with the hopes of capturing up to 50,000 metric tons of CO_2 per year, the equivalent of carbon emissions from nearly 11,000 passenger cars.[12]

◆ Alphabet became carbon neutral in 2007 and in 2017 became the first company of its size to match its total electricity consumption with renewable energy. By 2030, Alphabet plans to become the first major company to operate full-time on carbon-free energy.[13]

◆ Unilever is another global company making great strides across its many brands (Axe, Ben & Jerry's, Dove, Breyers, et al.). More than 25 of its brands are 100% sourced from sustainable materials. It has also set a goal of cutting its environmental footprint by 50% and becoming carbon negative by 2030.[13]

IBM's Efforts to Accelerate Sustainability

It comes as no surprise that a company like IBM would have many sustainability efforts in place. Among them is its IBM Sustainability Accelerator program, which supports environmentally at-risk communities around the world through technologies such as AI and hybrid cloud.

The company has a variety of active engagements in the areas of sustainable agriculture and clean energy. For example, through IBM's partnership with The Nature Conservancy Centre (TNCC), it is helping farmers in India achieve sustainable farming practices by reducing their practice of burning crops. The area of focus, known as the "breadbasket" of India, is a massive contributor of food, producing approximately 40% of the country's wheat and 30% of its rice. At the end of each harvest, farmers often burn crop residue as a quick and inexpensive way to clear the fields and ready them for the next harvest. This practice, however, produces air pollution and degrades the soil. Farmers, along with government officials and the community, sought to change the process. By applying advanced data analytics and accessible mobile technology, IBM and TNCC are addressing this process by promoting sustainable agriculture practices that can help protect this community from pollution and climate change. At the center of this effort is the CRM Connect, which offers valuable intelligence to farmers, agriculture sector leaders, and decision-makers. More than 1,000 farmers are using this technology solution to eliminate crop residue burning, and by 2024, the teams are aiming to engage with 12,000 farmers.[14]

I had the pleasure of speaking with Justina Nixon-Saintil, vice president and chief impact officer at IBM, who leads the company's Corporate Social Responsibility (CSR) efforts globally and oversees impact initiatives like this one. Justina shared with me some of IBM's best practices that ensure its CSR work is deeply embedded into the core of the business.

"What makes our CSR effort successful is that it's not siloed in the organization, but rather embedded throughout the company for greater impact. It's aligned with our business strategy, leverages IBM's core compe-tencies, and not only has the full support of our CEO but IBMers as well."

Justina noted the importance of mapping sustainability programs to three core strategic elements: leverage IBM's expertise (technology and knowledge) to effectively address an issue; answer the needs of its custom-ers and their community; and align with employee passions by giving them an opportunity to learn new skills and address meaningful societal issues. This approach builds a foundation for success on multiple fronts.

Sometimes one of the biggest challenges of initiating an effort like this is determining where to focus. IBM's process offers a smart blueprint others could follow.

"We use a very specific strategic process when identifying where to launch our efforts. The first is we often select markets where IBM has a significant presence and a large employee base. Since we are already engaged in that community, this effort provides an opportunity to further strengthen that. We also choose markets that IBM would like to expand into, as it helps the company establish a presence and support the community. Governments want to see companies invest in communities before they're allowed to do business there, so our CSR efforts showcase our commitment to bettering them. We also identify markets where our sustainability efforts can support national agendas like mitigating climate change or skilling peo-ple so they're not left behind by new technologies. Supporting national agenda items helps generate support from the government and community, as well as forge important local partnerships."

This strategic process infuses the CSR effort into the very heart of the organization, as it is aligned with core aspects of the business. "The effort is really part of the DNA of our organization and has a huge impact on engage-ment. We saw through our annual engagement survey that our employees' awareness of IBM's social impact in the community is directly correlated with higher levels of employee engagement. Our employees seek to be involved in impact programs, as it helps them develop new skill sets around technologies like the cloud and AI, as well as be involved in a meaningful effort that impacts society."

A Global Recruiting Company's Innovative Approach to Sustainability

Here's another inspiring example of a company that is doing its part to help thwart climate change. Award-winning global works solutions company Aquent is a forward-looking, innovative organization with a passion for delivering its clients the talent, technology, and services needed to excel in today's business climate. The company services major brands such as Google, Microsoft, Facebook, Merk, McKinsey & Company, indeed, Kaiser Permanente, and United Healthcare.

Aquent applies its spirit of innovation and unrelenting drive to its sustainability effort. It has made a bold commitment to achieve a carbon negative status – the first major firm in its industry to do so. After Aquent hits its milestone of becoming carbon neutral, the company will work to erase its entire carbon footprint of 35 years. Meeting this aggressive goal requires definitive changes to how the company operates now and into the future.[15]

As a service-based organization that does not manufacture products, Aquent's carbon footprint was primarily comprised of office utilities, employee commuting, business travel, and technology systems. Using EPA guidelines for carbon generation, Aquent calculated its global carbon footprint including internal staff and talent for the past few years. After collecting all of that data, it established a benchmark in 2019 that it generated nearly 12,000 tons of carbon, the majority of which was caused by staff and talent commuting to offices.[15]

In 2021, the company had reduced its carbon footprint by 59%. This was during the COVID-19 pandemic and a pivotal time in which Aquent let go of many of its offices, adopting a virtual-first work environment for all staff and most of its talent. In that year, the company generated just more than 4,800 tons of carbon.[15]

That carbon reduction trend accelerated to a full 80% in 2022, as the company took on the first of many solar projects, which came online that year. Combined with its other sustainability efforts, Aquent's carbon footprint reduced to approximately 2,500 tons.[15] In addition to funding multiple solar projects, the company also moved its data facility to one powered by hydroelectric power, which saves approximately two tons of carbon emissions annually. The company also began providing its staff with more efficient computers that use significantly less kilowatts per hour.[15]

Aquent Q&A

I spoke with Aquent CEO John Chuang to provide readers with insights into the company's strategy and philosophy around its successful sustainability efforts, and to share best practices, lessons learned, and the impact this initiative is having on company culture.

Q: As a recruiting company, why did Aquent decide to invest in its sustainability effort?

A: For starters, we believe climate change is a critical issue and that businesses must be part of the solution as opposed to part of the problem. We don't believe companies should wait for a legislative directive to step up.

Moreover, our sustainability effort is a true reflection of who we are as an organization. If we had to pick one word to describe our company, it would be pioneer. We're always interested in innovation and the way we fundamentally compete in the marketplace is through that innovation and by being different. For example, we were the first company to offer temporary employees benefits back in the '90s *before* the gig economy, and we were the first staffing company to offer training on a large scale. With that type of innovation at our core, we saw a sustainability effort as not only good for the planet, but also just a good business fit. It gives us a competitive advantage because we wanted to stand out as a service company that doesn't add to our clients' carbon footprint. In fact, we're just the opposite. If you hire us, we actually lower your footprint. That's a unique competitive advantage.

Additionally, our sustainability effort attracts and retains our employees. Our employee base and staff are truly of like mind about the problem of climate change, and there's a lot of pride in Aquent's innovative strategy to be part of the solution. It's a rallying cry we unite around.

Lastly, this effort makes financial sense for us. The hidden gem in all of this is that we're not losing money whatsoever with our climate initiatives. We've structured them in a way that makes good financial sense for us. It's not charity; it's part of our business.

Q: How did you go about building Aquent's sustainability plan?

A: Like all good plans, it started at the top. I was passionate about pursuing this path because I knew the effort was perfectly aligned with our culture and would be a huge differentiator for us. We set very aggressive goals because, to me, this is not about doing something because it looks good. This is about taking action that will have meaningful outcomes. My thinking is if we're going to do this, let's be awesome and do it faster and better than anyone else. So, with that, we set out to become carbon negative as quickly as possible. I wanted this to be a true differentiator; a high quality program with real impact.

Q: Tell us more about your views of a high quality program.

A: I think there are a lot of efforts out there that have questionable quality in terms of really eliminating carbon. Some companies buy credits, others plant trees and, quite honestly, some just do these efforts because it looks good, but the quality might be questionable. We decided we were not going to take the easy way out. We are going to do it the right way and have real, measurable outcomes and impact.

Q: What does it take to deliver on a high quality plan like this?

A: It takes many parts of the company to deliver on this. For starters, we needed so much data that we didn't have in order to calculate the carbon we're using both today and in the past. We never tracked that before, so IT, engineering, and data experts needed to get involved right at the outset to gather that data and establish a place to store it, as data is an essential piece of the puzzle and the plan. In fact, everyone involved had to expand their knowledge and responsibilities, but that's what's fun and what our company enjoys. We embrace learning new things and tackling new problems. It's really just part of our culture, so this effort fit right in. We also created a sustainability/ESG department and hired someone to lead this effort. It's been critical to have someone on board whose sole focus is to coordinate efforts and shepherd everyone involved as we moved through our strategic plan. I have to say that everyone is fully supportive and proud of this effort. It's incredible.

Q: What are some of the key elements of Aquent's sustainability plan?

A: One of the most significant things we did was to close many of our offices and adopt a virtual-first work environment for our staff and most of our talent. This started during the pandemic and what a lot of people don't realize is that the hidden benefit that remote working delivers is massive carbon reduction. Remote working alone has enabled us to drastically reduce our carbon footprint by nearly 80% over the past three years. This massive reduction made us realize we could not only become carbon neutral, but also set a goal to become carbon negative by eliminating our historic footprint. Now, as a service company, we are fortunate that our employees can do their jobs remotely. Obviously, a company that manufactures goods would need to adopt a very different strategy.

The other big initiative was to take on solar energy projects. We decided to do solar because we wanted to implement high quality initiatives that would have a significant impact in reducing carbon emissions. We weren't just going to buy carbon credits because they don't reduce carbon. We chose solar because it has a meaningful impact on carbon reduction. Also, solar projects are accessible, the right scale for our organization, and offer economics that fit our business.

We selected efforts to invest in based on those that would have the biggest impact. For example, we choose solar efforts that replace a conventional energy source like coal or oil. We have several projects in Indiana because that state uses a lot of coal to generate power. To learn about which solar projects to invest in, we either worked with a solar developer or found ways to get into the deal flow. Obviously, we had never done anything like this before, so we had to learn the process.

Our first project was providing solar energy for a kombucha factory. The company was great to work with, and its owner is very conscious about the environment. Because of our effort, the company's power is now 50% solar. We also provided solar energy for Allstate University's architecture program. The school is a big champion of solar and did not have the funds to do this project, so that has been another satisfying effort for us.

We also have a very interesting project for a dairy farm in Ohio. It's a fantastic story. This is a fourth generation farmer and the previous generations farmed in the Netherlands. The owner originally wanted to open his dairy farm in the Netherlands, but the country didn't want to use any more land for this type of farm. The authorities told him to set up a farm in Eastern Europe and he didn't want to, so he searched for another location and found what he needed in Ohio.

There were two primary needs to find the right location for his dairy farm. One is he needed abundant water because each cow drinks 30 gallons of water a day. This farmer has 1,000 cows, so that's 30,000 gallons of water a day! He also needed to be in close proximity to whoever is purchasing the milk because it has to be transported. The location in Mt. Sterling, Ohio fit the bill.

This farmer values sustainability, so it was a perfect fit for our project. The farm's biggest client is Dannon Yogurt, and the owner wanted to be the first dairy farm in the Dannon family to be powered by solar energy.

Here's an interesting challenge we tackled on this effort. Dairy farms consume an enormous amount of energy because of the massive volume of water and food cows consume, along with the process required to move water, food, waste, and milk around. One of the biggest issues is that milk comes out of a cow at approximately 101 degrees, but it needs to be delivered to Dannon Yogurt at only 36 degrees. Typically, the way farms decrease the temperature is to send it through pipes that go through groundwater, which reduces the temperature from 101 to 60. Then, a different, energy efficient and sustainable solution was needed to bring the temperature down to 36 degrees. We looked into several options to cool the milk, but all of them had an issue that made them unworkable. For example, if the farm used lithium-ion batteries, they would have to replace them every three years. Or, if the farm used a typical refrigeration system, it would require too much power and solar wasn't an option because the cooling happens at night when the sun can't power the system.

We were determined to find an answer and worked with the farmer on a very creative solution. In other parts of the world such as in New Zealand, farmers use an ice bank to cool milk, which is essentially sending milk through a bank of ice cubes to cool it down. We were passionate about solving this issue and scoured the US for an ice bank system. We found one that was used for air conditioners, but it had never been used for food production. We convinced the manufacturer to adapt the ice bank by using the right stainless steel, food grade materials, etc. The ice bank is currently in production, and the end product will be the first system in the US used to cool dairy products.

We're really excited about this effort! It shows how you have to embrace problem solving and get many people in your organization involved like engineering and IT to come up with innovative solutions. Many companies might have walked away from this challenge, but we were motivated by it. In fact, we're going to get a tax credit for it because it's made in the US.

We also have other efforts underway, including providing solar energy to a Honda plant in Ohio.

Q: Are there any lessons learned you'd like to share?

A: One of things we learned along the way was to choose solar projects in states with the regulatory framework to support it. If there are no regulations, you have to negotiate with local utility companies, which is a painful and incredibly slow process. If the state government is pro solar, the utility companies will play ball, and it makes the entire effort so much more efficient. We also chose projects where we would eliminate the most carbon. So, those two elements – state regulations and big carbon reduction – led to the best results.

Another thing we learned, which I mentioned earlier, was the amount of carbon data you need to do this correctly. To determine your carbon footprint, you need data on so many things, such as where your employees work, how they get to work, whether they carpool, take public transportation, etc. So, we had to gather all of the data to get a true sense of our footprint. We also had to calculate backwards because we wanted to eliminate our historic footprint. That required a lot of time and effort, but it has been completely worth it. This data enabled us to ask and then answer the important question: *How can we develop a better, more sustainable process involved in how we make work happen?*

The other important piece of advice is to not take the easy or inexpensive way out. For example, companies can invest in carbon credits, which is a convenient solution, but it really doesn't have much of an impact. Businesses spent around $100 million on carbon offsets alone just last year, but those investments hardly move the needle. If you're going to do this, do it right and in a way that will have a meaningful outcome.

Lastly, I would say we had to learn a lot about different taxes and tax incentives our company was eligible for, and it was important to hire a tax advisor and attorney with an expertise in energy contracts.

Q: Any mistakes you made along the way that others can learn from?

A: One of those was that we miscalculated the time it takes to implement a solar project. So, anyone embarking on that type of effort should factor that in. We also initially looked at solar projects that were too small and wouldn't have as much of an impact. In addition, we miscalculated our carbon usage initially. So, those are a few things we learned along our sustainability journey.

Q: What is Aquent's long term sustainability plan. What's next?

A: Once we eliminate our carbon footprint, we plan to go carbon negative. Getting there means staying on top of new technologies that can help us reach that goal or accelerate our ability to get there. That means our IT staff is very focused on new technologies for carbon capture, etc. We also need to get better at training our sales force to communicate the new value equation this brings to our brand. We now offer the tremendous benefit of being a sustainable company our clients can partner with, which can help them reach their sustainability goals. We believe that's a tremendous advantage we bring to our market segment and, more importantly, a critical effort we're doing to help our planet.

Tech for Good Takeaways

IBM and Aquent are two inspiring stories that underscore critical components of sustainability efforts.

- ◆ Justina Nixon-Saintil (IBM) shared the company's smart strategic model, which ensures its sustainability efforts are deeply embedded within the organization. The company aligns its sustainability effort with its core business strategies, leverages its core competencies (technology and knowledge), and answers the needs of communities/ customers. This ensures the effort is not siloed, but a true reflection of its DNA.

- ◆ Justina also gave us insights into IBM's framework for identifying where to launch an effort. The company chooses markets where it has a presence and employee base, or regions where it would like to expand into, and aligns its efforts with items on the national agenda so the programs garner support from local governments and citizens.

- ◆ The IBM story also demonstrates the tremendous impact these efforts have on employee engagement. They realized that employees' awareness of IBM's social impact in the community is directly correlated with higher levels of employee engagement.

- ◆ John Chuang's (Aquent) inspiring story illustrates the importance of aligning efforts with the core of your brand attributes. Aquent's effort reflects its spirit of innovation and unrelenting drive to do meaningful things that differentiate the company and have a positive impact on the world.

- ◆ Aquent's sustainability efforts are another example of the importance of having a passion for problem solving. Rather than take an easy way out in sustainability by, for example, investing in carbon credits, Aquent invests in high quality, high impact projects that really move the needle in terms of carbon reduction. When the company hit roadblocks as it was embarking in new terrain, it didn't quit or take a short cut that could undermine the effort. Instead, the company persevered, found solutions to the problem, invested the time and money required, and got on the right track.

◆ Doing something good for the world was also a powerful thread woven into Aquent's culture. People from many areas of the company are involved, passionate about the effort, and embrace contributing to the good the effort delivers. The sustainability effort became a rallying cry and a source of immense pride.

◆ The Aquent example also underscored the importance of breaking free from traditional thinking and roles, taking on new responsibilities and challenges, and evolving to a new path. The company's effort required new responsibilities and priorities for everyone from the CEO to the CTO to the CFO.

CHAPTER 4

Innovations for a Healthier Population

Although the healthcare industry may be one of the final frontiers for technology, this current wave holds the potential to truly revolutionize the practice of medicine on multiple levels, including diagnosing and treating diseases, better management of patient data, and new models for the delivery of healthcare services. While this industry has been historically slow to embrace technology, in no small part because of rigorous testing requirements and strict regulations, the COVID-19 pandemic illustrated how quickly this sector can mobilize and adapt to unprecedented new situations. Creating a vaccine to a novel virus in record time and the explosive adoption of telehealth are two powerful examples that demonstrate what can be accomplished when the need is dire.

A Medical Renaissance

The healthcare industry's ability to quickly pivot during this time opened doors for the adoption of technology across many aspects of healthcare, and many are predicting a phenomenal time ahead in the field of medicine. In the *New York Times Magazine* article, "Suddenly, It Looks Like We're In a Golden Age for Medicine," biochemist, Nobel laureate, and pioneer in CRISPR technology Jennifer Doudna describes this period as "an extraordinary time of accelerating discoveries."[1]

I spoke with Peter Durlach, CVP, chief strategy officer, Microsoft Health and Life Sciences, who has spent decades at the intersection of healthcare and technology. Working early on with healthcare innovations like the AI-powered radiology reporting program PowerScribe, Peter has seen firsthand the impact technology has on both medical practices and healthcare outcomes. I asked Peter how he sees the future playing out, given the state of innovation today.

"While I can't predict exactly where the tipping point will be in medicine and healthcare, what I can say is that the scale and velocity of what's taking place in healthcare right now is unlike anything I've seen before. And, it's not just from generative AI, although that's a big part of it. This has been building for years. This intersection of advancements in biology, cloud computing, and AI are all coming together, giving me confidence that we're going to see some amazing things. Just look at what we did during the pandemic, creating a vaccine at that scale. You don't need any more proof than that."

One organization that has created an entire ecosystem of innovative organizations delivering leap-forward solutions to transform health is Flagship Pioneering. Founder and CEO Noubar Afeyan, who is also co-founder and board chairman of COVID-19 vaccine developer Moderna, is currently working on several pioneering companies developing breakthrough biotech/healthcare solutions, from gene writing technology, to innovations in the development of protein drugs, to entirely new ways to detect diseases before their onset. With a passion for preemptive health and medicine, Noubar shared his views of the current healthcare system and the tremendous potential to deliver a new level of healthcare focused on protecting/improving people's health *before* they get sick.

"The healthcare industry is essentially a misnomer. It should be called sick care because the focus has been on treating sickness vs. preventing diseases. The question is how can we change to truly transform human health? The notion of detecting pre-disease conditions vs. early or late stage diseases and to preempt the onset of disease is an exciting area that would dramatically change both the cost and life impact of healthcare. For example, the healthcare industry has been successful in detecting stage three and four cancers, but what if we could detect the disease much earlier? We have an effort in place looking to do 90-95% sensitivity detection of stage one cancer. And the cool part is that we're finding *stage zero* cancer. This process is about imagining a world free of disease and pioneering a path toward that goal."

This is one of many leap efforts at Flagship that could revolutionize our approach to healthcare. Other efforts are underway across the healthcare landscape to deliver advancements in areas such as immunotherapy, CRISPR gene editing technologies, next-generation trials treatments for breast, lung, and rectal cancer, mRNA tools to help with other diseases, weight-loss drugs, drug development paths powered by machine learning, as well as other vaccines to protect people from the most difficult infectious diseases.[1] Chapter 11 explores biological systems innovations in the healthcare arena such as CRISPR, immunotherapy, and cellular rejuvenation.

There is also a plethora of emerging digital technologies that hold the promise to reshape several aspects of medicine, from how to diagnose, treat, and manage diseases to better management of patient data. Some examples of this include the Internet of Medical Things (IoMT), which includes medical devices and applications that are connected to cloud computing platforms. IoMT offers benefits such as monitoring and treating chronic health conditions, empowering people to better manage them through devices and wearables. Boston Scientific Corporation is a major player in the global IoMT market, offering remote patient monitoring and implanted medical devices. GE Healthcare and Johnson & Johnson are also significant companies in this space.

Along with those behemoths, there are many smaller innovators that are breaking new ground. One is Openwater, which is working on a breakthrough wearable device that will provide an alternative to radiation treatment and surgery in treating brain tumors. Identified by *Newsweek* as one of the "medical marvels disrupting healthcare," the device is currently being tested on mice. This innovative device sends beams of ultrasound to target and destroy cancer cells, with healthy cells remaining intact.[2]

Another is a company called Whoop, which develops an advanced fitness and health wearable that allows people to monitor their recovery, sleep, training, and health. Its app acts as a personal digital fitness and health coach, providing actionable feedback based on the user's data, behavior, and goals.[3]

One of the most challenging aspects of healthcare is managing the vast stores of patient data. Mismanagement of this data can have devastating outcomes, including wrong diagnosis and a failure to effectively manage and treat patient conditions. Cloud computing and data analytics can address this issue by providing medical professionals with real-time access to important patient data, including medical history, diagnoses, treatments, etc. Microsoft, Amazon Web Services, Consensus Cloud Solutions, UnitedHealth, and Athenahealth are among the many players in this burgeoning space.

We can't mention innovation without saying AI in the same breath. AI and robotics are among the most powerful and potentially transformative technologies to watch in this realm. One application of AI that is already starting to have a major impact involves the administrative end of healthcare, which has been a massive burden on the system, not only from a cost perspective, but also its impact on physician burnout. AI is emerging as a powerful tool that can streamline healthcare workflows and address these issues, automating many tasks and freeing up the time of physicians and nurses so they can focus more on patient care.[4]

Diagnostic imaging that leverages AI is also rapidly gaining scale and holds tremendous promise in delivering better outcomes in healthcare. In this application, AI amplifies the results of early stage screening. "About 80% of all medical pathways start with an image, along with lab data," said Peter. "We've relied on the human eye to look at the image, but this can be dramatically amplified by AI technology, which looks at the pixels. We're seeing an early indication of this in dermatology, as well as in radiology involving the heart, brain, and lungs."

Peter described a Microsoft offering in this realm, the Precision Imaging Network, which is a platform that has third-party imaging AI models that are FDA cleared to run on it to look at this image data and see things the human eye can't.

"It can quantify things in the anatomy that's almost impossible for a human to see," said Peter. "So, for example, this could involve seeing and quantifying calcification in your arteries or fat that's building up, delivering a much better predictive for early stage cardiac disease. This type of diagnostic work that combines quantitative data that's hidden in the pixels with clinical pathways is also done for the brain and certain cancers, and we're starting to see some really amazing results."

A recent report noted that AI can identify those at the highest risk of developing pancreatic cancer up to three years before diagnosis.[5] These deep learning medical tools analyze unstructured data (images, blood work, EKGs, medical history, etc.) to facilitate radiology diagnoses.

While voice recognition has been around for decades, it's an early AI breakthrough that continues to deliver incredible benefits in healthcare. For example, the Dragon Ambient eXperience (DAX) Copilot can listen in to the entire conversation between a doctor and a patient (with the patient's consent), record it, transcribe it, and then use large generative AI models to convert that multi-party conversation into a summarized, structured draft clinical note, as if the clinician had dictated it, but it's all done with AI.

"What the system can deliver is just breathtaking. Physicians typically spend twice as much time documenting as they do taking care of patients," said Peter. "This cognitive load of keeping track of what they have to document is a major cause of physician burnout. Ambient eliminates that burden. It's listening and doing the work for you. It's the number one thing that AI is helping with at scale today in the clinical setting. Speech applications like this are the tip of the spear, especially because our technology is the most evolved in this realm, given the long history that we've had in this space."

Another AI area that is becoming entrenched in medicine is robotics. This technology has transformed surgical procedures by providing a powerful tool to surgeons that extends their capabilities for better precision in the OR.

I spoke with Catherine Mohr, president of the Intuitive Foundation, the corporate Foundation of Intuitive Surgical, which makes the da Vinci surgical robot, to get her views on how robotics is giving surgeons powerful new tools to enhance their capabilities in the operating room. To date, more than 60,000 surgeons worldwide have used the da Vinci system in more than 10 million surgeries. Catherine's vast experience of seeing firsthand the tremendous benefits technology brings to the field of medicine makes her a big believer in how today's innovations can enhance outcomes for both patients and doctors (see Figure 4.1).

Catherine spoke to me about the common misconceptions around robotics and the importance of understanding how this technology is a tool for augmentation. "What's often misunderstood is how robotics work in surgical procedures. Robotics don't replace surgeons; they are not autonomous in surgery," said Catherine. "What they do is augment a surgeon's capabilities for better surgical outcomes. Robotics work as a powerful tool for surgeons, enhancing their vision of a patient's tissue by empowering doctors to see in wavelengths human beings can't see. This extended capability allows doctors to zoom in on a tumor, for example, which enables better accuracy in removing it. They also change the scale of a surgeon's movements when operating, empowering them to be much more precise. Essentially, robotics extend the limitations of a surgeon's senses, delivering greater precision and better outcomes."

In addition to her work with da Vinci Surgical Systems, Catherine's future-forward efforts with Intuitive Foundation include research and development programs to advance medical education around the world and apply novel technologies to reduce the global burden of disease.

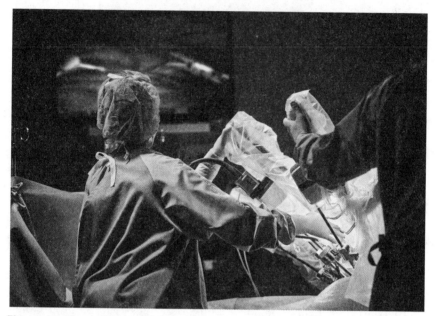

Figure 4.1 The da Vinci surgical systems are designed to help surgeons perform minimally invasive surgery. Da Vinci systems offer surgeons high-definition 3D vision, a magnified view, and robotic and computer assistance. They use specialized instrumentation, including a miniaturized surgical camera and wristed instruments (i.e., scissors, scalpels, and forceps) that are designed to help with precise dissection and reconstruction deep inside the body.[6]

©2023 Intuitive Surgical Operations, Inc.

One of those efforts includes addressing the lack of surgeons globally and its impact on patients, which all too often results in death when people don't have access to needed surgery. This initiative involves studying whether candidates at the fellowship exam level who don't have easy access to traditional medical school environments could learn procedures such as surgeries through simulation models.

"The experiment will include some students trained fully in traditional methods and others will have a hybrid where part of their apprenticeship will be what I call self-directed learning," said Catherine. "We can look at pass rates and examine the quality of learning in one way vs. another."

If successful (Catherine said it will take 10 years to study this and show whether or not this approach is ethical and responsible), it could address the lack of surgeons in the world and provide better care to patients living in areas where access is limited. This is one example of how technology can be applied in the future to open new doors for those who wish to study medicine, and potentially answer the need for more surgeons and greater access to healthcare in under-served communities.

From the Digital Divide to the Great Equalizer

Another area of innovation that is having a direct impact on the quality of life for billions of people is assistive technologies. These technologies and devices are designed to help the 2.5 billion people who have physical or mental disabilities such as those who have suffered a stroke, have autism or dementia, or are senior citizens. They help this significant portion of our population live fuller and more independent lives by giving them access to critical aspects of life that otherwise may be unattainable.

As with the other areas we've explored, technology has been evolving for decades to deliver breakthroughs in this realm. Among the many offerings included in this category are adaptive keyboards, which can feature higher level keys for better access or braille keyboards. Voice assistants like Amazon Echo enable people to use simple voice commands to do a range of tasks like calling people, sending texts, getting news updates, setting alarms, etc. Smart watches with braille not only enable people to tell time, but have connectivity features with smart devices, enabling wearers to receive and send messages, make calls, and receive notifications. Another AI-powered invention is smart glasses, which can help those in an electric wheelchair to control its movements by head changes. As with other smart devices, they can be connected to send/receive messages and calls, as well as get notifications, etc. Smart canes are another example of assistive technology.[7] A company called WeWalk makes these devices, which "detect above-ground obstacles and incorporates navigation functionality, as well as voice feedback that describes what the user is walking by and descriptions of other nearby destinations like shops and restaurants."[8] These are a few examples of the many technology-powered tools available today to help improve the lives of billions of people who face limitations.

John Samuel, who began losing his eyesight during his first year of college, shared his inspiring journey with me and discussed how technology has become a powerful tool for those with disabilities. While John struggled with losing his sight as he was building his career, he learned firsthand the barriers people with disabilities face. More importantly, he also learned how removing those barriers, in his words, "removes the disability."

That awakening led him to become co-founder and CEO of Ablr, a division of LCI, a nonprofit organization headquartered in Research Triangle Park. Ablr is a disability inclusion and accessibility business that was founded with a mission to remove barriers for people with disabilities, helping them to access critical aspects of life, including employment. John explained how TOMS shoes (which is built with the social impact of buy one/give one pair of shoes to those in need) inspired the formation of Ablr.

"Instead of giving a product to people in need, I sought to create tech-based jobs for blind people." Currently, Ablr is helping blind people in the North Carolina (Research Triangle Park) region secure work. His goal is to prove the model in this region and expand it to other areas, bringing a highly valuable service to help enhance the life and livelihood for blind people.

"Technology is the greater equalizer for people with disabilities because it removes barriers, opening doors to equitable access to critical things in life like education, employment, entertainment, and e-commerce," he said.

John described how screen reader technology (or text to speech software) were an absolute game changer for him because they gave him access to critical daily tasks such as email, search, research, e-commerce, etc. Today's screen readers are AI-enabled tools that provide customization in tone, speed, and audio conversion into multiple languages.

"Prior to using screen readers, I was literally making fonts on my computer 24x so I could use what little eyesight I had left at that time to read a few letters on the screen at a time," John explained. "Once I started using screen readers, it opened the world of accessibility to me."

When asked about the state of today's technology, John emphasized the need for the industry to include people with disabilities in the design phase of innovations as opposed to being an afterthought. "By incorporating the needs of those with disabilities at the start of developing an innovation, it will help eliminate unconscious biases, and make the product function better for this population right out of the gate."

MIT Solve's Mission for Social Impact

MIT Solve has created an open innovation marketplace comprised of inspiring innovators from around the world who are developing technology-driven solutions. Through its social impact challenges, Solve finds the best solutions from anyone, anywhere, and then brings together MIT's ecosystem and Solve supporters to fund and scale these organizations, enabling them to deliver transformative impact in under-served communities around the globe.

I spoke with MIT Solve Executive Director Hala Hanna, who gave me an overview of this inspiring organization and its portfolio of nearly 300 tech for good innovators. Hala emphasized the importance of bringing together a diverse community of problem solvers in order to tackle world problems. "Imbued in our philosophy is that no one institution alone has all of the answers and that we need to widen the problem-solving table to include more voices, experiences, grit, and passion. That approach is the fundamental underpinning of our mission."

One of the many innovators in MIT Solve's community is Access Afya, which offers people living in informal settlements in Nairobi a micro-clinic, which is "a standardized clinic in a box model that delivers chronic care, family planning, lab testing, child immunizations, and nutrition, pre and post-natal care, general outpatient consultations, first aid, and more."[9] The company also offers an app that helps its patients manage their health over the phone. "The clinic actually fits in a backpack of the health workers who are trained to deliver healthcare to these informal settlements with the average cost of a visit at around $4. So, the technologies this company is using are bringing critical healthcare services to an under-served community," said Hala.

Another MIT Solve innovator is GLOBHE, which uses drone technology to detect and predict hazards like malaria outbreaks. Every year, malaria affects approximately 220 million people, putting nearly 40% of the global population at risk for this deadly disease. Natural hazards created by climate change also pose threats to public health. Through its 9500 drone operators and "crowddroning" platform used in 140 countries, GLOBHE collects data on demand, which is used to help prevent dangerous situations. For example, malaria outbreaks can be avoided by finding infected mosquito breeding sites before they become malaria-transmitting mosquitoes, and residents can be warned of drought before it results in a wildfire. The technology can also detect cracks in a bridge before it collapses.[10]

Tech Reshaping the Healthcare Model

Today's technology is also creating an entirely new model for the delivery of healthcare. Telehealth practices, which exploded during the pandemic, were a catalyst for this new medical paradigm; a harbinger of a new healthcare landscape that is on the horizon. Keith Figlioli, managing partner at the investment firm LRVHealth, who has spent the past 20 years in technology and healthcare, sees a transformation in this area of healthcare coming down the pike.

"What we're seeing right now is the completion of wave one in healthcare, which is essentially sunk investment in technology without any demonstrable ROI. To date, this investment has been in necessary areas that had to get done in order to unleash the next wave of technology. This is all about to take off into what I call wave two, which is starting now and will bring very exciting changes that will dramatically impact healthcare in the next 10–20 years. It truly will be a digital transformation, delivering on what we call Care Anywhere, which will provide people with multiple models to both practice care and receive care, as analog, digital, and hybrid experiences all come together."

Keith explained how the model has already started to change, with newer practices emerging that help to address the scarcity of clinics and provide alternative options for physicians, which could help address burnout. "There was a time back in the '70s, '80s, and '90s when a doctor would graduate Harvard Med School and there was essentially only one place they went to work if they lived in Boston, which was MGH. Today, there's a proliferation of new brands offering new options, like Omada Health, a digital behavioral health company, or Oak Street Health, which cares for older adults. Today, doctors working at these places not only have the admiration of their peers, but also their envy. These new brands are creating an entirely new field for the practice of medicine."

Keith made an analogy to the digital disruption of retail and believes healthcare will have a similar trajectory. "In the early days of e-commerce, big box retailers had no idea what to do with digital, so Amazon and other brands were created. Eventually, the industry figured out the model to deliver a physical experience plus a fully immersive online experience all in one. That pattern will eventually happen in healthcare and deliver on the Care Anywhere concept, which will meld physical, digital, and hybrid into a profoundly better experience for consumers."

Tech for Good Takeaways

The various interviews and examples in this chapter illustrate additional key components of what's required to deliver on the promise of this era.

- As Noubar Afeyan (Flagship Pioneering) wisely pointed out, it takes imagination to deliver on the full capabilities this wave of technology offers. In the case of Noubar's biotech companies, this is about imagining a world free of disease, asking the right "what if" questions about delivering better health, and then pioneering a path to get there. Our world needs more of this approach: more passionate leaders who ignite their imagination of what could be, more curious thinkers asking the right questions, and more innovators who then strive to find breakthrough answers to those questions.

- Catherine Mohr (Intuitive Foundation) underscored the importance of letting go of misconceptions around technology. There is so much of that happening around generative AI right now. For example, robotics in surgery does not replace surgeons, rather it augments what surgeons do, giving them better precision and more successful outcomes. Naturally, we must be mindful of the guardrails needed to ensure technology isn't weaponized against us, but we must keep an open mind to the benefits today's breakthroughs can deliver.

- Hala Hanna (MIT Solve) spoke to the critical element of widening the problem-solving table by filling its seats with a broad range of experts. This type of collaboration unites a range of knowledge, experience, and perspectives, from technologists, scientists, ethicists, humanitarians, marketers, and investors, who together can help create breakthroughs that solve today's issues.

- John Samuel (Ablr) emphasized the importance of including the right people when designing a product, so the right elements are baked in from the beginning. In his case, he pointed to including people with disabilities when designing a product to eliminate any unconscious biases.

CHAPTER 5

Timing Is Everything

History is punctuated by moments in time when the right elements come together that change the trajectory of our world. I believe we are standing at one of those moments now; a time when we must ask the right questions, apply our imagination, and seize every technology to improve the human condition. It reminds me of what the Ancient Greeks would call *kairos* "a time when conditions are right for the accomplishment of a crucial action: an opportune and decisive moment."[1]

As mentioned in Chapter 1, all of the ingredients are aligned to make this a defining point in time: world problems reaching a tipping point, evolved technologies to address these issues, a financial community investing in these solutions, and a growing base of our brightest minds who are passionate about solving these humanitarian struggles.

The toolbox used by this cohort of problem solvers is filled with the powerful technologies we've noted, such as AI, robots, sensors, chips, quantum computing, CRISPR technology, cloud computing, IoT, etc., which have the advanced capabilities to deliver the kind of breakthroughs we need now. In many cases, it's the integration of these individual tools that's creating a force capable of solving bigger and more complex issues. For example, AI and IoT combine to deliver applications that save energy; sensors and cloud computing unite to monitor clean water projects for people in need; and AI and data automation are being used to protect coral reefs.

"This is an incredibly important moment in time, as technology has finally evolved to this exciting tipping point when we can deliver leaps forward," said Patrick Wheeler, executive director, Center for Digital Strategies at The Tuck School of Business at Dartmouth. "Breakthroughs like generative AI, which have been evolving to this point for years, are a transformative piece of the puzzle that give us the capabilities to unravel the mystery of things and solve big problems."

Among the many potential outcomes of today's evolved technology is that it delivers on the concept of adjacencies. This is essentially how a discovery in one application can be quickly leveraged in other areas to augment successful outcomes across many disciplines.

This is particularly true in the field of medicine. "There's so much excitement about the quantity and speed happening around today's innovations, and there are really interesting adjacencies taking place around medical technology in areas that seem unrelated," said Catherine Mohr. "For example, if someone finds a way to sequence DNA faster, that might allow us to sequence another critical application, like making a vaccine in real time faster. Or, that same technology could be applied intraoperatively into a wound bed when a tumor is removed so there will never be a positive margin again."

As we look to the future, those innovations in medicine happen beyond the adjacencies of the here and now. "If you take any given field – immunology, agriculture, you name it – you can take everything that's known, draw a circle around it and that's the circle of adjacency. Beyond that circle is where the adjacencies will be 5 to 10 years from now and that's where the leaps will come from. To get there, you have to be willing to go to unreasonable places, and iterate over and over again to pioneer that path of future innovation," said Noubar Afeyan.

The New Imperative: Find Your Company's Soul

The technology we have now and will have in the not-too-distant future put the power in our hands to better our world. With this tremendous opportunity comes responsibility. Organizations – no matter the size or the vertical – must find ways to leverage these innovations to enhance how they operate and what they bring to society.

This is a transformative journey that is essentially about finding your company's soul and creating key initiatives around it. This concept was central to my last book, *Authentic Marketing: How to Capture Hearts and Minds Through the Power of Purpose*. This purpose-driven mission is about determining who you are as a company, identifying what good you can contribute to the world, and making a plan to deliver on that outcome. *By having a purpose that is fueled by today's advanced technologies, it will serve as a powerful catalyst to augment and accelerate outcomes for stronger and more meaningful impact.*

Embarking on this effort requires asking the right questions and letting go of some of the traditional orthodoxies in business that can constrain breakthroughs. In the last section of this book, we'll provide a detailed path forward on how to get started. Here, we'll look at a few key elements that provide the primary pillars of a framework for your effort.

KEY QUESTIONS

What do you want your legacy to be?

I opened the book with a story about this question, which is where I always like to start the conversation. Answering this first critical question will help you find your company's *raison d'être* and determine how it can have a positive impact on humanity. When you answer this, you'll discover what's in the soul of your company.

I shared how Sam Allen of Deere answered this critical question. Here's another example of how an entrepreneur, innovator, and creative found his path. Swalé Nunez's revelation came at one of the biggest moments in his career to that point, when he was on stage addressing the world via a global livestream in front of a crowd of 6000+ people in attendance to launch a device for a leading tech hardware manufacturer. "I realized in that major moment of my life that I wasn't at all connected to the product I was selling. I walked off stage and thought, here I am, this kid from a developing country and I have this opportunity for the world to hear my voice, a moment I had envisioned as a child, but the context of the message I thought I'd be sharing wasn't the same as the one I actually shared. This was my big turning point."

Swalé left the corporate world and started his fascinating journey as a creative entrepreneur, founding a company called Enoem, a creative conduit that enables individuals to reconnect with their creativity and helps companies facilitate transformative innovation through human-centered design. He also started a company called Iuncta, which through its privacy first e-commerce checkout, is pioneering a better, more equitable online shopping experience that is powered by user identity. The company is working to empower people to take back control of their personal data/digital identity and derive value from it via brands they interact with online. "This form of tech for good reflects the passion I have to build solutions that prioritize people over the products built for them to use and delivers on the concept of human-centered design," said Swalé.

The story of Aquent also illustrates this concept. Innovation is at the very soul of this company, along with a passion for being part of the solution to today's problems. The combination of those elements was brought to life in how the company approached its successful sustainability effort.

What actions can you take that reflect what's in your company's soul?

Next, you need to think through answers to this question by imagining the various ways you can bring this legacy to life. Could your company use technology to transform the goods and services you bring to market in ways that would solve a problem or deliver better outcomes for people or the planet? Are your customers struggling to overcome a hurdle that you could help them solve through one of today's innovations? Think about Deere's powerful mission to solve the ever-growing challenges farmers face and how it continually leverages advanced technologies to deliver new solutions.

Another way to fulfill this is by starting an initiative that could help solve an issue in your community or helping an under-served community get access to essentials like food, education, or healthcare. Think about Ablr's mission to help the blind community, and below you'll find other inspiring examples, such as an initiative by Dell Computer and a company called Unima.

One important question every organization must ask is, are we doing everything we can to help in the fight against climate change? In Chapter 3, we highlighted several examples of companies taking this type of action and dove deeper into IBM and Aquent's efforts. Ask yourself what actions your company can take to create a meaningful sustainability effort with high quality outcomes.

How can technology accelerate and augment this effort?

This part of the process involves exploring which combination of technologies will fuel the delivery of your mission. For example, AI is augmenting outcomes across just about every application it's applied to, and data can often be used to provide information that can help deliver better outcomes. Find those technologies that can accelerate your mission.

One note about technology is that finding the right ones is never a one and done process. As technologies evolve, you should continue to incorporate them to ensure you are delivering the best outcomes possible. Think about the Deere story and how the company has continually invested in advancements in technology to ensure it is providing farmers with the best possible solutions to help them in their plight to do more with less.

The book has illustrated a variety of paths on how companies are leveraging technology in ways that positively impact our world. Deere demonstrates how a company transformed its entire mission around this, and

Aquent showed how a company can do its part in the fight against climate change.

Below are a few examples that illustrate other paths, from major brands that have a specific project involving tech for social impact, to start-ups built from the ground up with this type of mission.

Bringing Internet Access to Under-Served Communities

While most of us take internet access for granted, it's hard to imagine that almost half of the world's population goes without. To address this, Dell developed a creative solution, called Solar Community Hubs. These tech stations bring internet access to under-served communities, connecting them to the digital world and providing access to critical things like education, work, and healthcare. The hubs are old shipping containers converted into classrooms that use solar power, energy-efficient Dell technology, and air-cooled servers, providing user stations and networking technology that allow up to 40 people at a time to use the technology. The space also can be used for training or as an internet café. The hubs are used by micro and small businesses, offering not only jobs and education, but also telemedicine services via the internet.[2]

Diagnostic Testing for All

Nearly 50% of the world's population doesn't have access to diagnostic testing for illnesses such as tuberculosis. Unima set out to change that by creating a technology that enables people to achieve rapid diagnostics at the lowest possible cost and outside of the laboratory setting. The company is delivering equity in health by bringing this valuable service to people living in even the most remote places in the world.[3]

Cloud Computing for Bees

When you think of Oracle's cloud computing, the last audience you would imagine it helping would be the bee population, but that's one of the ways the company's technology is being applied for good. The bee population is in rapid decline, which threatens our very food supply. The World Bee Project launched a global honeybee monitoring effort to gather data and implement efforts that improve pollinator habitats, create more sustainable ecosystems, and improve food security. The World Bee Project database feeds data into the Oracle Cloud, which uses analytics tools including AI and data visualization to provide new insights into the relationship between bees and their varying environments. These new insights can be shared with farmers, scientists, researchers, governments, and other stakeholders.[4]

AI to Prevent, Detect, and Fight Wildfires

Protecting rainforests from the devastation of wildfires is a major focus in the fight against climate change. The Brazilian Amazon, the single largest tropical rainforest in the world, was devasted by more than 3,000 fires in one day in August 2022 alone (according to Greenpeace). Umgrauemeio is on a mission to stop this. The company uses AI to prevent, detect, and fight these wildfires.[5] This breakthrough earned the company a Top Innovator award from the World Economic Forum, which honors innovative solutions to the world's most pressing issues as outlined by the UN Sustainable Development Goals (SDGs).[6]

Re-Imagining the C Suite

One of the fundamental behavioral changes businesses must take is to look at the executive team through a different lens. This is about aligning company leaders with values and goals to ensure the organization is focused on not only profit, but also on ethics, morality, and purpose.

Starting at the top, the CEO will spearhead answering those key questions to identify the company's path of using tech for good. The other critical priority for today's CEO is the process of re-imagining how the executive team should evolve to deliver on this mission.

We'll begin by looking at how to retool the function of today's CTO because that position plays an essential role in this era. This executive's job must include identifying those technologies that are best to fuel the company's mission to impact humanity. In addition, the CTO must evaluate not only whether or not the technology is effective, but also ensure it is used ethically and in constructive ways that are not detrimental to people and the planet. An example of this is that if the CTO identifies AI technology that will be used by HR for recruiting, the CTO must ensure there are no inherent biases in the system that could work counter to a fair and equitable hiring or promotion process. Technologies must also be evaluated to ensure they are energy efficient and optimized to minimize the company's carbon footprint and do good for the environment. The CTO should also ensure the technology has been sourced from an ethical, reputable company that practices sustainability.

If the company is a developer of technology, the CTO must lead efforts to ensure the applications of its innovations are thought through, both in terms of the positive and negative impacts they can have on society. Tech for tech's sake is no longer enough. Potential negative consequences must be explored and policies put in place, so technologies aren't weaponized against us.

The CFO's role must evolve to determine how to make the right investments so the company can deliver on this mission. That means taking a broader view of the types of technology and sustainability efforts in which the company invests. For example, if a company's goal is to do everything possible to support the fight against climate change, the CFO should make investments in technology that reduce the company's carbon footprint, deliver greener equipment and infrastructures, minimize value-chain emissions, reduce energy consumption, etc.

The CMO should continue to focus on customer experiences, as I would argue that's now a permanent mainstay of marketing. Putting a company's tech for good strategy at the core of the customer experience will be a powerful element that will create deeper connections with customers, as it will enable them to "see" firsthand your core values and the good you bring to the world. In my last book, I talked about how this moves you from story-telling to *story-doing*. This effort should be leveraged across paid, earned, owned, and shared channels, whether it's a video posted on LinkedIn, a blog post, or a sponsored story in a key vertical publication. This storyline should also be the lead element of communications delivered by the CEO, whether that's focused on employees, investors, or customers.

There should also be new members taking a seat at this table. Many companies have already appointed a chief ethics officer to focus on maintaining ethical practices in products and across the workplace, as well as ensuring efforts reflect the company's values and are compliant. Another new role to consider is a chief humanitarian officer, whose role would be to deliver on the mission of the company and its contribution to humanity. Chief innovation officer is another new role, which would focus on finding innovative new solutions to today's problems.

Re-Inventing How We Work

In addition to retooling the C suite, companies should also re-architect their work environment to ensure it is optimized to deliver on the promises of this era. For starters, that means ensuring your company's mission – and its values – are clearly communicated and reinforced so all employees are engaged in them and inspired by them. That will not only give employees a north star to follow every day, but also attract and retain today's employees, who are motivated to work for organizations that contribute good into the world.

Successful work environments also require a problem-solving culture and teams comprised of a diverse set of talents – from tech to marketing to

HR – all working toward the same end. This team will leverage the power of technologies like AI to do lower-level tasks, freeing them up to do higher-level thinking.

"I think the piece that is really necessary here is that we need to remake how we work together, creating teams with diverse skill sets who can collaborate, ask the right questions, explore answers from multiple angles, and set out to see what's possible in solving today's problems," said Patrick Wheeler. "This structure has been successful in the past to change the course of our world. We are on the cusp of that type of transformation right now, and these types of organizational changes will serve as a catalyst to pivot and lead us to what's next."

These types of behavioral organizational changes are fundamental to thrive in this new era. Tech for good is so much more than your grandfather's CSR. It is not simply about giving back. Philanthropic efforts will always be important, but this is much bigger than simply writing a check. This is about finding your mission to have a positive impact on the world and retooling your organization to deliver on it.

Innovation and the Moral Corporation

While we've explored the world-changing outcomes this wave of technology promises to deliver, it's just as critical that we address the concept of responsible innovation. This involves enabling innovation to thrive, while working hard to ensure negative outcomes are averted. Chapter 16 will delve into this in greater detail, providing a path for businesses built around the three Es: ethics, engagement, and evolution. Here, we'll take a brief look at this critical issue through the timely lens of what's happening with AI.

As we move out of the last wave and into this one, the Silicon Valley mantra of "move fast and break things" is no longer acceptable. The previous wave served as a cautionary tale of the damage technology can deliver, with Facebook serving as the poster child. While it empowered every user with a platform to share their voice and provided a vehicle for social connections, in the wrong hands, it was leveraged for misinformation and propaganda that almost broke our democracy. Bringing an agnostic platform to market with the mindset of how it's used is "not my problem" cannot continue, as the stakes keep getting higher.

What the world grapples with in this new era is how do we learn from mistakes like these. How do we proceed in a manner that puts an ethical lens on our inventions so we more fully understand their potential impact? What processes do we need to put in place to ensure new technologies are used to benefit our society and not to the detriment of our world?

These types of questions and the debate about how technology can impact our world is now in full rigor around generative AI/ChatGPT. The potential magnitude of this innovation is so tremendous it's actually hard to get our collective minds around it. Bill Gates described the latest developments in AI as "revolutionary as mobile phones and the internet."[7] Many others have described the technology as "bigger than the printing press or the splitting of the atom."[8]

Conversations are taking place in every corner on how this breakthrough could change our society in both profoundly positive and negative ways, with many believing generative AI poses an existential threat to humanity. The concern prompted an open letter signed by hundreds of AI experts, tech entrepreneurs, and scientists, calling for a pause of the development and testing of AI technologies more powerful than GPT-4 so that risks can be studied.[9] Scientists and technologists also issued the following warning statement about AI's threat to human extinction. "Mitigating the risk of extinction from AI should be a global priority alongside other societal-scale risks such as pandemics and nuclear war."[10] AI was also the subject of a recent Ted Talk attended by the global elite. When asked about their views on AI, they responded with ambivalence, finding it to be both tantalizing and terrifying. They're tantalized because of the breakthroughs AI and generative AI can deliver, and terrified because AI also poses threats, some say at the existential level. At the event, University of Washington Professor Yejin Choi said that AI systems need to be "re-architected and taught both common sense and human values."[11]

These types of efforts and discussions are healthy because they are igniting conversations and actions around the concept of responsible innovation for not just ChatGPT, but for every breakthrough. We must explore an innovation's full potential, both the positive and negative, and then determine the guardrails needed to ensure it is harnessed for good and not to the detriment of society.

Esther Dyson, a journalist, investor, and philanthropist who for decades was one of the most sought-after tech industry analysts, has urged the need for new thinking from the tech industry. At Techonomy's TE22 conference, she said that tech and venture capital's "addiction to big exits and big profits is fostering a culture of short-term thinking and a dearth of socially minded leadership."[12]

I spoke with Esther about how the current business model needs to change. "Today, we are surrounded by business models that enable the worst behavior, so how do we create models that enable good behavior? One problem in the model is that their marketing is often very different from their delivery. So, how do we create a model that ensures companies deliver more transparency to make those distinctions clearer? For all the companies I invest in, we make sure they stick to their vision in terms of how they treat employees, as well as deliver on the products they create. If we could move toward a world with greater transparency, we could better determine which companies are actually doing good, and which ones are using their employees and manipulating their customers," she said.

This involves establishing what I call the moral corporation – a company that operates every day and in every way from a core of strong ethics that drives its policies and procedures, and builds a culture around doing the right thing. An essential element of this type of ethical framework is delivering on this concept of responsible innovation, working to ensure technology delivers positive outcomes for the greater good, while ensuring potential negative impacts are reviewed, assessed, tested, and averted.

Reid Hoffman, co-founder of LinkedIn and current partner at Greylock, is a technology optimist and a big believer in the power of tech for good. In a podcast with *Harvard Business Review*, Reid posed the types of questions tech companies must ask about their offerings. "I think that the question is you say, well, how does this affect the human condition? What does it mean for different individuals? Are there bias issues? Are there things where it creates some kind of bad social impact? And you have to ask these questions."[13]

While we must ask these types of questions and work hard to address the negatives, we must also ensure we are not stifling innovation and its potential to do so much good. In his substack, Mark Andreessen wrote a piece, entitled "Why AI Will Save the World," emphasizing how this technology holds the promise to "make everything we care about better." Andreessen explains that AI's ability to profoundly augment human intelligence is central to the potential and enormous good it can do, including the creation of new medicines, paths to solve climate change, further decoding the laws of nature for more scientific breakthroughs, as well as pushing the arts into a golden age through AI-augmented artists and musicians.[14]

Andreessen's points illustrate the kinds of amazing outcomes that can emerge if we focus on ensuring this technology serves us well. This reminds me of something Michael Dertouzos said to me in the early days of the tech industry. He said technology should be our slave; it exists to serve us and positively impact humanity. His thinking is precisely the mindset we must adopt, as it will enable us to seize this Kairos moment.

PART 2

The Potential for Great Leaps

CHAPTER 6

The Seventh Wave of Modern Computing

I remember so clearly the day Michael Dertouzos, then director of the MIT Lab for Computer Science, came to my office to introduce me to a British scientist named Tim Berners-Lee. This was back in 1993, and the purpose of their visit was to share a new innovation Tim had developed. While he was working at CERN, the European Particle Physics Laboratory, Tim invented something he was calling the World Wide Web. This was made possible in part through his development of HTML, the hypertext markup language that enabled a "web" of documents to be viewed by browsers.

While Tim's original intent was to build a platform that readily enabled information sharing between scientists in universities and institutions around the world, clearly this technology was destined for a much larger purpose. Seeing the transformative potential of this invention, Michael excitedly shared his views of how it would enable a time when we could buy and sell things online, get online advice from a doctor in another country, and readily share digitized pictures and videos. In that moment, I could envision how this technology could change literally everything.

That's one of many disruptive innovations that has served to catapult us into the next wave of computing. Over the course of the past six waves of computing, from the 1940s to today, technology has evolved from a massive machine housed in a back room of a large corporation or government organization, to something so ubiquitous we barely even know it's there. Today, technology is the enabler of just about every aspect of our life, from automating every major business function, to maximizing the efficiency of

59

complex energy production and distribution systems, to managing our health records and flagging potential health issues, to tracking our steps for the day, identifying a song we're listening to, and serving up answers to literally any question we could imagine.

As the seventh wave of technology is upon us, our innovations have finally evolved to have an even greater and more meaningful impact by helping to address some of the most pressing societal problems we face today. Part 1 highlighted many of these, and in this chapter, we'll take a deeper dive into a few of the technologies or technology categories that hold the greatest promise for impact. By no means am I implying that these are the only important technologies today, but the ones we explore below bubble up time and again as having great potential to transform the world around us.

Before taking a deeper look at these, it's critical to understand the waves of computing that have taken place over the past several decades, and how technologies have evolved and matured to what I believe is creating this watershed moment.

The Seven Waves of Technology

"If I have seen further, it is by standing on the shoulders of giants."

When Sir Isaac Newton wrote that famous metaphor, he summed up the essence of what science and technology are all about: that breakthroughs come from collective learning, from building on discoverers of the past. Technology is a powerful story of evolution; every invention builds on the one before it.

Think about AI alone, which dates back to many key events in the 1950s, including Alan Turing's seminal paper, called "Computing Machinery and Intelligence," and the Dartmouth Conference, a think tank event attended by early AI pioneers who convened to discuss "synthetic intelligence." Over the decades that followed, AI has had many starts and stops, including a boom in the 1960s and a bust in the 1980s. Now, AI is finally coming of age as the tsunami of generative AI is literally transforming everything it touches.

I've lived through many of AI's ebbs and flows. One of my fondest memories was in the mid 1980s when Nicholas Negroponte, co-founder of the MIT Media Lab, introduced me to two pioneers in the field of AI, Marvin Minsky and Seymour Papert. Many consider them to be among the fathers of AI. They were both brilliant, funny, and highly charismatic, and it was fascinating to hear them discuss their deep studies on how computers learn. While they each had their own passions about AI, both saw how this technology could better the world. Marvin was focused on how machines could be developed to replicate a human's common sense/reasoning and be used to solve some of humanity's biggest problems. Seymour, who was a visionary around using technology to change how children learn, saw how AI could impact this process and his constructionism theory of learning, which is grounded in the belief that learners construct knowledge by actively building things such as a poem or an idea.

These guys were big thinkers who were way ahead of their time. They were part scientists, part philosophers, and all about finding ways to enable machines to learn so they could improve key aspects of humanity. As generative AI started to explode into the public consciousness with OpenAI's release of ChatGPT in the fall of 2022, I couldn't help but think how thrilled Marvin and Seymour would be to witness this technology finally coming into its own and deliver on their early visions.

What has enabled AI, along with other technologies, to arrive at this point in time is the steady evolution of technology that started to have a big impact in the 1940s and has continued and accelerated in every decade since. This chapter includes a brief history of the waves of computing that led us to our current moment, as well as stories of some of the amazing people I've worked with during these eras whose disruptive innovations left an indelible mark on our world and helped to push us toward the next breakthrough.

Wave 1: The Mainframe Era

Technology is so embedded in our lives it's hard to imagine a time when it was confined to computer rooms or data centers that primarily housed massive mainframe computers, often called Big Iron. These machines were launched by IBM in the 1940s under the astute leadership of CEO and Chairman Thomas Watson Sr. (pictured below), just as World War II was ending. Mainframes were very costly and mostly used for bulk data processing. They were used primarily by the government for processing censuses, as well as in large organizations for mission-critical applications requiring the analysis of large amounts of data with no down time and highly stable processing capabilities. These machines were the first powerful computers that could provide time sharing, multi-tasking, and virtual memory. I remember at one of my first summer jobs, punching a time clock that was connected to one of these big machines.

Photo credit: Yousuf Karsh

This was an era of centralized computing, in which data processing and storage were managed by one large computer. Mainframe computers set the stage for the many waves of computing that followed and are still in use today, operating as servers in many of the world's largest corporations, as well as in large banks, insurance companies, retail corporations, and government organizations. Amazingly enough, IBM remains the only provider of these massive machines today.

Among the many visionaries of this era was a woman named Grace Hopper, a computer scientist and mathematician who served as a US Navy rear admiral. She was among the first to program computers and is widely regarded as a leader in software development concepts, helping with the transition from primitive programming techniques to the use of sophisticated compilers. A true pioneer in this realm, she believed "we've always done it that way" was no reason to continue to do so.[1] It is precisely this way of thinking that has helped propel innovations throughout the many waves of computing.

Wave 2: Minicomputers

A smaller, more general-purpose computer, called the mini, was launched in the 1960s, disrupting the mainframe era. These computers were sold at a significantly lower price point than the mainframe. Offered by the likes of Digital Equipment Corporation (DEC), Data General, Wang, and HP, they were envisioned to broaden the impact of computing on business operations.[2] However, given their smaller sizes, lower memory capacity and computing capabilities, minicomputers were generally used for managed process control, data transmission, and switching operations rather than the higher-powered activities dealt with by mainframes such as large-scale data storage or processing efforts.

This era was chronicled in Tracy Kidder's famous book, *The Soul of the New Machine*, which tells the story of the development of the first minicomputer at the now defunct Data General. The book brought to the fore the plight of engineers, illustrating both their struggles and acts of heroism as they raced to deliver next generation technology against the odds. The book is described as the *Odyssey* of computing literary foundation in a blog post by Bryan Cantrill, an American engineer from Sun Microsystems. He wrote the passage below, which is a compelling articulation of Kidder's "why" behind the drive to innovate:

"...it is not merely about the specific people or the machine they built, but about why we build things—especially things that so

ardently resist being built...the engineers in the book repeatedly emphasize that their motivations are not so simple as ego or money... [It's] the opportunity to advance the state of the art, the potential to innovate; the promise of making a difference in everyday lives; the opportunity to learn about new technologies."[3]

While many have forgotten this era of computing, it was an important time, marking the transition away from mainframes and setting the stage for the next era of personal computing through its distributed computing model. During this time, computers were also getting customized for specific applications. For example, Apollo Computer and Sun Microsystems developed workstations for engineers, a movement that helped push this wave closer to the coming PC era. Software also began to emerge in this era, with the development of the operating system (UNIX, specifically).

DEC was a standout innovator in this wave, which introduced its PDP (Programmed Data Processor) line that was the most successful mini. The company also introduced a more sophisticated way to tie its minicomputers to terminals by creating a network that connected these computers together. DEC's leadership was firmly of the belief that dumb terminals should remain as such, but the company's vision for the future of computing would be challenged by other pioneers of the 1970s and early 1980s who were imagining how smaller, more accessible computing devices could be put into the hands of everyday users. I'll never forget the look on DEC Co-founder Ken Olsen's face at DEC World when Bill Gates as keynote spoke passionately about the emergence of PCs and the power they would give individual users. Gates clearly saw the disruption coming, one that led to the demise of this era of computing, as the world embraced a new, more democratic approach to computing.

Wave 3: Personal Computers and Client/Server

Gates's vision of the personal computing era came to life in the 1980s. This transformative wave was not just about business productivity and streamlining business operations, but now focused on personal productivity. It put the power of computing in a person's hand, forever changing how we work and live. Hardware advancements from major players such as IBM, Dell, Hewlett-Packard, and Apple were shrinking down machines – both in physical size and cost. During this wave, the client/server model of computing emerged, which allowed a client (someone on a PC, for example) to request data or services from the server (minis, mainframes, workstations, etc.), which would process the request. This efficient networking structure further moved computing to a distributed model, transforming how we worked and shared information. We use a similar model today, only now the server is the cloud.

This significant period would not have been possible without the software revolution, which was at the heart of the personalization push. The emergence of the software industry would eventually evolve to automate and disrupt just about every task imaginable. Microsoft was central to this. The company's Windows operating system enabled applications to run on top of it, empowering users to transform how they work, create, and play and, importantly, encouraged developers to create software applications that could run on the operating system. Eventually software became the lifeblood of computing as it was the great enabler unleashing the true power of computing technology.

Michael Dertouzos, Robert Solow, and Richard Lester were spot on in their book, *Made in America*, when they asserted the power of software and how the US's leading position in that arena created a golden age for our country. Software became a competitive advantage held by the US, as it was the leader and the largest developer of software, a position still held today.

During this era, I had the good fortune to work with Mitch Kapor, founder of Lotus Development (now part of IBM), and Jim Manzi, who was president and CEO and one of the early software pioneers. Mitch invited me to his office to preview Lotus 1-2-3, the first spreadsheet application that took off in the early 1980s. As he walked me through the software and demonstrated how it could automatically update numbers on a spreadsheet, I immediately thought of my grandfather, who was an accountant. My grandfather would tell me his painful stories of how a single change to one number would manually take him hours and hours to reflect that change throughout the entire ledger. 1-2-3 would completely eliminate that pain. This was the beginning of the world of application software, which brought with it massive efficiencies, eliminating tedious manual tasks like those my grandfather had to do. Today, we have apps on our phones, which are essentially software applications that enable us to do just about everything imaginable, like monitor our heart rate, identify a constellation, or create a photo collage.

As I think about how computing became so personalized, it's impossible not to also think about Steve Jobs. He illustrated how to personalize computing in a way that Gates and Microsoft had not done at the time. Jobs had a strong and compelling vision of how hardware and software needed to develop together and integrate seamlessly to delight users.

The first time I met Jobs, he was visiting Lotus Development to discuss the possibility of creating 1-2-3 for the Macintosh. I had never encountered a CEO with such a commanding presence, as well as such fierce clarity and determination around his vision. He was the first person who truly embodied the concept of CEO as brand, a model later brought to life by so many others, including Michael Dell, Scott McNealy, Jeff Bezos, Kim Polese, and Bill Gates. His imposing traits made Jobs the type of leader that led engineers to follow him anywhere. More importantly, they enabled him to realize his vision of making personal computing, just that, more personal. His breakthroughs in how we use computers and other devices to enhance both our professional and personal lives pushed the waves of computing just that much closer to the one we're in now, which is all about unlocking creativity, innovation, and impact through our use of technology.

Wave 4: Software and the Enterprise

While this segment of the industry has its roots in manufacturing dating back to the 1960s, the first ERP (enterprise resource planning) systems used by corporations across many core business functions began in the 1990s. This wave marked the disruptive move from closed, proprietary systems to open, standards-based software. Enterprise computing integrated disparate networks and applications into an enterprise-wide infrastructure, enabling information to flow throughout organizations and to other companies. These software systems manage functions like database management, customer relationship management, supply chain management, business process management, among other functions.[4]

So many major players emerged during this era, doing a land grab for a piece of this burgeoning marketplace. Among them are Oracle, co-founded by Larry Ellison along with Bob Miner and Ed Oates, to capture the database portion of the market; Peoplesoft, founded by Dave Duffield and Ken Morris, which focused on the HR segment; SAP, founded by Hasso Platner and four others, to dominate the global integrated finance ERP market; and Adobe, co-founded by John Warnock and Charles Geschke, which is currently working to own the customer experience end of this market.

What these companies delivered, which was missing from the last era, was the horizontal software that could help run an entire company. This systemic software was a powerful solution to help organizations effectively run vertical applications across all of its primary disciplines, from HR to finance to customer experience.

Wave 5: Web and Search

The birth of the internet was arguably the most disruptive innovation (until perhaps generative AI), marking a radical change to how we access and exchange information and knowledge. It was an exciting and transformative time that opened a world of opportunities. The one primary concern I recall during this time was primarily among old model businesses, which feared being left behind as this new paradigm took shape. I mentioned the story of Tim Berners-Lee, who not only created the World Wide Web and HTML document formatting protocol, but also developed the first web server and the first browser. Today, he continues to work at the MIT Lab for Computer Science.

After Tim laid the groundwork for this era, websites intended for use by the general public began to emerge in 1994. This created the emergence of browsers, igniting fierce competition from initial players like Netscape Navigator and Internet Explorer, and later Magellan, Excite, and Alta Vista. This set the stage for the big players of today – Chrome, Firefox, Safari, Bing, et al. More content created more user engagement generating a virtuous cycle where online user networks grew quickly and exponentially. With this growth, the proliferation of new content and links across the emerging World Wide Web created a challenge for how this information would be organized, indexed, and easily discoverable.

In the early 2000s, I met two young innovators, Sergey Brin and Larry Page, as they were just starting Google. Even in those early days, they had a very clear vision about the critical role search would play in our world, given the exponential growth of online information. They were among the visionaries of this era who could see how technologies were evolving and integrating to create entirely new, more convenient ways of doing just about everything, from communicating to accessing information. Their invention tapped into society's pent up need to "search" for information and get fast answers to questions. Sergey, Larry, and I discussed the potential power for internet search to transform how we understand the world around us and the incredible amount of knowledge being poured into the web at the time. I asked them if they thought we could ever search on our phones, so we could carry that capability in our pocket. Their response: "We'll get there." And, of course, we did.

The innovation within this period went beyond search. There were tremendous developments and disruptions across a range of industries, a mad gold rush of sorts, with companies seeking to bring industries online and create new markets enabled by the emerging internet. We experienced the craze of the dot.com boom . . . and its eventual burst. Brands like Pets.com and Boo.com came and went, but many started in that era are deeply entwined in our lives today.

This era changed everything about business as we knew it, even if many of the models wouldn't be proven out until many years later as other technologies advanced. Those that innovated and endured demonstrated the potential the internet had to upend existing industries and create entirely new ones. Just as Sam Walton invented Walmart as a destination where people could buy just about anything, Jeff Bezos wisely mirrored that concept in the online world with Amazon. He started initially with books by taking a bricks-and-mortar offering and digitizing the shopping/purchasing aspects of it, and then delivered those goods to customers. Bezos's longer-term strategy for Amazon was to expand far beyond books to become a better and more contemporary online version of Walmart, where customers could buy just about any good imaginable. Another smart move Bezos made was to articulate to investors that Amazon would lose money for years as he was building out this massive enterprise. This was an unusual and wise move, reflecting one of many of his smart strategies that offer a good lesson in entrepreneurial practices.

Pierre Omidyar founded eBay, a marketplace for people to buy and sell goods online. Where Amazon was providing a service directly to customers, eBay was turning its customers into both buyers and sellers, creating markets for everything from niche collectibles to electronics. Alongside the growth of platforms such as Amazon and eBay – just to name a few of the early internet pioneers – was the capacity to take and receive online payments. This became big business for companies such as PayPal, which digitized payments and enabled companies like eBay to experience rapid growth as buyers and sellers could more easily and reliably transact in this new commercial arena.

Over time, so many now familiar brands emerged, such as Warby Parker and Etsy, to dominate their place in the e-commerce space. Several brick-and-mortar brands, like Walmart, Target, and BestBuy, made successful transitions to become massive online players. And today, the web serves as an online version of just about everything that exists in the brick-and-mortar world, from shopping to education to healthcare.

Wave 6: Social Media and the Cloud Movement

This wave, which fully came into its own in the early 2000s, brought with it a transformative shift to how we connect, share, store, and access information as a society. Social media sought to digitize our offline relationships, bringing them into the internet era, enabling us to connect and communicate in ways that had not occurred in the previous waves. Social platforms ushered in a wave of new companies, enabling us to connect socially and professionally, and share everything imaginable, from personal stories, to professional news and ideas, to photos, videos, and music, etc.

One of the first social networks to launch was LinkedIn, which came on the scene in 2003 as a professional platform, providing a new way to connect, network, find employment and employees, as well as share information and thought leadership ideas. LinkedIn Co-founder Reid Hoffman was a firm believer that computing was evolving to digital destinations comprised of social communities and sought to create a platform for the professional world, an online digital water fountain of sorts, where people could convene, share ideas, and network. Today, this digital destination has grown to include more than 900 million members in 200+ countries.

A year later, Facebook (originally called thefacebook) started on college campuses and became a wildly popular social platform and today remains the largest platform with more than 2 billion users accessing it daily.[5] Reddit launched as a platform to share content and vote on the most popular stories. Twitter, now X, provided a platform to share short bursts of information (originally up to 140 characters, now 280, along with photos or videos). Tumblr gave us the means to share blog posts, and Pinterest marked an explosion of visual images, along with Instagram. Wikipedia was established as an online encyclopedia. Snapchat, TikTok, and so many other brands emerged and continue to define this online landscape of social sharing.[6]

While there have certainly been downsides to social media, as addressed in Part 1, this world-changing wave fueled entirely new ways to communicate, connect, share, and gain access to information and entertainment, both personally and professionally.

Soon after social media was established, the cloud was formed as a central data center that would make it easier and more efficient to access data anytime anywhere. Social media and other online sources created massive quantities of data, requiring a new and better way to store it. While this concept had been around since the 1960s (with time sharing and remote job entry), in the early 2000s it became our primary means to store and access data, as well as provide computer-related services. Amazon and a company called Rackspace were the first to enter this space. Companies like Microsoft, Google, and IBM, along with so many others, saw the opportunity and entered this space with their own flavor of cloud computing. The technology is transformative for both individuals, who don't have to carry all of that data around on their phones and desktops/laptops, as well as for companies as it provides a convenient and cost-effective way to store data and deliver computing services.

This era also saw the emergence of the "sharing economy," community-based online platforms that allowed consumers to provide, acquire, or share goods and services. Who would have thought that one of the largest taxi companies would own no cars and one of the biggest hotel brands would own no rooms? But brands like Uber and Airbnb emerged and quickly dominated their respective market spaces. This was an indicator of how technology was shifting to platforms that provided a place for individuals to share ideas, as well as goods and services in ways that unlock new types of value not possible before. This industry was enabled through big data and algorithms, and the ability for technology platforms to efficiently connect service providers with users. The players that succeeded in this space understood the critical role technology played in creating a competitive advantage and leveraged that to build their service model and brand.

Wave 7: Humanity

As illustrated in Part 1, technology has finally evolved and reached a tipping point in which it can address world problems. Advanced technologies, the immense speed of innovation happening today, and the power of developments in adjacent technologies or disciplines combine, giving us the capability to create novel solutions to a host of complex issues impacting mankind and the planet.

It's not only the individual technologies that are solving problems, but also the combination of technologies that are being integrated to produce powerful solutions. I heard that from Peter Durlach, who explained how the cloud, AI, and advancements in biology/genetic sequencing are coming together to solve issues in healthcare. Deere is using the combination of AI, cloud computing, computer vision, machine learning, and robotics in its solutions that help farmers maximize crop yields. And a post on Flagship Pioneering's website discusses how biology and AI are the "mutually enabling innovation engines of our generation, particularly so when combining forces," and that, "Moving forward, the exponential increase in biological data generation, computing power, and AI model performance will accelerate the pace of discovery and deepen our understanding of biological systems."[7]

Just as the global challenges we face are complex and interrelated (i.e., climate change impacts farmland and our ability to grow enough crops to feed the world, as well as causes many health issues), there's an interrelationship with today's technologies that are being integrated to solve those very issues. Complex problems, complex solutions.

The tremendous opportunity of this era brings with it massive responsibility, and the need to think and behave differently. The interviews and stories shared in this book illustrate how the power of embracing unorthodox thinking, sparking our imagination, asking the right questions, and igniting a passion for problem solving can unite to deliver amazing outcomes. These key components are drivers of breakthroughs in any era and are precisely what's needed today. This is the new model and new mindset companies must embrace.

In the next five chapters, we'll take a deeper look at some of the key technologies that are driving major breakthroughs in this era. We'll explore the brief history of each technology to understand how it has evolved to its current state and capabilities, and look at some of the key innovators along the journey of evolution to understand how their breakthroughs pushed technology to the next phase. Finally, we'll spotlight where the technology is today, look at current applications that hold tremendous potential, and get a glimpse into what may be on the horizon.

The technologies we're focusing on include AI/robotics, chips/sensors, quantum computing, new energy sources, and biological systems. What's amazing about all of these is their ability to be leveraged horizontally to address so many issues, from climate change to healthcare. The integration of today's technologies is delivering a level of scale, velocity, and break-throughs never before possible.

The chapters in this part of the book are designed to offer the C suite information about the tech tools available to them now or in the near future that hold the most potential to transform how their organization impacts the world.

CHAPTER 7

AI Enriching the Human Experience

I'm going to lead this chapter with AI because it's clearly having its moment right now, as generative AI and the chatbot based on the technology, OpenAI's ChatGPT, take the world by storm. The noise around this innovation is almost deafening, with narratives ranging from AI will save the world to the technology will destroy us. It brings to mind the Greek mythological figure called Prometheus, who stole fire from the Gods and gave it to humanity in the form of technology.[1] This figure represents the progress and peril of the advancement of knowledge and technologies, "an avatar of both the liberating power of knowledge and the dangers of technological overreach."[2]

As we look back in history, there have always been versions of those narratives, with naysayers expressing concern about robots taking over the world to techno-optimists envisioning AI solving all kinds of problems. Many articles on AI's history point to the fact that the general concept has been swirling around for considerably longer than many of us may realize, potentially dating back to ancient or medieval times, bringing back another story from ancient Greeks. Stanford University classics scholar, Adrienne Mayor, suggests that the ancient Greek story of Talos, a giant bronze man built by Hephaestus, represents a mythical but artificial being created by the Gods.[3]

For most of us though, AI as we know it was officially born in the 1950s. Since that time, AI has been on a rollercoaster of fits and starts, mostly driven by either funding or the fact that computing power had not evolved enough to fuel its capabilities. As mentioned earlier, Alan Turing, known for cracking the German's Enigma code in WWII, wrote the paper "Computing Machinery and Intelligence," which posed the question, "Can Machines Think?" He developed the Turing Test, aka the imitation game, with the purpose of exploring the presence or absence of intelligence in computers.

The Dartmouth Conference was also held in the 1950s. This was a seminal event that established AI as a field of study and set in motion a path for research and innovation around this technology. During this pivotal conference, scientists and researchers convened to discuss a range of subjects relating to AI, such as natural language processing (NLP), machine learning, algorithms, etc. At the close of the conference, the concept of synthetic intelligence was coined as artificial intelligence. Two brilliant computer scientists and early pioneers in AI led this conference, Marvin Minsky and Jack McCarthy. The Dartmouth Conference had a significant impact on the trajectory of artificial intelligence, as it helped establish this technology as a field of study and encouraged innovation in this realm.

Following the conference and through the mid 1970s, AI had a boom period. For example, in 1958, McCarthy and colleagues developed the LISP AI programming language, which is one of the oldest programming languages and is still in use today. The conference also precipitated research labs in AI at major universities and research institutions such as MIT, Stanford, and Carnegie Mellon.[4]

Optimism around AI was extremely high during this timeframe of the 1950s-1970s, along with expectations of what it could deliver in the near term. And while some innovations were beginning to prove this out, computing technology was not yet powerful enough to deliver on those expectations. Computers simply didn't have the storage or processing power necessary to bring AI visions to fruition. These obstacles led to a dark period for AI, as interest, funding, and research dried up for at least a decade.

This led to the winter of AI in the late 1970s and 1980s. There were, however, some areas of progress during this time. The most significant was the development and eventual adoption of expert systems, which helped to thaw AI's winter in the late 1980s. These systems emerged as the "new thing" and it was estimated that a full two thirds of the Fortune 500 companies used them daily.[5] Expert systems demonstrated AI's capabilities in delivering real world, practical applications in business and other areas. Still in use today, expert systems contain a database of expert knowledge to offer advice or aid in decision-making, ultimately simulating the judgment of behavior of a human being. However, they also had inherent limitations around processing unstructured data like natural language or images. This led to the leveraging of technologies such as natural language processing, which uses AI to enable computers to understand natural language (unstructured data) as humans do, as well as computer vision technology, which allows computers to identify and understand images (objects and people).[6]

In the 1990s and 2000s, advancements in AI started to deliver on many of the initial goals for this technology. Dragon Systems speech recognition software came to market, underscoring how AI could be used to interpret spoken language. These breakthroughs happened as computing power increased, finally enabling leaps in AI capabilities.

In the early 2000s, the emergence of big data helped propel AI to the next level. While previous advancements had been made in the areas of NLP and computer vision technology, they were limited by the quantity of available data. But now big data removed those obstacles, giving access to huge quantities of data that came from sensors, company operations, social media, and a wide range of other public and private sources, all of which fed and trained machine learning algorithms. Data storage and processing technologies also advanced, fueling the use of big data, as well as the development of new algorithms and deep learning that enabled accurate predictions.[6] These advancements led to widespread application adoption across a variety of industries, including technology, banking, marketing, and entertainment.

The 2010s brought a host of AI breakthroughs, many of which we use every day. For example, Apple introduced the virtual assistant Siri, Facebook developed DeepFace facial recognition, Google introduced technology to identify relationships between words (Word2Vec) to ultimately detect synonyms, and Uber started its self-driving car pilot program. Microsoft introduced the Turing Natural Language Generation generative language model, and Open AI released GPT, which paved the way for future LLMs and generative AI interfaces, including ChatGPT.[7]

Generative AI Finally Reaching the Promised Land

This brings us to today, clearly an unprecedented point in AI's history. Even before the launch of ChatGPT, there were other impressive advances in this decade, most notably the University of Oxford's development of an AI test to quickly ID COVID in the ER. However, ChatGPT is undoubtedly transformative, called by many the biggest disruptive technology of the century. It has captured the attention and imaginations of just about every audience in the world – the general public, business sector, governments, the medical and education communities, among so many others. This is definitely another one of those massive disruptive moments in history – like when the internet was born – when a technology has the potential to change the trajectory of everything it touches.

The important perspective to have about this current phenomenon is that the most recent breakthroughs in AI are the result of decades and decades of evolving technology, of innovations like machine learning and neural networks that have been built upon by many generations of innovators. The technology just finally reached a tipping point that enabled it to more fully deliver on the promise of AI. A really interesting fact is that when OpenAI released ChatGPT, it was in no way expecting it to be massively disruptive in any way. In fact, many company scientists say they were completely surprised by its impact. This was in large part due to the fact that the technology is simply an updated version of *GPT-3.5, which OpenAI released months before ChatGPT.* It was viewed internally as a "research preview," a "more polished version" of two-year-old technology and the goal was to work through some potential flaws by getting public feedback.[8] Clearly the feedback OpenAI received was swift and unprecedented. When OpenAI released ChatGPT in November 2022, it rocketed to 1 million users in just 5 days.[9] Unfathomable.

To provide a quick definition of generative AI, it is a form of artificial intelligence that uses models or algorithms to produce a variety of new content, including text, images/visuals, videos, music, or voices from the data it is trained on. It was first invented in the 1960s by Joseph Weizenbaum. ChatGPT, which is based on generative AI, offers breakthroughs in writing essays, emails, and poems, for example, in creating images, explaining computer code, translating languages, and even in telling jokes. Among the many reasons this technology has become a technology phenomenon is that it's incredibly easy to use and generates human-like results fast.

ChatGPT, along with a plethora of other AI technologies, is being used across just about every industry imaginable, including healthcare, pharmaceuticals, finance, customer service, marketing/advertising, education, automotive, and so many others. When used in the right way and in the right applications, the technology holds the power to augment humans and enhance what we do, serving as a co-pilot – as Microsoft calls it – making our jobs and our lives easier and delivering breakthroughs in critical areas like medicine and energy efficiency.

While there are many promising outcomes happening now or on the horizon across these industries, there are naturally concerns ranging from unemployment to the technology taking over the world. These underscore the critical point that this latest generation of AI presents the world with both tremendous opportunity and tremendous responsibility. While AI holds so much promise in so many areas, there is also significant fear and uncertainty. While this is a complex equation, what's certain is that we need to proceed with a combination of vigilance to ensure safe and responsible use of the technology and vigor around pursuing innovations that can help humanity. A deeper look at how to put this technology on a path of good is explored in Chapter 16.

However, for now, I'll quote Deloitte's Human Centered Approach to AI report, which I think nicely summarizes the mindset and approach we should adopt regarding this technology:

> *"A human approach to AI is necessary to enable the kind of customer and workforce experiences that respect our humanity, sustain a level of empathy, and earn a measure of trust. Respect for these essential elements of being human is essential to realize positive applications – and positive outcomes – of AI in experience."*
> — Amelia Dunlop, chief experience officer, Deloitte Digital[10]

Leaping Forward with AI

When I look at AI applications available now, in the works, or in the not-too-distant future, I have found amazing potential for tremendous breakthroughs in so many realms, from improving business efficiency to delivering climate change solutions to advancing healthcare to enhancing education. I've cited many examples in earlier chapters, and this one includes others that underscore this point. These just scratch the surface of what is underway in this realm, but it gives a sense of the magnitude of potential.

Impacting Education

While there are concerns that ChatGPT could replace people in their jobs and increase unemployment, it is also believed that this technology can help people with less education gain more skills so they can better compete in the marketplace. Many also see benefits the technology can deliver in the world of education. Bill Gates is among them, seeing tremendous potential in ChatGPT to help close the education gap for millions of students. In Gates's "Unconfuse Me" podcast featuring Khan Academy CEO Sal Khan, he noted how AI chatbots could provide feedback on essays and help with how to write more clearly and with better reasoning. It also helps teachers "imagine new lesson plans and support students with personalized education."[11]

I had the pleasure of speaking with several executives in Deloitte Consulting's Higher Education practice, who also contribute to the firm's Future of Work Institute, which focuses on elevating the current and future workforce with the human-centered skills needed to thrive in an era of continuous change. I asked them for their perspective on how AI is currently impacting higher ed and how it will evolve this area in the future.

"We're talking to a lot of different universities across the globe about the power of AI and the impact this technology will have," said Tamara Askew, principal at Deloitte who leads Deloitte's AI in Higher Education capability. "There are so many ideas about how we can use this technology, and we're already starting to see the impact of AI on our education system. There are learning/tutorial tools like Khanmigo (Khan Academy's AI powered tutor for students/assistant for teachers), as well as tools for grading, writing, and interactive learning. They're starting to be integrated into Learning Management System environments, and that's going to end up being just table stakes," she added.

Tamara emphasized that the more critical element involves the shift in how higher education prepares students for success in the workforce, and the role AI can play in that important change.

"I think the bigger piece involves answering questions like how do we keep the students from losing their ability to think creatively, to get them to think outside of the box and be adaptable?" said Tamara. "Those types of attributes are going to be tantamount to success in the future. We're not relying on AI to do everything for us. We're relying on humans, and AI is a powerful tool that can really help people on that journey. So, we need to have those creative skills to get the most out of these tools, and to really maximize our interactions with these tools."

Roy Mathew, national practice leader for Deloitte's Higher Education practice, gave a perfect example of how universities can meld today's tools with students' creative skills. "A professor at a top research university in the US asked students to write an essay using ChatGPT. When they arrived in class, the professor then instructed students to apply their creativity and imagination to make the essay better. This exemplifies how human skills can be applied to enhance what an algorithm creates."

Cole Clark, managing director in Deloitte's Higher Education sector at Deloitte Services, addressed another critical role AI can play in terms of leveling the playing field around skill development for lower income individuals.

"I think a lot of low income individuals lack a lot of the basic skills necessary to achieve academic success," Cole said. "Schools such as Southern New Hampshire University, Western Governors University, Grand Canyon University, Liberty University, and University of Maryland have been using AI and machine learning for as long as a decade to assist students with tutoring, coaching, and tailored interventions. As the technologies have evolved, these schools use it in more meaningful ways. These innovations augment regular instructions and provide academic support at scale because, as an example, Western Governors University has 140,000 students to support. It's a pretty daunting task to have a human involved in the interventions necessary to keep all of those people on track, so these technologies are really critical in enabling the school to deliver that type of support at scale."

Transforming Science

In the realm of science, AI's potential is also enormous. Eric Schmidt (former CEO of Google) in a recent LinkedIn post noted a couple of great examples of how this technology is transforming "how science gets done." For example, scientists at McMaster and MIT are using an AI model to ID an antibiotic for what the World Health Organization is calling "the world's most dangerous antibiotic-resistant bacteria for hospital patients." The post also mentions how a Google DeepMind model can control plasma in nuclear fusion reactions to help make the clean energy revolution more of a reality.[12] In this post, he also emphasizes the need for government regulations that minimize risks, for large datasets that will help scientists move forward on innovations and for investments in projects that deliver "high social returns."[12]

Advancing Medicine

As mentioned throughout the book, AI is becoming widely regarded as a key technology ingredient in solutions that will help improve our health. For example, it is being used to help with early diagnosis of diseases, as well as in the development of breakthroughs in biotech involving cell and gene therapeutics. Biotech labs throughout the world are applying machine learning and AI to break through gene therapy roadblocks. These technologies can help reduce time and money in the development of gene therapy products and techniques, such as those done with CRISPR gene editing. They deliver on the promise of precision medicine or personalized medicine, which optimize the outcomes of therapy by tailoring them to people's genes or molecular profiles. Flagship Pioneering has several innovative companies leveraging AI and digital biotech work to deliver breakthroughs, including Valo Health, which is working to reduce the time and cost of discovering a novel drug candidate.[13]

The podcast, *Possible*, hosted by Reid Hoffman and Aria Finger, featured Siddhartha Mukherjee, a cancer physician, researcher, and author, who is an expert on the forefront of medical discoveries around diseases like cancer. He discussed exciting possibilities involving AI and the early detection of cancer.

"So, can we use new technologies, potentially generative algorithms, to figure out people who are at higher risk? Do we screen them differently? Do we find early cancers? Does that help? Big, big, big questions will be answered in the next decade or so. In the field of cancer treatment . . . the exciting thing [is] . . . not just the immune system, but the body's entire natural physiology to act against cancer. That ranges from new medicines that unleash or reactivate the immune system to recognize cancer CAR T cells . . . the use of diets in combination with drug therapies to potentially attack cancer cells . . . and the use of new technologies . . . that have been fast forwarded by AI to find new medicines, new drugs against cancer. And so all of that . . . in the arena of cancer treatment, is where there's a lot of exciting stuff going on."[14]

Dhruv Suyamprakasam, founder and CEO of virtual healthcare company iCliniq, extols the virtues of ChatGPT to reduce the administrative burden in healthcare, describing AI as an "ally" for physicians. He points to the physician shortage (according to the Association of American Medical Colleges, the US will face shortages of 37,800 to 124,000 physicians across all specialties and subspecialties within the next decade) and physician burnout from administrative work.[15] This combination is threatening our healthcare systems. Suyamprakasam believes AI can be leveraged to help on a variety of levels. The technology can assist physicians in patient education, be used for medical research to summarize findings, and help physicians summarize visits with patients, as noted in Chapter 4. These are just a few of the many potential applications within the healthcare space that may transform how diseases are treated, how healthcare is administered, and how health outcomes can be improved.

Fueling Sustainability

Forrester Research's report, "Generative AI will Supercharge the Green Market Revolution," points to the "immense potential" of this technology in sustainability efforts. For one, generative AI can automate several processes, such as automating a "carbon footprint calculation, monitor emissions in real time, and generate timely recommendations, including what-if scenarios and even net-zero pathways."[16]

The report notes that AI holds the promise to accelerate research on new approaches for sustainability. This is already happening in agriculture. This is exemplified in Deere's 2017 acquisition of Blue River Technology and its integrated computer vision and machine learning technology. These offerings enabled Deere to deliver precision agriculture and the ability to farm sustainably, helping farmers reduce the use of herbicides by spraying only where weeds are present.

AI is being applied to help with other sustainable efforts as well. For example, smart sensors and AI can reduce water consumption by 40+ percent.[16] Generative AI is also being used in the design and manufacturing of sustainability products by providing teams with rapid prototypes that enable them to simulate offerings quickly and expedite production and testing. All of this holds the promise to accelerate the development of solutions to help mitigate climate change.

I spoke with Alan Trefler, founder and CEO of Pegasystems, who has a long history with AI, beginning when he attended Dartmouth in the 1970s and was involved with projects that taught computers to play chess. He shared his perspective on the enormous impact AI is having in multiple arenas.

"There's been tremendous change in the last decade," he said. "If you look at what's going on in agriculture, there is micro-planting that really optimizes every square meter of the field, which is really quite remarkable. In pharmaceuticals, AI is applied to figure out how proteins fold and improve the ability to create new medications. And in healthcare, AI can help keep track of patients or do a better job of diagnosis by pairing radiologists with machine learning and machine algorithms. In software development, there are now tools that go way beyond simply churning out code to helping unlock innovation and creativity in the application development process itself. And, those are just the beginning. All of those applications are going to get radically more extreme in terms of the benefits we see from them."

Entire books could be written about just one of these examples, but these samplings highlight the tremendous work underway across every field imaginable in which AI accelerates outcomes, augments our work, and serves as a "co-pilot" to enhance our ability to address problems and deliver leap forward solutions.

Robotics Enhancing Humanity

While robotics and AI are related, they are essentially two separate fields. They overlap in that some robots incorporate AI as the brain that instructs them on how to operate. These technologies share the similarity of being human-like or performing human-like tasks. Robotics are physical technologies that are programmed to carry out many functions humans would normally do. For example, they can perform menial, repetitive tasks (like the robotic arm in an assembly line) or more complex, high-level tasks that augment people's capabilities (like the robotics surgical system). AI involves computer programs/systems that emulate the human brain and can learn, solve problems, and carry out functions that typically require human intelligence.[17] The technology is often used in robots that perform more complex tasks.

The origin of the word robot comes from a Czech word "robota," which essentially means forced labor.[18] This brings me to the thinking of two people I've admired in my life. One was a mentor I've referenced several times in this book, Michael Dertouzos, the MIT professor who served as director of the MIT Lab for Computer Science. As mentioned earlier in this book, he said to me many times that technology exists to serve us; to be our slave. The other is my most admired philosopher, Aristotle, who believed the human condition was largely dependent on what machines can and cannot do and that if machines could do more for us, we would be freer.[19] This thinking is the driver behind innovation in both the realms of robotics and of AI.

As we look back in the history of robots, this technology actually dates back to ancient civilization, but modern-day robots began during the industrial revolution. During the early twentieth century, the engineering capability was developed to create machines that could be powered with small motors and the first human-like machine, a humanoid, was developed.[20] The first applications of robots were in factories, which performed manufacturing functions that automated tasks humans were doing, creating less work.

The first digitally operated robot, called Unimate, was invented in 1954. This hydraulic arm, developed to lift heavy loads, is considered to represent the foundation of the modern robotics industry.[20] Unimate worked on a General Motors assembly line in New Jersey. Over the next two decades, more advanced robotic arms were developed that incorporated cameras and/or sensors. In 1966, Stanford Research developed the grandfather of self-driving cars and clones, which it called Shakey. This was the world's first mobile intelligent robot that combined AI, computer vision, navigation, and NLP.[21]

The 1990s also brought several advancements in the field of robotics. In 1995, da Vinci Surgical Systems was invented, bringing robotics into the operating room to help augment surgeons' capabilities and deliver better patient outcomes. Kismet was also developed, the first robot with "social" features such as the ability to react to our emotions and express its own. The RoboTuna was also built by a doctoral student at MIT in 1996 to study how fish swim in the water.[22]

In 1997, the world witnessed the famous chess game in which world champion and grandmaster Garry Kasparov was defeated by IBM's Deep Blue chess playing program. This major milestone gave us a glimpse into the tremendous capabilities of this technology. The Sojourner was also in operation that same year, a small robot performing tasks on the surface of Mars as part of the Mars Pathfinder mission. It was shut down after only 83 days in operation.[22] And in the early 2000s, another robot was put into orbit, which was an arm used by the space shuttle. Robots were invited into our homes in 2002 with the invention of Roomba®, robotic vacuums developed by iRobot.[22]

Today, the field of robotics is growing exponentially, as robots are put to use across multiple industries and applications, from manufacturing to military to medicine. In some cases, such as in manufacturing, robots perform menial and repetitive tasks that free up people to do higher level and more creative jobs. In medicine, they augment a surgeon's capabilities for better patient outcomes. Robotics are also delivering amazing outcomes in prosthetics, using neural networks that enable people to move the limb and even feel through the protheses.[23]

One of the most moving stories in my lifetime around this technology was when it enabled the professional dancer, Adrianne Haslet-Davis, who sadly had part of her left leg amputated following the 2013 Boston Marathon bombing, to dance again. MIT professor Hugh Herr and his Biomechatronics Group at the MIT Media Lab built an amazing bionic ankle prosthesis for Adrianne, which remarkably gave her the ability to dance again. At the end of Herr's TED Talk, Adrianne danced her first performance since the accident. It was the most inspiring and emotional TED Talk I've ever seen. I encourage you to Google it and watch the video. It will not only move you emotionally, but also bring to life the amazing things this form of technology is doing for humanity.

Robots are in use today across a broad range of menial and sophisticated tasks. For example, they are used in kitchens for food preparation, but also play an important role in renewable energy, reducing energy consumption and waste. Robots also have long been used by the military, performing everything from surveillance to warfare activities.

One fascinating example of how robots are helping the planet is a pilot project between ABB Robotics and the non-profit organization Junglekeepers, which is focused on protecting the Amazon rainforest and reversing its mass deforestation. ABB's cobot YuMi automates seed planting in a jungle laboratory, expediting this time-intensive task, making it more efficient and scalable. The effort leverages ABB RobotStudio® Cloud technology, in which experts "simulate, refine, and deploy robotic programming in real-time from 12,000 kms (or nearly 7500 miles) away in Sweden."[24]

"This pilot project was important to not only prove out the concept, but also to see how the machinery dealt with the climate, where it is 98–99% humidity and 95 degrees Fahrenheit, essentially an extremely difficult environment in which to operate," said Marc Mustard, ABB's global head of content and brand. "We were delighted to learn that the YuMi cobot was capable of running for several hours a day, every day without any issues in that environment. The results were great, as we managed to accomplish in around two hours what would normally take a week of just solid manual labor of planting pots. We're working with them now to see how we can help in the future."

The promise of what robots can deliver in medicine is another phenomenal area. For example, microrobots may be used to travel through blood vessels and deliver therapies like radiation or a medication to a specific site. Robotic endoscopic capsules can be swallowed to monitor the digestive system, gather data, and send diagnostic information to healthcare providers. Overworked nurses can get some relief from robotic nurses that can do tasks like digital entries and drawing blood. There's even hope that medical robotics can replace antibiotics by using "nanorobots with receptors to which bacteria adhere and can be used to attract bacteria in the blood stream or in sites of local infection."[25] Advancements in robotics will continue to evolve, as robots are developed with greater cognitive capabilities by leveraging sensor technology, machine learning, and AI.[26]

Helen Greiner, who co-founded and served as president and chairman of iRobot, the company that invented the Roomba® vacuuming robot, shared with me her life-long fascination with robots, as well as her views on the important role robots play in our world.

"I saw *Star Wars* when I was around nine and fell in love with R2D2. He's been my muse. He saved the universe and was so much more than a machine. Since then, I always wanted to build things that are more than machines. And at the end of the day, they kind of come to life, right? We saw that with Roomba. When people bought them, they'd buy them as appliances, but when they get them home, they're like, oh, this is like a pet. So, they start naming them and formed a bond with them. One study showed that 66% of people actually named them."

I asked Helen for her perspective on the fear concerning AI and how she thinks about the latest innovations in AI and robotics. "Unlike many people in the world, I don't worry about what robots can do, I worry about what they can't do. There are so many things robots should be doing and sometimes the technology isn't there yet. But I think it's coming and it's coming very quickly, which is why it's such a wonderful space. There are just so many jobs that aren't getting done because they're not able to be done yet with robots. Just think about all of the mundane tasks you do around the house – folding laundry, putting the dishes away. These things take time that people could be spending with their kids, investing in their career, or just doing a favorite hobby like gardening."

Rather than worrying about AI and robots taking over the world, Helen expressed her concerns around more practical and pragmatic matters that should be addressed. "I think focusing on things like safety around robotics is hugely important. Take for example the drones we use. They could drop something on someone's head and hurt them. And as the robots get bigger and are able to do more things in the world, safety will be even more paramount. Just think about robotic cars driving around. I think we must focus on doing everything we can to make sure these inventions are as safe as possible."

Helen's wise words underscore the essence of what the world struggles now with technology and generative AI specifically. As noted, this breakthrough has created yet another watershed moment in history in which technology is transforming just about every aspect of our world. As this chapter illustrates, the potential for this technology to deliver so much good is massive. Moreover, as AI is integrated with other technologies, it fuels the ability of our innovations to solve many problems that were previously unsolvable. However, this technology has also raised key concerns and complex questions, as the world seeks ways to deliver on the concept of responsible innovation to ensure this technology is used to benefit humanity vs. working against it. You'll read more about efforts underway in this realm – and what your company can do to establish the right balance of vigilance and vigor around this technology – in Chapter 16.

CHAPTER 8

Chips and Sensors Everywhere

Silicon has been described as "the humble mineral that transformed the world."[1] This abundant natural substance is at the heart of today's semiconductor chips, which power everything imaginable in our world, from smartphones and MRI scanners to internet data centers, robots, and safety features on our vehicles. The story of chips is one of constant innovation and disruption. Over the years, chips have continued to shrink in size while growing exponentially more powerful. The chips we use today operate like miniature tech superheroes that can execute literally billions of instructions per second.[1]

While it's hard to imagine a time without these tiny powerhouses, let's take a quick look back at the evolution of this technology. Prior to chips, computers were powered by glass vacuum tubes, copper wires, and other electrical components. They were huge, incredibly slow, and required massive amounts of energy to operate. ENIAC, which was launched in 1946, was the world's first general purpose computer comprised of those elements. It included 18,000 vacuum tubes, miles of copper wire, and required 150,000 watts of power to operate.[2]

But in 1947, a breakthrough at Bell Labs changed all of that with the invention of the transistor, a far better mouse trap for the flow of electricity because it moved through solid material. This enabled the use of smaller circuits that could be turned on and off and use less energy. This discovery was developed by two researchers under the guidance of William Shockley and was the foundation for the invention of the silicon transistor in 1954.[2]

Shockley knew he was onto something and recognized this transistor would transform the world of computing. He started his own company and enlisted Robert Noyce, a physicist from MIT, and Gordon Moore, a chemist from Caltech.[2] Within that year (1957), several engineers from the company left to start Fairchild Semiconductors, which is widely considered to be the first Silicon Valley start-up. There, the innovation engine churned, as breakthroughs enabled integrated circuits to get smaller and smaller, while increasingly more powerful. The first had a single transistor that could perform one logic function and by 1968, the company's transistors on its integrated circuits numbered more than 1000. It has been called the "greatest example of economies of scale in history."[2]

The now famous Moore's law was born, in which he predicted that the number of components on a chip would double every two years. Moore knew the critical role chips would play in our world, likening them to the "sun" of our solar system. For nearly 60 years, Moore's law proved correct, but many are now predicting its demise.

Other familiar brands entered this market, including Texas Instruments, founded in 1951, which evolved to become a pre-eminent semiconductor manufacturer. Another major pioneer in the semiconductor space was National Semiconductor, which was founded in 1959 and was acquired by TI in 2011. It was known for power management chips and easy-to-use analog integrated circuits.

As the industry continued to grow at a healthy clip, it fueled Fairchild's expansion, which had 30,000 employees nearly 10 years after its founding.[2] At that time, 95% of its chips were used for military and space applications.[3] In an effort to create a more nimble organization that could keep pace with this industry, Moore and Noyce left to establish their own start-up, called Integrated Electronics, later shortened to Intel. There, the first CPU (central processing unit) was invented, a game changer that was essentially an entire computer on a chip. Intel launched its now famous 4004 chip in 1971, which changed the trajectory of computing and technology. As Ted Hoff, who invented the chip, said, Intel "democratized the computer."

Moore's law continued to prevail, as chips continued to get faster and smaller, eventually making computers more affordable, not just for office use, but for home/personal use as well. This marked the beginning of the PC era and Intel's dominance in the chip space. This paved the market for dominant players like IBM, which flooded Intel with orders. Microsoft launched to address the software side of this emerging industry and Intel was *the* standard for Windows-operated PCs. This time period was all about the race to amp up chips' power and increase the number of steps they could perform per second.

Parallel processing came into play, as multiple CPUs were put to work inside computers, enabling many tasks to be performed at once. As the industry continued to evolve, specialized chips emerged, which are chips designed to handle very specific types of applications. Intel's "off the shelf" chip model did not meet requirements for specific applications, and many companies now have internal chip design teams who produce this technology for their specific needs, such as running their massive data centers. Companies like Amazon and Microsoft have these, along with Google and Tesla, which have designed chips suited to specific needs within their organizations.

Eventually, the cost of continuing to further miniaturize transistors was a burden on chip manufacturers and the industry consolidated. As the PC era was winding down, the smartphone market emerged. In a major misstep, Intel passed on the opportunity to produce Apple's iPhone chips, failing to recognize the massive opportunity emerging. Like so many innovations before it, smartphones were the next disruptive innovation that would dominate the market.

Powerhouses in the Chip Ecosystem

Many companies recognized this enormous opportunity. Samsung was the first to move in, developing the chip for the first iPhone. Taiwan Semiconductor Manufacturing Company (TSMC) also capitalized on this burgeoning market and became a manufacturer of chips designed by customers. Today, TSMC and Samsung manufacture the vast majority of semiconductor chips, with more than 61% and 11% market share, respectively.[4] Intel continues to manufacture chips in the US.

ARM is another major force in this space, designing chips with less power that were optimized for use in mobile phones. The company led this ecosystem involving TSMC, Samsung, Qualcomm, MediaTek, and others, operating almost like the sun within the cellular solar system. Its power efficient CPUs fuel smart, AI-capable devices such as smartphones, as well as chips used in vehicles and data centers. The company was also among the first to recognize and capitalize on the opportunity to supply chips for the Internet of Things.[5]

A Dutch company called ASML has also played a critical role in the industry. As a lithography equipment maker, the company enables the mass production of semiconductor chips used by every major chip company. Its innovative technology enables chipmakers to produce products that are faster and more powerful and energy efficient. Today, ASML builds 100% of the world's extreme ultraviolet lithography machines, without which cutting-edge chips would be impossible to make.[6]

There are a number of other powerhouse brands leading the semiconductor industry. Qualcomm is an innovator in wireless and mobile communications systems that has shaped the evolution of smartphones and contributed to technologies such as 5G. It designs semiconductors, which are then manufactured by companies like Samsung and TSMC. In the book *Chip Wars*, author Chris Miller explains, "Companies like Qualcomm might not have survived if they'd had to invest billions of dollars each year building factories. They're wizards at cramming data into the radio-wave spectrum and devising ever-more-clever chips to decode the meaning of these signals. . . . It was a good thing they didn't have to try to be semiconductor manufacturing experts, too."[7]

A massively dominant force in this space is NVIDIA, founded in 1993 and currently valued at more than $16 billion. An innovator in computer graphics and AI technology, the company invented the GPU (graphics processing unit), which ignited the PC gaming market, redefined computer graphics, and fueled AI, playing a key role in the development of the metaverse. This darling of the semiconductor industry develops some of the world's most advanced chips, systems, and software for AI, which is transforming industries worth trillions of dollars, from gaming to healthcare to transportation to applications that are transforming society.[8]

RISC-V Democratizing Innovation

Another player that is helping to level the playing field with chip technology is RISC-V International. The company is a global non-profit that's the home of the RISC-V open-source instruction set architecture (ISA), specifications and stakeholder community. The RISC-V open architecture enables design freedom and open collaboration, reducing costs of innovation and allowing the community to share technical investments.

Company CEO Calista Redmond likened the story of RISC-V to that of the early days of Linux, the open source, community-developed operating system. "In the early days of Linux, there was a common concern, which was that every piece of hardware had to come with a licensed piece of software. That was frustrating to folks in the market who wanted freedom of choice and didn't want a vendor lock-in. RISC-V is similar to that, providing an open architecture that offers choice and design freedom. Even though there are 50 architectures, only two brands own about 99+% of the market, which were ARM and Intel."

Calista explained that RISC-V's design freedom opens doors for new communities and countries to get into the game. "RISC-V has completely leveled the playing field. It's the most open architecture for anyone to engage on and there are more design houses on RISC-V now than any other architecture in history. So many regions and countries are viewing RISC-V as a way to bring forward their digital economy and participate in the game." Calista added that entire countries like Pakistan got 3,000 people together and launched RISC-V as its national architecture, and India is embracing it as well.

Micron Technology is another major brand in this space, which specializes in memory solutions for vehicles, servers, and computers. Apple is one of its largest customers. Another player is Analog Devices, which does data conversion, signal processing, and power management technology, providing solutions for digitized factories, mobility, healthcare, climate change, and to connect people.

Chips Powering Today's World

As this story underscores, semiconductor technology is another great story of evolution. Today's chips are like nano-sized, turbo-charged versions of the original invented back in the late 1950s. They now come packed with billions of transistors, capable of executing billions of instructions per second. The smallest transistors on the market are now hitting the 3 nanometer mark, a length equivalent to 15 silicon atoms.[9] And, while chips continue to get smaller and more powerful, they are produced at a scale that's almost unfathomable. I'll quote Chris Miller here again as he put it best: "Last year, the chip industry produced more transistors than the combined quantity of all goods produced by all other companies, in all other industries, in all human history. Nothing else comes close."[10] Wow.

Without question, this tiny technology is the backbone of our digital world – the brains powering just about every aspect of our lives. Chips are used in PCs, data centers, smartphones, as well as in routers and switches that form the backbone of the internet. They enable the plethora of IoT devices, from wearables to smart appliances like washing machines and dishwashers. They also allow for the collection, storage, and monetization of data, which enables companies like Google, Facebook, Uber, and Airbnb to exist. Our vehicles are loaded with chips to provide safety and convenience features. The government has long used them in military systems. Trains, medical systems, banking ATMs, LED bulbs, and digital cameras are also all powered by chips. This list just scratches the surface, but it gives a sense of how ubiquitous this technology is in our world.

While we rely on chips for all things electronic/digital, there are naturally challenges that must be addressed. One is that while the silicon industry has enabled the growth of data on everything and everyone, it also comes with the risk of potential hacks. This will be the next level of government regulation to ensure the right data gets *only* to the right person.

Another major challenge in the semiconductor industry that emerged during the pandemic was the supply chain issue. Initially, this problem created massive chip shortages, which had a tremendous impact on the automotive, medical device, and electronics industries, among so many others. This issue later evolved to the flip side when the industry ended up with a glut of chips (memory chips in particular), as production ramped up only to be met by a slowed demand from a weakened economy.

In spite of these issues, the semiconductor industry continues to expand, with experts estimating it will be valued at more than $1 trillion by 2029. The growth will largely come from consumer electronics, as the world continues to embrace phones, wearables, and other devices. Other growth areas come from AI, the Internet of Things, and machine learning.[11]

Fueling Tech for Good Efforts

Chips play a massive role in tech for good efforts. For example, they are central to the decarbonization and clean energy movement, as they improve energy efficiency and are critical to renewable energy sources. For example, chips are transforming how energy is used, managed, and produced. They are used in power management systems and smart electrical grids. Chips also power many of our smart appliances that help reduce energy consumption. They are also a key component in many renewable energy sources such as wind turbines, solar farms, and other forms of clean energy. This helps reduce the carbon footprint by minimizing the greenhouse gases from fossil fuels. They are also central to electric vehicles.

However, while chips can help fight the battle of climate change, manufacturing them is also a big contributor to the problem. Semiconductor manufacturing leaves behind a massive carbon footprint, with some estimates reporting that it contributes as much as 31% of global greenhouse gas emissions.[12] It also requires huge quantities of energy and water, and creates hazardous waste. The issue is well known and documented, often called the dirty little secret of the industry. As such, manufacturers like TSMC are pledging to reach net zero emissions in the future. That's a concern to stay vigilant on.

Advancing Healthcare

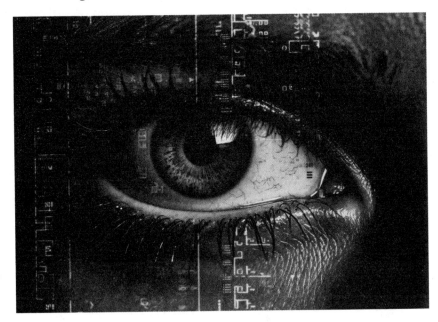

Chips are also powering amazing advances in healthcare through medical devices. For example, they are used in wearables in combination with sensors, which can monitor things like heart rate, temperature, blood pressure, and brain wave activity. The data collected can be sent directly to healthcare providers so they can monitor patients and assist with diagnosis and make more informed decisions about treatment. Chips are also used in implants such as pacemakers and insulin pumps to manage a variety of medical conditions. They are also integral to a variety of diagnostic devices to detect and diagnose a variety of health conditions.[18] Many are small enough to be used in remote locations where traditional medical equipment may be scarce. They are also central to imaging systems like X-rays and MRIs, improving accuracy for better diagnosis.[13] Chips are also used in customized drug delivery systems, which are customizable and programmed to release drugs in a specific dosage at a specific time to optimize outcomes and minimize side effects.[14]

Calista Redmond, CEO of RISC-V International, spoke to the amazing advances technologies like RISC-V can amplify in the world. "A technology like RISC-V can help realize the promise of so many important things – like accessing a remote doctor or specialist who has the expertise to treat a condition, opening doors to education for kids and adults that might not otherwise have that opportunity, helping farmers improve their methods, and enabling remote workforces to exist. These are just a few of the societal benefits this technology can deliver. These types of positive impacts really light up our truth and drive our pursuits."

Sensors, Life's Detectors at Work

Sensors are another tiny invention that brings big breakthroughs across just about every aspect of our lives, automating everything from turning on a light when you walk into a room, to monitoring your steps on your cell phone, to enabling smart cities to efficiently manage energy consumption. Although the first sensor dates back to the 1800s and was used to measure temperature in a specific type of thermostat, this is yet another technology that has taken the world by storm as of late.

Sensors essentially measure a change or event and transform that information electronically so it can be read and computed. There are sensors that monitor temperature, proximity, pressure, water quality, smoke, infrared, motion, humidity, images, among other elements. In our lives, this helps us monitor everything from our heartrate, blood pressure, temperature, oxygen saturation, respiration rate, and other bodily functions.

Today, sensors are literally everywhere you look. Our cars are loaded with them to detect everything from when the windshield wipers should turn on, to whether or not we're driving too close to another vehicle, as well as monitor functions in the vehicle from the coolant system to the oil pressure to speed. Other forms of transportation, from buses to trains to airplanes, are also loaded with sensors. In planes, they measure air pressure, speed, tilt, among other things.

Our connected computing devices like smartphones use them to track our steps, monitor the direction we're moving in, assess our positioning (like a compass), alter the phone's brightness, and so much more. They are in smoke and carbon monoxide detectors, in our appliances like dishwashers, washing machines, and refrigerators. Energy devices and medical equipment also incorporate these helpful detectors.

Some of the explosive growth behind the proliferation of sensors came as the Internet of Things became the internet of *everything*. Like chips, sensors and software are central to that capability, powering their capability to monitor and detect changes. Think about how wearables work. They can detect a change in your heartrate, body temperature, calorie intake, step count, sleep quality, etc. They are also at the heart of connected medical devices. One example is a subcutaneous system that monitors and records glucose levels in diabetic patients; another is a pacemaker for people with irregular heartbeats. Ventilators, catheters, dialysis machines, and surgical equipment also use sensors.

As the world evolves to "smart" everything – appliances, cities, homes, grids – sensors are the brains enabling this. IoT sensors are at the heart of this, helping to reduce energy consumption, generate renewable energy, and measure carbon consumption and waste. Smart agriculture, as we addressed with the Deere story, is another example of how sensors can help deliver sustainability and help farmers maximize their yields cost effectively.

While chips and sensors are among the smallest disruptive forces in our world, these tiny powerhouses are at the heart of so many innovations today. Not only do they bring conveniences in how we live, help us stay safe, offer efficiencies in manufacturing, they also deliver on tech for good efforts in climate change, medicine, and feeding the world. I'm excited to see how these technologies continue to evolve and become infused into our daily lives to enhance how we live, work, and play.

CHAPTER 9

The Promise of Quantum Computing

Like other futuristic technologies – such as flying cars – quantum computing has been touted to have a major transformative impact on our world when it arrives. Leaders in the pharmaceutical industry are optimistic that quantum computing may accelerate by years the process of discovering new drug compounds, delivering potential medical breakthroughs that could positively impact millions of lives. Climate scientists and meteorologists see potential in quantum computing to more accurately model how the globe's climate patterns may evolve or to predict with greater precision if and where extreme weather events may occur. Numerous other potential use cases are being explored across industries, from advanced manufacturing to banking, security to materials science. Quantum computing currently exists as potentially transformative in beneficial and problematic ways. While there are tremendous potential benefits for quantum technology to do good, it is important to consider the potential risks inherent in quantum computing. Such powerful computational capabilities have the capacity, for example, to unpick some of the foundations of modern security by rendering existing encryption technology obsolete. Some experts worry that the race by countries to create a computational edge through quantum could be like a new arms race, not dissimilar to some concerns we read about regarding artificial intelligence.

Similar to artificial intelligence, which has grown in fits and starts over the years but is now having a prominent moment heralded by generative AI, quantum computing has been building for decades. It is a technology that has long been on the horizon, but is potentially now becoming a reality as several technological advancements enable these powerful machines to achieve their computational wizardry. Established computing industry players such as IBM and Google along with venture-backed upstarts in Europe, Asia, Australia, and the US are experimenting with a range of quantum solutions that are delivering early versions of these computers for testing and exploration. The world may soon have a quantum moment that not only may seem to bend the laws of physics, but could positively impact some of our most complex challenges.

What Is Quantum Computing Anyway?

Quantum chandelier

Before we dive into quantum computing's history, I want to address a more fundamental question: What exactly is quantum computing? Most of us have a passing familiarity with the computers that power our day-to-day lives – whether the laptops in our bags or the smartphones in our pockets. At the most simplistic level, a series of semiconductors and memory chips combine to process bits of information that can either exist in an on or off state – a zero or a one – switched on or off by passing electricity through circuits. The flipping of these tiny switches enables the computation and storage of information at increasingly complex scales depending on the size of the machines involved. The zeros and ones that flip on or off (depending on the task) run or support almost every aspect of our modern lives.

Where classical computing deals in bits – a clear binary between a zero and a one – with millions or billions of transistors being flipped between these states, quantum computers operate based on quantum bits or qubits.

Qubits can exist as both a zero or a one at the same time, effectively existing in multiple states simultaneously. In quantum physics, this state is called superposition – the idea that particles can be in two places at the same time. It is these unique properties that give quantum computers the amazing potential to solve incredibly complex problems so much more quickly than classical computers. Instead of having to determine every single calculation as would be the case with the computers we use today, quantum computers have the capacity to engage with larger datasets and puzzle out the near infinite number of possible states that qubits might be in. The most important aspect of quantum computing for us to understand is that quantum physicists and entrepreneurs believe these machines have the capacity to crunch much more rapidly and at much greater scale incredibly complex problems, including many that are difficult to solve today with classical computers or supercomputers.

Companies are exploring different hardware approaches to make quantum computers. Like many deep tech development efforts, it is not yet clear which technologies will perform the best or scale most effectively. The first commercially available quantum computer, D-Wave One, was built on quantum annealing technology, which is designed to solve optimization problems. Some companies, such as IBM and Rigetti, are pursuing quantum computers using superconducting materials. Other companies, like PsiQuantum and Xanadu, are exploring how photons may be able to create quantum states to store and process information at quantum scale. There are several other technical approaches that have attracted interest and have research teams and venture dollars hard at work.

Much like classical computers, quantum computers are not simply hardware. The emerging quantum computing ecosystem consists of both hardware and software that are evolving in tandem, similar to how today's computing capabilities have been evolving since the 1970s. The complex and emerging quantum hardware described briefly above requires software innovation to unlock the technology's potential. There has been an explosion of activity within the quantum software industry over the past five years, which coincides with advancements on the hardware front. A plethora of software start-ups are working to build algorithms required to operationalize the quantum hardware systems. These software capabilities will be essential for end users to seamlessly hook into, experiment with, and exploit the power of the underlying quantum devices. So, it is not just the complex physical devices themselves that are required to realize the potential benefits of quantum. We also need easy ways for users to interact with quantum computers to develop and test algorithms that may solve real-world problems.

We may be on the cusp of quantum computing developments that could reshape some of the world's most difficult problems. For years, much of this innovation and the underlying scientific research have been done in labs around the world, from commercial labs at firms like IBM, to research labs at Oxford University. A mixture of in-house research scientists, professors, postdocs, and programmers have been exploring the technical possibilities of quantum computing. Given the complex nature of technological development, the hardware and software haven't been ready for prime-time exposure to end customers. However, innovative companies are now starting to showcase quantum machines in a variety of settings. Some are housed in those same research institutions. Others are being connected to classical computers in a hybrid attempt to pair classical and quantum computing offerings. While others still are being installed in data centers that power much of our modern lives. Through each of these approaches and many others, these emerging machines and their associated software are more accessible than ever, enabling exploration and experimentation.

A Brief History of Quantum

Quantum's present promise can be traced back to debates among the leading minds in theoretical physics from the early twentieth century. A very brief history of quantum's rise would be incomplete without mentioning some of the most famous names in the history of physics itself. In the 1920s and 1930s, Albert Einstein and Niels Bohr explored how the subatomic particles that comprise everything in the universe behave or should behave. At the heart of these discussions or theoretical disagreements was the inherent unpredictability of these particles and the concept of entanglement "in which two particles, no matter how far apart, behave in ways that, while individually random, are too strongly correlated for the particles to be acting independently."[1]

One of the more important moments within this period was the Solvay Conference on Physics, which was held in October 1927 (see Figure 9.1). The Solvay Conferences first commenced in 1911 and focused on large, unsolved problems in physics and in chemistry.[2] During the 1927 conference, which was the fifth conference held, the attendees explored the then recently developed quantum theory. Einstein and Bohr were in attendance. This conference, still held today with the 2022 focus on Physics of Quantum Information, is regarded as one of the most important early discussions on quantum theory. It was the venue in which Einstein sought to convince other leading physicists, through his thought experiments, that the quantum

Figure 9.1 This photo taken during the 1927 Solvay Conference shows many of the era's most notable physicists. Seventeen of the twenty-nine attendees of the conference were or became Nobel Prize winners. Included in the photo are the likes of Max Planck, Marie Curie, Albert Einstein, Paul Dirac, Max Born, Niels Bohr, and Werner Heisenberg.

mechanics theory of the time was incorrect, with Bohr countering Einstein's arguments.[3]

Shortly after the Solvay Conference of 1927, the physicist Erwin Schrödinger developed one of the most famous thought experiments in physics, which subsequently became known as Schrödinger's cat. This thought experiment was a means of trying to understand one of the principles described earlier – quantum superposition. This is the idea we explored in relation to the qubit, where the qubit may simultaneously exist as a zero or one at any given time. Schrödinger sought to explain this paradox by way of analogy where a cat would be placed in a sealed box along with a flask of poison and a radioactive substance connected to a Geiger counter. His thought experiment ran that when the Geiger counter picked up the radioactive substance, the flask with the poison would be shattered and the poison would then kill the cat. From the perspective of a bystander observing the sealed box, the cat could be considered simultaneously both dead and alive at any point in time. However, when one opens the box, the cat is either dead or alive. This thought experiment sought to illustrate the behavior of atoms, in effect the behavior of the qubit that could potentially be a zero or a one depending on when one sought to measure or observe it.

While Einstein, Bohr, Schrödinger, Werner Heisenberg, and Paul Dirac debated both the physics and mathematics of quantum in the early 1900s, the modern era of quantum exploration in relation to computers really only started in the 1970s and 1980s, coinciding with advancements in classical computing. Similar to the set of eminent physicists in the 1920s and 1930s who explored quantum physics principles, a group of physicists and mathematicians during this time developed theories and pushed one another to explore the potential for quantum principles to be applied to computing. These academics and theoreticians spanned much of the globe, from Moscow to Oxford and Cambridge to Boston.

One physicist who is credited with advancing the field in the late 1970s and early 1980s was Paul Benioff of the Argonne National Laboratory. He explored the potential for quantum computing, and his research yielded a seminal paper in 1980 that focused on a quantum model for a Turing Machine, which is essentially a computing machine that takes a series of rules and computes a desired result. Benioff's research and writing explored how computers could be capable of operating within the laws of quantum mechanics as they were understood at that time.

Benioff's initial publication and a subsequent paper published in 1982 coincided with Russian mathematician Yuri Manin's hypotheses on the possibility of quantum automation or a quantum computer, and Nobel Prize winning physicist Richard Feynman's exploration of simulating quantum systems. In 1981, Feynman delivered a keynote address entitled "Simulating Physics with Computers," where he proposed that a quantum computer had the potential to simulate quantum states in ways that classical computers, given their binary zero or one operations, could not. Feynman subsequently spent time in the early 1980s collaborating with the Thinking Machines Corporation, a supercomputer manufacturing company that developed out of research from MIT.[4] During this period, Feynman worked with Thinking Machines to explore supercomputer development and the potential structure of quantum computers. The engagement between Benioff, Manin, Feynman, and others formed the theoretical basis for quantum computing as a potential alternative to classical computing.

From these early conceptual beginnings, research and theorization rapidly accelerated with David Deutsch, a fundamental physicist affiliated with Oxford University who developed a paper on quantum algorithms in 1985. This paper proposed that a quantum algorithm could be exponentially faster than any possible classical algorithm. The basic idea was that it should be possible to develop a universal computer, an extension of the type conceptualized by Alan Turing. However, Deutsch's algorithm would be underpinned by the fundamentals of quantum physics that could not be reproduced by Turing's conception of such a machine. Deutsch believed that quantum physics would naturally lend itself to being applied to computation but in powerfully different ways to how classical computing works.

In the 1990s, the quantum computing space saw dramatic advancements both in the theories that underpinned potential computing capabilities and in emerging quantum hardware. Deutsch continued his theoretical exploration, proposing in 1992 with Richard Jozsa, a mathematician and theoretical physicist, a quantum algorithm that was one of the first examples of how quantum processing could solve problems infinitely faster than classical computers.[5] Shortly after in 1994, Peter Shor, who had recently completed his PhD at MIT and accepted a position at Bell Labs, developed what has become known as Shor's Algorithm. This quantum algorithm focused on how to find the prime factors of an integer. Prime factorization is at the heart of much of our present-day digital security with public key encryption. It is not easy to factorize prime numbers, particularly large ones. However, Shor's Algorithm became viewed as one of the first and, over time, one of the most promising quantum-related algorithms. It has potentially significant implications for cryptography since Shor's Algorithm can factor large numbers much more rapidly than classical computing-based algorithms. A flurry of additional algorithms followed. In 1996, Lov Kumar Grover, while at Bell Labs, created a database search algorithm using quantum principles to accelerate search capabilities.

Shortly after, in 1998, researchers across a set of US laboratories and academic institutions developed the world's first quantum computer, which could be fed data and generate an output. Isaac Chuang at the Los Alamos National Laboratory, Neil Gershenfeld of MIT, and Mark Kubinec of the University of California at Berkeley were credited with this breakthrough. At the turn of the millennium, new computing systems were developed with Geordie Rose and colleagues starting D-Wave Systems, which is widely credited as one of the first quantum computing companies. In 2001, IBM and Stanford utilized a 7 qubit quantum processor, which was the first to implement Shor's Algorithm, successfully factoring 15 into its prime factors.

Commercially available quantum computers followed relatively quickly in the 2010s, with D-Wave One being the first. In 2016, IBM made the leap of providing quantum computing capabilities through its IBM Cloud offering. Before the decade was out, Google's quantum computing team announced its system had achieved quantum supremacy. This term, coined by California Institute of Technology professor of theoretical physics John Preskill, described quantum's capacity for exceeding classical computing's capabilities. Within a relatively brief period of time, quantum computing evolved from theoretical possibilities in David Deutsch's seminal 1985 paper, to small, rudimentary prototypes in the late 1990s, to numerous companies seeking to embed quantum capabilities with classical computing technology.

The Emerging Potential of Quantum Computing

Over the past decade, innovation in quantum computing hardware and software has accelerated. I was fascinated by my conversation with Olivia Lanes, PhD in Quantum Physics, global lead and manager for IBM Quantum Advocacy, in which she highlighted both technical challenges with the classical computing paradigm and the genuine excitement and enormous potential for quantum to deliver rapid advancements in everything from medicine and biotechnology to applied materials sciences.

"Moore's law is dying and new power and efficiencies will come from quantum computing," Olivia shared with me. She added that the capacity for quantum computing to "increase computational power substantially, making the computational space that you have to perform algorithms and run computations exponentially large has applications across a wide range of technological and social challenges that we face as a society today."

Her views are reflected in the myriad Fortune 500 companies and venture-backed start-ups that are innovating in the quantum space. In early 2023, McKinsey & Company published an insight piece highlighting that "investors poured $2.35 billion into quantum technology start-ups in 2022" across a range of quantum focus areas.[6] It is not only early-stage investors that have boosted their interest in quantum opportunities, but also governments around the world continue to fund the science behind this technology, and are increasingly investing in projects that hold the promise to deliver national quantum advantage. In 2023 alone, the United Kingdom announced a £2.5 billion quantum initiative, the National Quantum Strategy, while Germany launched a €3 billion program to develop a universal quantum computer. These are some of the numerous national initiatives along with private investment within the quantum space. Both public and private backers are pursuing applications that have the potential to enhance socio-economic, technological, security, and other priorities around the globe.

While the overall size of existing quantum computers remains a constraint, emerging case studies and use cases are becoming more prevalent. With the emergent technology in the hands of more users, particularly larger organizations, customers and developers can see how the technology could solve difficult challenges in the future. The number of potential applications and prospective benefits are too numerous to explore in depth, but there are three areas that strike me as potentially exciting and positive: life sciences and drug discovery, energy systems and climate change, and advanced manufacturing.

Quantum's Promise in Drug Discovery and Life Sciences

One problem set that quantum has often been touted to impact in a positive way is the drug discovery process. Currently, pharmaceutical and biotechnology firms invest billions of dollars and many years trying to bring to market new drugs or therapies. These discoveries happen at a molecular level, making the capacity to model out interactions at that level critical for accurately predicting how complex interactions within the body may unfold. Utilizing classical computers, as we have done for decades, to model and predict potential new drugs is limited by our current computational capacity.

Research scientists at Imperial College London have been experimenting with how quantum computing methods may enhance drug design methods such as molecular docking and RNA folding prediction. Researchers are excited by the potential capacity for future quantum systems to "simulate interactions between molecules more authentically" and "accelerate high-throughput screening of drugs, [handling] previously elusive complex biological systems."[7] Dr. Shang Yu at Imperial College London highlights that quantum computers may be able to "accelerate the launch of new drugs, reduce R&D costs, and bring more and better treatment options to patients."[7]

D-Wave Systems, one of the early pioneers of quantum computer technology, believes that life sciences is an area of particular promise for quantum computing. The team at D-Wave highlights that beyond more efficient identification of relevant molecules, there are opportunities within the wider research and operating activities for life sciences firms. For example, "crunching 'big data' from clinical studies" may enable more targeted disease treatments or highlight previously unknown or difficult to discover "connections between specific genetic features and human disease."[8]

Quantum's Potential in Fighting Climate Change

Where quantum computing may potentially enhance global health through more rapid and personalized drug discovery, industry, researchers, and campaign groups see quantum as a potential ally in the fight against climate change. The multifaceted challenge of combating climate change and adapting the world's energy systems requires potential interventions across many complex value chains. Recent research and analysis by Deloitte's consulting arm identified several areas where quantum has the potential to bolster international efforts to address climate-related challenges. For example, Deloitte highlighted that quantum computers may excel at simulating complex physical systems, particularly chemical simulations that could more rapidly advance catalyst development, reducing energy or resource requirements in the process.[9]

The co-founder and CEO of PsiQuantum, Jeremy O'Brien, believes that quantum computing will transform chemistry. Given the importance of advancements around chemistry and materials science to develop low-carbon technologies, this should mean that quantum computing could play a major role in deepening and accelerating the energy transition. For example, O'Brien explained in a 2022 interview with McKinsey that it should be possible to replicate how microbes make ammonia under normal conditions, and "[w]e know it should be possible to replicate the function of this enzyme using an artificial catalyst, but we simply can't simulate the stability of the naturally occurring enzyme with normal computers."[10] A breakthrough like this would mean that natural gas could be replaced with water as a source of hydrogen, enabling comparatively inexpensive ammonia production that could be used to power ships in the coming decade.[10] As part of PsiQuantum's vision, O'Brien believes that quantum computers should play a pivotal role in solving complex challenges such as climate change, and has established this as a primary use case for the company's quantum capabilities.

While quantum may play an instrumental role in modeling out molecular breakthroughs that may increase how much batteries can store or what fuels can be created in ever greener ways, mitigating climate-related risk and adapting our energy systems will happen within complex physical and social systems that are challenging to model. Everything from more accurately modeling weather forecasts, to simulating how different energy production and transmission systems may develop or shift over time will require greater computational power. These are areas where quantum computing's power may more rapidly and with greater fidelity simulate scenarios that engineers, policymakers, local communities, and others can take advantage of. Scientific researchers, policymakers, and the energy industry are increasingly exploring how quantum computing capabilities could enhance local energy grid performance, improving security of the power systems while also increasing their resilience. While the research and simulations are in their infancy, there is excitement that in the future quantum systems could conquer challenges that are difficult to model with conventional computing.

As an example of how energy systems may be improved through quantum computing, the co-founder of ParityQC Wolfgang Lechner and a group of academic and industry researchers explored how the electric grid will need to be adapted in order to manage electric vehicle demands. Working with EDF, a large energy producer in France, the team explored how quantum algorithms could best manage the electric power systems, taking into account cost, electric vehicle loads, user needs, and buffer requirements to keep the grid stable.[11] PASQAL, a quantum hardware company, and ParityQC, a quantum architecture company that develops blueprints and an operating system for scalable quantum computers, evaluated how quantum algorithms compared to classical algorithms when assessing grid management issues for electric mobility and smart charging for electric cars. While based on a small-scale dataset, this type of experiment highlights the potential for quantum to address real-world challenges, which could significantly improve complex energy systems.

Quantum's Potential to Transform Manufacturing

Advanced manufacturing industries are exploring how quantum computing may reshape the very materials that keep airplanes in the sky. In my discussion with Olivia Lanes, she noted a complex engineering challenge that Boeing collaborated on with IBM, utilizing IBM's quantum capabilities. The focus of the work was to explore ply composites that become critical parts of an airplane's wings and other components. Olivia highlighted that nearly 100,000 variables can be factored into a ply's design, which is simply too large for classical computing capabilities to manage effectively. The IBM and Boeing teams worked together to explore 40 variables through IBM's quantum computing capabilities, demonstrating new methods for simulating and evaluating how ply layers could be developed most efficiently. This was the largest such simulation on a quantum computer at the time of the experiment.[12] *Note: The Boeing example was drafted before the company's issues surfaced. I chose to leave it in because it's a powerful example that illustrates the tremendous potential quantum has to revolutionize manufacturing.*

While this is a proof of concept of sorts, it highlights how such simulations for larger quantum computers in the future hold the potential to analyze and optimize 100,000 variables – a nearly impossible task today. These types of simulations may reduce the time and cost in modeling out the most attractive materials for aerospace products such as planes and satellites, while creating more robust materials that can enable planes to fly safely over longer distances and at lower operating costs.

In another aerospace materials advancement, Rolls-Royce, NVIDIA, and Classiq, a quantum software start-up, designed and simulated the "world's largest quantum computing circuit for computational fluid dynamics (CFD)."[13] The focus of this work was to explore how a combination of classical and quantum computing could be used to design jet engines. The teams researched how to more efficiently develop the complex engines that power leading aircraft. Classiq focused on the development of quantum algorithm designs, an important enabler for end customers such as Rolls-Royce and quantum hardware manufacturers. These types of quantum algorithms will enable specific domain expertise to be applied to real-world technical problems.

Quantum's Potential Machine Learning Entanglement

Many researchers and industries believe that quantum may empower artificial intelligence and machine learning capabilities. Some of the companies I touched on earlier see potential for quantum computing to enhance today's machine learning models, and scientific researchers are hopeful that the intersection of these two technologies will unlock subatomic secrets.

For example, Rigetti, a California-based quantum computing company, is exploring how quantum machine learning could enable financial institutions to make better decisions with their vast amounts of data. The company was recently awarded an innovation grant by the UK's national innovation agency (Innovate UK) "to improve current classical machine learning techniques used by financial institutions to analyze complex data streams."[14] Working in combination with Standard Chartered, Amazon Web Services, and Imperial College, the consortium hopes to identify whether quantum machine learning methods could enhance how banks more efficiently serve customers.

Scientific researchers are eyeing potential advancements with quantum machine learning that may help them better understand the building blocks of matter and our universe. At CERN, Europe's particle-physics laboratory, researchers believe that quantum machine learning may help them identify subatomic particles in the Large Hadron Collider.[15] Other researchers are optimistic that quantum's computational power may enable the detections of "correlations in . . . data that would be very difficult to detect with classical algorithms."[15]

The Promise of a Quantum-Powered Future

Quantum computing capabilities have advanced dramatically since their modern conception in the early-to-mid-1980s. In the past decade, and particularly in the past five years, the number of hardware and software companies working to realize the potential of quantum computing has grown considerably. From small-scale proofs of concept, such as the Boeing collaboration with IBM, to research on quantum's potential to speed the energy transition, there is growing confidence that quantum could be transformative in addressing many of our most pressing challenges. Increasingly, there is hope within industry that this ambition is being matched by technological advancements within the quantum computing field itself. While it will still be some time before quantum computing becomes the de facto computing framework governing our technology horizons, there are more opportunities today to gain exposure to quantum's computing promise. And as more organizations explore what quantum may mean for their industry or problem area, we may find that we accelerate more quickly to our quantum-powered future.

CHAPTER 10

Sustainably Powering Our Future

Few challenges or goals are more consequential for our society than the energy transition. Across almost every industry I work in, sustainability and energy transition are important topics of discussion among CEOs, chief communications officers, and leadership teams. Companies such as Deere & Company, as described in Part 1, have sustainability and climate resilience at the core of their corporate strategy and day-to-day operations. Many other organizations are increasingly focusing on how they can positively impact their supply chains and key stakeholders with the environment, sustainability, and more efficient energy consumption in mind.

Technological innovation was at the heart of how our modern energy systems powered economic growth in the nineteenth and twentieth centuries. With the 2050 climate goals of keeping global warming to 1.5°C and the imperative of empowering a growing world population, further technological advancements will be central to sustainably and responsibly powering the next century of global growth (see Figure 10.1).

Many of us are already accelerating the energy transition – hopping into an electric car or switching to a renewable home energy supplier. Around the world, technological innovation has been making transportation more sustainable, grids greener, and products more environmentally friendly. While these technologies are relatively recent additions to our energy landscape, many are gaining momentum and having impact. In 2010, solar electricity panels – also known as solar photovoltaic panels or solar PV – were 0.8% of total global power capacity.[1] By 2020, solar PV was 9.4% of global

Figure 10.1 Solar energy has grown dramatically over the last 15 years. Solar PV panels, such as the ones pictured above, are now seen on homes, businesses, and fields around the world.

power capacity – a massive leap in both absolute and relative terms. According to the IEA, "utility-scale solar PV is the least costly option for new electricity generation in a significant majority of countries worldwide."[1] There have been huge technological advances in solar PV alone that have enabled this impressive growth. And solar is just one type of technology that has increasingly changed the energy landscape over the past decade and will shape it going forward. In 2023, the IEA reported that there was a "50% increase in renewable energy capacity to almost 510GW in 2023, the fastest growth rate in two decades."[2]

Many energy experts have explored the complexity of our global energy systems – from markets to policies to politics. And a lot has been written on fossil fuels, the largest contributing factor for the need of the energy transition. I have chosen to focus on showcasing some of the impressive technological advancements that have built our current energy system before exploring the exciting technological possibilities that may shape this century and beyond. As we will see in this chapter, given the scale of the challenge and uncertainty of which technologies may contribute the most, the capacity to reach net zero by 2050 requires exploring numerous solutions simultaneously. Even considering that uncertainty and need for a wide range of solutions, I'm hopeful that you'll be humbled by the impressive array of energy innovations as I have been while researching them.

A Brief Look Back at Energy Systems

From the world's first hydroelectric power station developed in Cragside, England in 1878, to the US's first power station built in New York City (the Pearl Street Station), the late 1800s saw a tremendous burst of innovation in energy systems in both the UK and the US. The innovations weren't solely focused on power generation itself. The development of centralized power generation capabilities created the need to distribute that energy. Pioneers such as Thomas Edison, George Westinghouse, and Nikola Tesla battled, in what became known as the War of the Currents, to come up with ways of effectively distributing electricity to street lamps, homes, and businesses.[3] From this competition and innovation, the likes of Edison General Electric, which became General Electric when it was floated as a public company, and Westinghouse Electric were founded and powered the development and distribution of electricity across the US.

Early Experiments with Renewables

In the early 1900s, generating plants became larger and more complex. They also began incorporating new fuels, such as gas, to produce electricity. However, what struck me about the early developments of power generation was not the trajectory we're all familiar with – increased use of coal, oil, and gas. I was impressed by the number of experiments involving renewable sources.

In 1904, Piero Ginori Conti, in the Tuscany region of Italy, experimented with using geothermal energy, which is drawn from the earth's crust, to power several light bulbs. Known in Italian as "La Vallee del Diavolo" or "Devil's Valley," the region has a lot of volcanic activity. With his proof of concept successful, a short nine years later on the same site in Larderello, Italy, Conti launched the world's first geothermal power station. After becoming operational in 1913, the plant has continually produced geothermal power through today.[4]

Energy from the earth's crust wasn't the only renewable source that innovators explored. Frank Shuman, an American engineer and inventor, explored the possibilities of harnessing the sun's rays to generate electricity. He built his fortune in safety glass – a form of glass with wire mesh in it. Some of the properties of the glass also inspired him to explore if that same glass could transform the sun into energy. He developed a system where "reflectors were placed around insulated boxes, which were built on swivels so the reflectors could follow the sun's path during the day."[5] By concentrating the rays on a water vessel, the steam generated would turn an engine.

In 1913, Shuman headed to Egypt to demonstrate the potential for his sun engine. The 55 horsepower (41kW) solar energy station in Maadi, Egypt impressed the British Consul-General – Lord Kitchener – who is reported to have seen the potential for the technology to improve irrigation and agricultural productivity in Sudan and Egypt.[5] This was, in essence, a proof of concept for solar energy.

Feats in Engineering and Physics Advanced Energy Systems

During World War I, oil as a transportation fuel had a dramatic impact on land and at sea. In the immediate pre-World War I period and through the 1950s, there were a number of advancements in processing fossil fuels that played a pivotal role in today's energy systems. One innovative area was the liquefaction of gas. When compressed to liquid, the liquid takes up 1/600th the volume of its gas form. In 1912, the Cabot family began construction of a liquefied natural gas plant in West Virginia, which became operational in 1917.[6] A few decades later, the first commercial liquefaction plant was built in Cleveland, Ohio in 1941 for storage of natural gas. And on January 25, 1959, the first liquefied natural gas carrier – the Methane Pioneer – set sail from Louisiana bound for England.

During this time, we also pioneered splitting atoms. During World War II and the years that followed, we unleashed energy through nuclear reactions. By splitting uranium atoms through a process called fission, heat is produced that can rotate a turbine and generate electricity. In the US, the exploration of how to harness fission started in earnest with the Manhattan Project and, subsequently for civilian energy purposes, through the creation of the Atomic Energy Commission (AEC) in 1946. The first civilian nuclear reactor was built in Idaho and generated nuclear-powered electricity on December 20, 1951 while the Shippingport Atomic Power Station became the first commercial nuclear power station in 1957.[7]

Moving electrons has become an increasingly important part of our everyday lives, as has storing energy. Throughout the twentieth century, advances in battery technology impacted everything from our transportation systems to pacemakers to computing capabilities. At the start of the twentieth century, Thomas Edison sought to commercialize the nickel-iron battery invented by a Swedish scientist, Waldemar Jungner. At the same time, Jungner himself opened a factory to produce nickel-cadmium batteries that became popular due to the rise of portable radios in the early twentieth century. By the middle of the century, a Canadian chemical engineer, Lew Urry, had invented the disposable alkaline battery that became incorporated into many new electronic devices. Starting with research in house at Exxon in the early 1970s and ending with Sony commercializing the technology in 1991, the advent of the rechargeable lithium-ion battery made possible our "on the go" lifestyle through its use in laptops, mobile phones, and tablets.[8] The trio whose research led to the invention – Akira Yoshino, John Goodenough, and M. Stanley Whittingham – shared the 2019 Nobel Prize in Chemistry.

Throughout the twentieth and early twenty-first centuries, we generated energy at a scale unprecedented in human history, enabling the growth of ever larger cities, the birth of auto and air travel, and the creation of many modern conveniences. To do so, we compressed gasses, split atoms, and moved electrons, delivered by feats in both physics and engineering.

What we have discovered over the past three to four decades is that the structure of the energy system we developed has created serious challenges, as the fossil fuels powering our lives are having the dire impact of warming the planet. However, recent advancements and technologies that may be on the horizon could reshape our energy systems in ways that may be as profound for future generations as the fossil fuel system has been in the last century.

From the conversations I've had with leading venture capital investors, technologists, and energy researchers, it is clear we likely have many of the technologies today to speed a sustainable energy future. From Shuman's proof of concept in the Egyptian desert in 1913 to the present day, we have seen solar energy become one of the most cost competitive forms of electricity generation. Further out on the development curve are potential technologies that go a step beyond just harnessing the sun's rays or the wind's gusts to create the very reaction on earth that powers the stars – fusion. Between the established technologies and cutting-edge research and development, there is an impressive array of innovations now and on the horizon that may help decarbonize our energy systems and the products we use, enabling a greener and more sustainable future.

The Electrification Challenge

While there are so many energy areas to explore, there are two main areas I've chosen to focus on as we look toward a more sustainable energy future: electrification of transportation and electrification of our power generation grids. These will be at the heart of a lower carbon world. A third set of innovations we'll explore at the end of this chapter may play a valuable supporting role, potentially reshaping how we decarbonize everything from our air to the industrial processes that make many products we consume.

Imagine Life in a Greener Future

After a busy week of meetings up and down the California coastline, you step off an electric vertical take-off and landing vehicle – a passenger drone – that has whisked you with zero carbon in flight from San Jose to just north of the Golden Gate Bridge. From there, you step into your electric car and hum to your house, where you plug in to charge your car's battery from the invisible solar panels integrated into your roof tiles. In this scenario, your house only uses the solar tiles as backup generating capacity because the recently operational fusion reactor near San Quintin powers the whole region with reliable zero carbon energy. The mix of solar, wind, and fusion energy has created a decentralized electrical grid that delivers greater energy resilience, lower costs, and cleaner air. Direct air capture units in and around San Francisco ingest CO_2 that we haven't yet removed from the energy cycle, enabling production of greener concrete and environmentally friendly polymers that go into local building materials and manufacturing start-ups.

I am guessing that for some of you, aspects of the vision I just painted may feel familiar – an electric car and battery storage at a house or workplace. Other elements such as electric air travel, direct air capture (DAC) technology, or fusion may sound like they're out of a sci-fi movie. While work is underway on the more futuristic innovations in this scenario, which I'll explore in this chapter, many of the experts I've spoken with believe that several technologies we have already developed such as solar and batteries are likely to go a very long way to decarbonize our lives.

While speaking with Andrew Beebe, managing director at venture capital firm Obvious Ventures, I was struck by his optimism around solutions to the energy transition we have in today's technological toolkit. "Although I'm excited about some of the innovations on the horizon, I'm really energized by many familiar solutions like wind, solar, and lithium-ion batteries, which can have a dramatic impact on our move to cleaner energy," Andrew said. "I think that if we can scale out everything we have already designed and come up with a few innovations in other key areas, we will make impressive progress."

Among the technologies that may turn out to be transformative when and if they come to pass are fusion, where we recreate the physical process by which the sun produces energy, and DAC, where carbon is literally sucked directly from the air. Those technologies, and a few more we'll explore below, have existing research teams, businesses, and projects focused on how to bring them to life.

While we know that not every technology will be successful, what's promising is the scale and pace of technological exploration underway on how we electrify and decarbonize our energy systems. It's truly exciting and holds potential to have a far-reaching and long-lasting impact on how we live, move, and consume.

The EV Movement

Automobiles aren't a uniquely American obsession. With car ownership levels skyrocketing around the globe, decarbonizing personal transportation is an important part of the energy transition. The rise of EVs has been rapid. Much like what we saw with the increase of solar PV for power generation, EVs have risen rapidly across North American, European, and Asian markets. Plug-in hybrid EV and battery EVs have increased from about 100,000 sold in 2012 to nearly 26,000,000 on global roads in 2022.[9] According to the International Energy Agency, approximately "70% of the global stock of electric cars in 2022 were [battery electric vehicles]."[9]

A recent study by Ricardo Energy & Environment for the UK's Department for Transport looked at the greenhouse gas contribution of different automobile types on the UK's roads. The headline finding was that in 2020 EVs were estimated to save upward of 65% greenhouse gas emissions compared to a similarly sized gas-powered vehicle.[10] The report showed that those greenhouse gas savings are likely to increase as batteries improve and as the UK's electricity grid becomes greener. While studies have shown that production of battery EVs causes more pollution in comparison to internal combustion engine vehicles, this difference is likely to narrow over time.[11]

China has been a considerable source of the battery innovation and EV production, as well as a source of consumer demand for EVs. In 2022, the International Energy Agency reported that China's domestic market "accounted for more than 50% of all the electric cars on the world's roads, a total of 13.8 million."[12] This has been fed by a virtuous cycle of domestic production incentives, homegrown electric car brands, and domestic value chains in critical EV components such as the batteries. According to the *Financial Times*, BYD—China's leading electric car maker—sold 526,000 battery EVs, eclipsing Tesla's production for the fourth quarter of 2023.[13] In the battery space, Contemporary Amperex Technology Company – or CATL – is now the world's largest battery manufacturing company. Based in Ningde, China, it has become a critical supplier of both the Chinese domestic EV industry, as well as international car manufacturing industries in South Korea, Europe, and the US.

The growth of higher quality EVs and energy-dense batteries will likely intensify the adoption of EVs. This will have the benefit of electrifying our roads, not only cars but also trucks that transport goods over long distances. Additionally, we are likely to start seeing EVs hovering above our heads in the not-too-distant future. Companies such as Joby Aviation and Archer have been working for years to electrify air travel in the form of eVTOLs or electric vertical take-off and landing aircraft (see Figure 10.2). In 2023, both Joby and Archer made progress on their certification efforts with the United States Federal Aviation Administration. This means that both companies are inching closer to introducing flying electric cars into commercial use, potentially heralding the start of a more sustainable aviation future across a wide range of aircraft types.

Figure 10.2 New forms of transportation are likely to reshape both urban and rural environments. eVTOL vehicles, such as the one pictured above, have the potential to play an important role in green transportation.

Electrifying Our Power Systems

Increasingly adopting EVs will decarbonize transportation, but without greening the grid we won't reap the full benefits of EVs on our roads. With more vehicles to plug in, we will need more green energy to supply them. As mentioned earlier in the chapter, the growth of renewable energy sources has been dramatic over the last 10-15 years. Wind, solar, geothermal, and other renewable sources have played an impressive role in beginning to shift the way in which our electrical grids generate power. Technologies such as solar PV and wind are proven, and we can expect that additional innovation within these technologies will continue to lower their production costs and increase their efficiency in turning the sun's rays or wind's gusts into energy. When combined with battery innovations that can store renewables, we could suddenly store and then discharge sustainable energy, which would be transformative.

Solar Energy Advancements

What types of innovations could we expect in areas such as solar PV? Solar panels are made out of photovoltaic cells. These cells are placed between layers of materials such as silicon, which have conducting capabilities, and can create an electric field when sunlight hits the panel. However, the amount of sunlight that solar panels can convert into electricity is limited by the silicon in the cells themselves. In 2023, there were advancements in boosting the efficiency of PV cells by including a semiconductor, perovskite, on the existing silicon cells.[14] Researchers believe that it should be possible to continue boosting efficiency beyond today's PV cell capabilities, meaning that ultimately electricity production costs can be driven down further while boosting the amount of energy PV cells and panels generate.

Some researchers also believe they are on the cusp of solar breakthroughs that draw inspiration from plants. Building on ideas first explored by chemists in the 1960s, a range of companies now believe that dye-sensitized solar cells could be the next big thing, particularly for our electronics. The cells convert light in a manner similar to plants, which means they should be much more efficient even indoors and could "attach to the wall with little more than some removable adhesive."[15]

Batteries as the Missing Link

As researchers and businesses explore how to boost energy output and lower existing renewables technology costs, other organizations are exploring how to make the most of a sunny day or prepare for a cloudy one. Unlike fossil fuel-based power plants that can reduce or increase the amount of energy they generate based on the amount of fuel they consume, the sun, wind, and tides can be unpredictable. An incredibly sunny day might yield an abundance of electricity generated by the solar panels on your house or at a solar PV power plant, but if that electricity doesn't get used it simply dissipates.

This is where batteries come in, big ones. Battery technology will enable individuals, neighborhoods, or regions to store excess energy produced through renewable energy sources that cannot be used at the exact time the energy is produced. Large-scale batteries could maximize renewable energy generated and empower consumers over where and when they utilize this energy.

Batteries may be the missing link that enables our electrical grids to go completely green. Because of this, battery research and innovation is a rich field. There are many competing models for how large-scale batteries could help store the energy generated by renewable sources – from fancy metals to familiar elements to water. Given the overall demand for batteries, a range of competing technologies may cater to different use cases.

For example, Invinity Energy Systems manufactures vanadium flow batteries, which is an alternative to the now dominant lithium-ion batteries. Invinity's innovation is to store "energy in a liquid form, which is pumped around large tanks and passed through a 'cell' to convert it into power when needed."[16] Invinity's technology has been piloted as part of the Energy Superhub Oxford (ESO), "Europe's most powerful electric vehicle charging hub."[17] The installation of Invinity's battery, as part of Energy Superhub Oxford, was the UK's largest flow battery put into operation.[18]

In the US, ESS Inc. is developing batteries that can store energy from renewable power generation using simple materials such as iron, salt, and water. Current ESS batteries are assembled into shipping containers, making them both modular and easy to move around. The innovation at the heart of the ESS approach is the separation of the energy storage part of the battery from the power producing part.[19] ESS believes that this separation reduces degradation of its batteries over time, potentially enabling the batteries to last 25 years vs. the 10-year operating life of conventional batteries.[20] Solutions such as ESS's have the capacity to bring more resilient power systems to remote or underserved regions, enabling increasingly decentralized power generation and microgrids to sustainably serve smaller communities.

In Portugal, a Spanish company – Iberdrola – is experimenting with water batteries. By drawing excess power from local wind and solar farms, the company pumps water to a reservoir nearly 7km up a mountain.[21] Given the amount of power being generated, it may be possible to store nearly 21GWh of electricity in this reservoir, which could be used to power 2.4 million homes in Portugal for a full day. When the sun goes down, the pump in the reservoir can be turned into a turbine, generating power.[21] It is not just the Portuguese who believe that water batteries may be a valuable link in the renewable value chain. China, Australia, the US, and the UK are all exploring or building out capacity.

Decentralized and Optimized Grids

Distribution of renewable energy sources along with reliable and scalable energy storage solutions create the potential for a much more decentralized energy system. Today, most people and businesses rely on energy from a central production source, a power plant not too far away from their home or workplace. Power plants are often very expensive to build and operate, and they represent a single source of potential failure. If the plant goes down, your lights go off until it is functional again. In a world where the sources of power generation are more distributed, that could mean local areas would build and manage power generation and distribution solutions that are considerably less expensive, offer redundancy, and are more responsive to local demands. This decentralization could lead to a revolution – and, in some respects, a simplification – of how we power our communities.

In the UK, Octopus Energy is at the vanguard of building the decentralized grid of the future. As 2023 drew to a close, Octopus Energy became the UK's largest power supplier.[22] Octopus invests in renewables generation, and it has developed and licensed its customer management system to other utility companies and real-time data to optimize supply and demand on its network. CEO Greg Jackson said that Octopus "[has] machine learning and algorithms running over . . . so that we can better forecast minute-to-minute consumption and generation, [and] match them together."[23]

One of Greg's mantras is that renewables combined with Octopus software and analytics create a more decentralized energy system, giving consumers greater control over not just their energy consumption but how to optimize energy production. Firms like Octopus see themselves as the service providers that enable this more decentralized energy world. They are working to speed the delivery of renewable and sustainable energy to more consumers and empowering them with the data and energy infrastructure to have greater control. For example, your battery EV can power your house, and solar panels can charge the car battery and local home batteries. This may mean there will be no grid in sight. It may be some time before this is how we all generate and consume our energy, but these types of decentralized or closed ecosystems may be on the horizon.

The Promise of Fusion

A bit further out, we may soon see the glow of an entirely new power source – fusion. Fusion is how the sun generates energy, and scientists have been exploring whether it is possible to create this reaction on earth. At the most basic level, fusion is two nuclei coming together to form a single, heavier nucleus. In this process, energy is released and there is no carbon created. Also, unlike nuclear energy production, there is no long-lived radioactive waste that is produced. Experts differ on when fusion may be a commercially viable source of power – 10 years, 15 years, or maybe 20+ years. While the timeline is difficult to pin down, there has been considerable and growing interest in fusion. Recent scientific breakthroughs have experts believing it's a matter of when and not if fusion connects to the grid.

In December 2022, the Lawrence Livermore National Laboratory in California achieved what is termed a "net energy gain" in a fusion experiment. This means that more energy was produced when creating a fusion reaction than went into producing the reaction, a potentially groundbreaking advancement. According to the *Financial Times*, "total private investment into fusion has now surpassed $6bn, with most of the funding coming since 2021."[24]

There are a number of technical approaches to fusion that some 43 private fusion companies are pursuing.[25] One such company is Commonwealth Fusion Systems (CFS). The company was spun out of MIT's Plasma Science and Fusion Center and uses large magnets to hold the deuterium-tritium fuel in place while the fuel is super-heated to a temperature hotter than the sun. CFS is building SPARC, a high-field tokamak.[26] A tokamak is "a machine that confines a plasma using magnetic fields in a donut shape."[27] If successful, SPARC would "pave the way for ARC, the first commercial power plant capable of feeding electricity into the grid, which is projected to be operational in the early 2030s."[28]

None of today's emerging fusion technologies is a sure thing; many approaches are likely to fail. However, Philippe Larochelle of Breakthrough Energy Ventures believes that "[s]ometime in the next decade or two, we are going to build the first commercial fusion reactor and then humans are going to spend the next 10 million years building better fusion reactors because fusion is really just an amazing energy source. The fuel is infinite, carbon free, and extremely cheap. . .you can build it anywhere and scale infinitely."[29]

Potential Future Decarbonization Innovations

So, we've electrified transportation and the grid. The technologies and R&D areas we have explored may, by themselves, lead to a more sustainable world. This is a world in which we meet the 2050 climate goals, keep warming to 1.5°C or less, and create even more novel sources of energy innovation.

When speaking with Alex Schindelar, president of Energy Intelligence, an energy research and analytics firm, he stressed that electrifying transport and the grid may be the most optimistic scenario. "If you can't electrify everything, we will likely remain reliant on fossil fuels for certain applications in the coming decades, which means that we will need to decarbonize the liquids mix that we use." Decarbonizing industrial use cases, shipping, aviation, these are potentially more complex challenges, and if these applications remain dependent on fossil fuel liquids, Schindelar highlighted "then technologies that extract carbon from the production process or the air may play a credible role. Ultimately, the scale of our decarbonization challenge will require pursuing numerous solutions simultaneously as no one energy source or decarbonization technology is likely to be a silver bullet."

As I touched on briefly earlier in the chapter, we could dedicate an entire book to the wide range of technologies that could decarbonize industry and manufacturing. There are, however, several potentially transformative technologies under exploration that could help to decarbonize our air or industrial processes. I'll touch on these briefly. They are not without their controversies (some believe they could incentivize ongoing polluting behaviors or that the technologies will never get to scale), but these technologies could potentially play a complementary role to wider climate resilience and energy transition efforts.

One I'd like to explore here is DAC, which is the concept that CO_2 can be sucked out of the atmosphere anywhere in the world. DAC is different from carbon capture, which generally tries to capture carbon at the point where it is most intensively being generated, like at a power plant. The amount of carbon in any bit of atmosphere will be much less dense than, for example, where flue gas leaves an industrial facility. This is why currently DAC is seen as an expensive way to decarbonize. Despite the current economic challenges of the technology, there are companies both large and small exploring its technical and commercial potential. Additionally, governments around the world are exploring how DAC could contribute to climate goals. The United States Department of Energy announced in August 2023 the first investment phase of a $3.5 billion effort to build four DAC hubs across the US in the next 10 years.[30]

Climeworks is a Switzerland-based DAC and storage company. The company developed Orca, which it deployed in Iceland in September 2021 and described as the "first and largest direct air capture and storage plant."[31] Orca uses large fans to pull air through large shipping container-sized boxes that the company calls collectors where CO_2 molecules collide with a filter and combine with a special molecule named an amine.[32] The carbon that Orca extracts from the atmosphere is "mixed with water and pumped deep underground, where it slowly turns into rock."[33]

Other companies also have big ambitions for DAC. Occidental has been engaged in carbon capture storage and enhanced oil recovery for years, which encouraged the company to consider exploring DAC. In 2019, Occidental began working with Carbon Engineering on DAC in an effort to deploy large scale projects.[34] In November 2023, Occidental and BlackRock formed a joint venture to develop a facility, named STRATOS, which would be the world's largest DAC plant and is a vote of confidence that this technology may scale.[35] The objective is to have the STRATOS plant in Ector County, Texas complete by mid-2025 at which point it can begin extracting 500,000 tons of CO_2 annually. Given that experts estimate the globe may need 23 billion tons of carbon to be captured by DAC annually by 2050, hopefully scalable solutions are on the horizon.[36]

Detractors contend that DAC and carbon capture technologies may encourage polluting industries to continue polluting or that they may be uneconomical in cost or energy terms. Despite those concerns, the technical ability for removing carbon from the atmosphere – at small scales – has been proven and there is energy behind demonstrating it can scale cost effectively.

Infrastructure Choices Shaping Future Energy Systems

There is considerable inertia within the energy industry to make the most of existing energy and industrial systems. This may bias technological progress toward energy solutions that fit today's infrastructure. For example, industry experts and others discuss hydrogen as a potentially attractive component of the transition. They believe it could have potential applications for oil refining and transportation.

As an example, Duke Energy has been exploring a green hydrogen production and storage system.[37] At a facility in Florida, solar energy produced by a Duke power plant will feed into the electricity grid, but a portion of the power will be passed to units that will split water into hydrogen and oxygen. The hydrogen will then be stored. Hydrogen can be used as an alternative fuel to gas in the power plant's turbines. A key component of the project is the capacity to retrofit a gas turbine so that either hydrogen or gas can power the turbine.

This type of retrofitting highlights the potential for existing infrastructure to be repurposed with renewables technology creating fuel further upstream in the power generation process. Fuels such as hydrogen, at least in the context of power generation, could enable existing infrastructure – from pipelines to power plants – to be used for longer periods with the types of retrofitting mentioned above. Skeptics argue that such approaches are inefficient in comparison to building out battery technology to manage peak demand needs. There is a tension – potentially a very expensive one – between moving fully to renewables to electrify the grid versus combining with or adapting existing infrastructure as part of the energy transition.

Navigating Our Uncertain Future

Although the components of a more sustainable energy future are fitting together, the exact shape of our future energy systems is not yet certain. Will we live in a completely decentralized energy world where the combination of battery EVs, solar PV, and potentially a breakthrough in fusion enables local communities to take much greater control over where and how energy is produced? Will centralized forms of energy production remain prominent, though retrofitted to include more elements of renewables? The stakes are high and the costs considerable, particularly against uncertain technology outcomes and complex political and regulatory environments.

Over even just the last 15 years, the progress we have made toward more sustainable transportation, power generation, and numerous other products and services is monumental. And the amount of ongoing innovation is humbling. While we race to scale many of the technologies that we know work and push to discover new technologies that we hope will plug existing gaps, we also recognize that there are many challenges ahead. Some of the technologies we are pursuing will not pan out. Our ambition to scale quickly may prove slower than we would like. The amount of coordination that will be required and the capacity to assess and evaluate trade-offs will not be straightforward.

I am optimistic though that the technology innovations we are seeing will be paired with an openness to innovate in how established industry leaders, upstart start-ups, government, policymakers, and campaign groups can collaborate to realize the ambition of our sustainable energy transition.

CHAPTER 11

The Surging Biological Systems Wave

As I researched and discussed biological systems, I was reminded of how many everyday challenges these systems help to solve. For many of us, when we think of biology, we naturally think about our bodies. We think about health or disease and the ways in which modern science and technology may improve our health or mitigate disease. While there are impressive biological challenges we need to meet for our personal and global health, biological systems impact nearly every aspect of our lives. From the food we eat, to the energy we consume, to the products we rely on, the engineering of biological systems has led to impressive innovations. There is enormous potential for us to engineer biological systems to meet some of our most complex challenges, but I would like us to keep in mind two important ideas as we explore: we are very early in our understanding of these systems, and biological systems can be analogized to the original information technology. These themes came through in some of my early conversations and research.

As I started to explore biological systems, I was fortunate to speak with Brian McGee. He is chief business officer at Anocca, a Swedish biotechnology company innovating in T-cell immunotherapy, and Brian has acted as an executive and advisor for large pharmaceutical firms and early-stage biotech companies. One of Brian's insights that really struck me was his observation of how early we are in our understanding of biology. "At the core of life sciences innovation is trying to reverse engineer how biological systems work. The technology of our biology has evolved over millions of years into phenomenally complex systems, and we are very, very early in the process of understanding how these systems truly work or can be unlocked."

As noted in Part 1, we had an insightful and inspiring conversation with Noubar Afeyan, the founder of Flagship Pioneering, a biotechnology venture building firm. He has also reflected on the ways in which biology is the original information technology platform. Noubar and his teams have developed groundbreaking companies such as Moderna, the biotechnology company that develops mRNA vaccines, including one of the first COVID-19 vaccines. In a talk that Noubar gave in 2023, he highlighted that "the original IT industry was actually biology, and it's a code industry . . . the DNA is the code, mRNA is . . . the software that gets made out of it."[1]

While many of us marvel at the progress we have made in medicine or our healthcare more broadly, I think it's valuable to keep Brian and Noubar's reflections in mind as we explore biological systems in this chapter. If we are at the very beginning of exploring the technology of biology and its applications to our world, it is humbling and exhilarating to think about what may be on the horizon. We may be experiencing a moment where various technologies intersect and enable some impressive leaps forward. Advancements in biology, AI, processing power – through chips or quantum – could have a profound, positive, and lasting impact for billions of people around the world in most every aspect of their lives.

The Modern Technology of Biology

Many of us are likely to have heard of terms such as CRISPR (Clustered Regularly Interspaced Short Palindromic Repeats), which enables gene editing. Perhaps some of us are familiar with cell therapy where new cells are placed into a body in the hopes of replacing a body's diseased cells. Others may know about plastics made from biological sources. An in-depth history of biology is well beyond the focus of this book; however, I'm going to include brief introductions to some of the recent technological advancements built off biology. Then I'll explore some of the companies and research groups innovating at the intersection of biology and technology.

Unraveling the Double Helix and Replication

While today's exciting developments in gene editing or biotechnology could be traced back to scientific advancements in the nineteenth century or even earlier, the big breakthroughs started in the 1950s. Researchers worked to understand how DNA – the molecule that carries an organism's genetic information – was structured. In 1953, James Watson and Francis Crick were credited with identifying the double helix structure of DNA. Their efforts built on the work of numerous scientists, including Rosalind Franklin's x-ray crystallography research. The Watson and Crick model identified that the four bases (the parts of the DNA that store information) are structured in two strands and wound around one another.[2] Scientists credit this model with explaining how DNA is able to replicate itself so consistently and accurately.

In 1958, shortly after Watson and Crick's double helix discovery, Arthur Kornberg identified an enzyme that explained how genetic material is accurately and efficiently replicated. Kornberg was able to determine how this enzyme, named DNA polymerase, constructs DNA from its components.[3] Kornberg was also the first person to synthesize DNA in a test tube.

Recombinant DNA and Antibodies

In the early 1970s, Stanley Norman Cohen, Herbert Boyer, and their team experimented with how to combine DNA from two different sources. In 1973, while working with different species of bacteria, they effectively cut open the DNA from one bacterium, inserted a gene into that DNA strand and reinserted the newly formed – or recombinant – DNA into another bacterium species.[4] Cohen and Boyer's work is regarded as having created the first genetically modified organism. The following year, they repeated the same process, this time inserting a gene from a frog into the bacterium. In 1980, they received a US patent for gene cloning.

Within this period, researchers also explored how to harness antibodies the immune system produces as a form of protection. In 1975, Georges Kohler and Cesar Milstein conducted breakthrough research that demonstrated how antibodies could be produced from a cell line to target a particular threat to the body.[5] This approach for generating monoclonal antibodies would eventually be used to treat different forms of cancer and played a role in combating COVID-19, among other applications.

Mapping and Cloning

Shortly after, Kary Mullis invented polymerase chain reaction (PCR). PCR can rapidly make millions or billions of copies of pieces of DNA.[6] This enables researchers to study DNA segments in much greater detail. The PCR technique pioneered by Mullis has been applied to everything from genome mapping, which I will touch on in a moment, to forensic investigations where tiny amounts of DNA may be present.

Throughout the 1990s, we saw a number of significant breakthroughs. Building on technology already developed, the US allowed gene therapy to be administered. A trio of doctors – R. Michael Blaese, W. French Anderson, and Kenneth Culver – developed an experimental procedure to treat a four-year-old girl with adenosine deaminase (ADA) deficiency, a rare immune disorder.[7] The therapy involved using recombinant DNA techniques to treat her condition and was the first instance of gene therapy in humans. A few years later, the US Food and Drug Administration approved the Flavr Savr tomato, which was the first genetically engineered food to be commercially developed for humans.[8] In 1997, Dolly the sheep was born, surprising the world. Dr. Ian Wilmut cloned a sheep using a mammary cell from an adult that he implanted into an egg whose DNA had been removed.[9] Suddenly, cloning human or mammalian life was no longer the domain of science fiction. Within the span of a decade, we moved from gene therapy in humans, to genetically modified organisms fit for human consumption, to cloning mammalian life.

As we entered the twenty-first century, there was an acceleration of "firsts" across the world. In 2001, Celera Genomics and the Human Genome Project announced they had completed a draft of the human genome. By 2003, when the project came to a close, the researchers who collaborated on the sequencing efforts had mapped an impressive 92% of the human genome.[10] By sequencing the genome, it meant we had developed a map of all the bases – the exact order of them – throughout our DNA. This detailed mapping was a breakthrough that set up future technological innovations addressing genetic mutations and enabling the delivery of personalized medicine.

We also marked another first – the first synthetic life form or organism with a synthesized genome. In 2010, geneticist Craig Venter and his team created a bacterium with an entirely synthetic genome they used to take over a cell.[11] At the time, the discovery prompted discussions about the potential for such technology to produce everything from vaccines to biofuels.

Editing the Genome

While we were mapping the genome, we also began exploring the possibility of editing it. Researchers in Spain, the US, France, and elsewhere identified ways in which enzymes could be programmed to cut or edit specific areas of genetic code. As mentioned earlier, this is called CRISPR, a biological technology that would enable researchers to "permanently modify genes in living cells and organisms and, in the future, may make it possible to correct mutations at precise locations in the human genome in order to treat genetic causes of disease."[12] By 2012 and 2013, teams at the Broad Institute, Harvard University, and University of California at Berkeley published papers on and worked to patent CRISPR-related technology (see Figure 11.1).

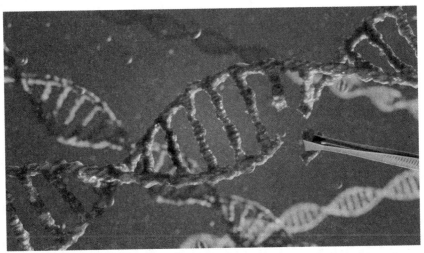

Figure 11.1 The CRISPR gene editing technology enables scientists to edit strands of DNA.

As we have seen, within a relatively short period of time, researchers have uncovered foundational and fascinating aspects of our biological technology. It began with the discovery of the fundamental hardware of our genetic code (DNA's double helix) and quickly moved onto determining the basics of how the genetic operating system ran (DNA polymerase). Shortly afterward, we began experimenting with blending together different sources of DNA. We explored the possibilities of genetic engineering and cloning. We synthesized natural genomes and, eventually, edited the code of life at the level of our genes. We have accomplished a great deal, and yet even for those closest to these innovations their counsel is that we remain very early in our understanding of – and the potential to positively exploit – the power of biology's underlying technology.

Key Biological Systems Enhancing Our World

These discoveries have formed the basis of rapid advancements in health, energy systems, and in the products we consume, to name just a few areas. Entirely new industries were spawned from these scientific advancements.

The modern biotechnology industry arguably has its roots in the mid-1970s with the founding of companies such as Genentech. By 2028, we are projected to spend nearly $900b annually on biotechnology products.[13] This industry has skyrocketed from zero to a thriving global market in the span of just over 50 years. More important than the market size is the impact of the therapies developed by biotechnology and other firms. From mRNA vaccines that were rapidly developed to address the COVID-19 pandemic, to drug therapies that alleviate the impact of autoimmune disorders such as arthritis, technological innovations leveraging biology have had a profound impact on our health.

To feed nearly 8 billion people, we consume enormous quantities of energy and water to produce the proteins, fats, and carbohydrates that sustain us. According to Breakthrough Energy, an investment vehicle founded by Bill Gates to accelerate the transition to net zero, meat production accounts for 15% of greenhouse gas emissions.[14] This is why organizations such as Breakthrough and many others around the globe are investing and hoping to scale cultivated meat projects and companies. These companies are exploring how to use stem cells to cultivate animal cells that look, feel, and taste like the meats we consume today; however, they are grown in labs as opposed to reared on farms. Investors and innovators believe this technology could dramatically reduce carbon emissions. This is one example of biological breakthroughs that may reshape how we feed and fuel ourselves.

The engineering of biological systems may also develop more sustainable ways of producing the chemicals and materials that enable our modern lives, as well as create entirely novel products that aren't in our markets today. Venture capitalists are increasingly backing companies that are experimenting with producing carbon-negative chemicals or attempting to create durable, sustainable materials from microbes.

The number of industries that biological systems may transform is considerable, but in the coming pages I will showcase examples across biotechnology, food systems, and energy and materials. As you'll see, there are many exciting and emerging technologies, as well as significant uncertainty around how those technologies may develop or scale.

Enhancing Human Health

Biotechnology clusters have been developing rapidly across the globe. There are established and world-leading hubs in cities such as Boston, Massachusetts and Cambridge, England, while Beijing and Bangalore are rising in Asia. The thousands of companies that are exploring society's most difficult health challenges are building on the foundational scientific breakthroughs we touched on earlier in the chapter. Across the globe, health issues such as cancers, immunodeficiencies, and neurodegenerative disorders present massive challenges for health systems and very personal challenges for the individuals affected. While many companies are racing to create cures for these conditions, others are exploring how to proactively remove the potential for the onset of these diseases.

According to the World Health Organization's Global Cancer Observatory, it is estimated that there were 18.1 million cancer cases globally in 2020.[15] Recent reporting from the *Wall Street Journal* has highlighted that cancer is affecting more young people globally, igniting concern around the cause of this rise in cases.[16] While these statistics are sobering, scientific researchers have been advancing cutting-edge technologies to combat cancers.

TCR-T Immunotherapy

One cutting edge technology is immunotherapy, which involves helping the body's immune system to detect and destroy cancer cells. This treatment has become more prominent in conjunction with traditional forms of cancer treatment such as chemotherapy or radiation. One area of increased focus is T-cell transfer therapy. T-cells are a type of white blood cell named lymphocytes, which are a critical part of the body's immune system that can help battle cancer.

What does T-cell transfer therapy aim to do? This immunotherapy works to turbocharge the body's ability to detect and destroy cancer cells. While there are different types of T-cell transfer therapies, the underlying concept is that doctors identify the type of tumor or cancer a person has, remove T-cells from the body, engineer those cells to respond to counter the cancer, and then reinject them to attack the tumor cells. Some of the therapies focus on the proteins found on the cancer cell's surface. These therapies are called CAR-T therapies. Others seek to attack the proteins within cancer cells and are named TCR-T therapies.

In my discussions with Brian McGee, he illustrated why immunotherapies such as TCR-T are so potentially transformative. "The really exciting approaches today are those that use the body's own systems to defend against disease. In the past, we used chemicals to interact with the pathways that cause disease, but now we can repurpose the building blocks of nature to fix disease or, potentially more interestingly, ensure that disease never develops in the first place."

One company focused on how T-cells may transform cancer treatment is Immatics. Based in Germany and Texas, Immatics focuses on TCR-T therapies, exploring how to identify the specific targets on and, importantly, in cancer cells for T-cell treatment. It then engineers T-cells that can respond to and destroy those target cells. Immatics believes that by being able to target the proteins both on and inside cancer cells, its therapies are likely to be more effective. In a recent company presentation, Immatics illustrated how therapies like CAR-T that focus solely on a cancer cell's surface proteins might mean that only 25% of the cancer's proteins are accessible. However, unlocking the interior of a tumor cell could open the remaining 75% of that tumor's proteins to potential treatment.[17]

Gene Editing

While CRISPR may be the most well known of the gene editing technologies, it is not the only technology that can edit DNA. CRISPR is being built upon to create gene editing capabilities that can edit longer strands of DNA, as well as individual bases within a DNA sequence. The potential impact could address a wide range of health issues, from inherited blood disorders to cardiovascular disease.

Some have described CRISPR as a pair of scissors that can relatively easily and quickly excise large portions of genetic code – multiple bases at a time. Base editing, in comparison, is the ability to make changes to a single base within a DNA sequence. Rather than cutting DNA, base editing chemically alters a base, turning it into another base.

Beam Therapeutics is a Cambridge, Massachusetts-based company focused on developing disease solutions through base editing. It highlights that many human genetic diseases are caused by a single mutation within a base. These so-called point mutations are potentially prime targets for base editing technology, the type that Beam is pioneering. Giuseppe Ciaramella, Beam's president and chief scientific officer, explained that "[m]any existing gene editing approaches are like 'scissors' that cut the genome. Base editors are like 'pencils' that enable erasing and rewriting one letter of the genome at a time."[18]

The technology leverages CRISPR, but it ensures that both DNA strands are not broken when there is an intervention. The company uses a base editing enzyme as means of chemically altering the base it wants to change. Base editing may have a host of benefits, and the most significant is the capacity to intervene on a base causing a problematic mutation without having any wider impacts on the genome. Initial areas of therapeutic focus for Beam include blood-related diseases such as sickle cell.

Longevity

Discovering ways to extend our lives has long been a human fascination. Today, numerous research teams are turning their scientific exploration efforts to deliver on this pursuit.

Many teams working to increase longevity are focused on a concept known as cellular rejuvenation. While not a spa treatment for your cells, that idea isn't too far off. The concept is that there should be ways to make cells more youthful, to reduce the ways in which cells degrade by understanding how genes express themselves (or don't) over time, and enabling greater longevity at the cellular level.

The Salk Institute, in 2022, announced that cellular rejuvenation efforts had reversed signs of aging in mice. The Institute, in collaboration with Genentech, demonstrated they were able to "effectively reverse the aging process in middle-aged and elderly mice by partially resetting their cells to more youthful states."[19] Scientists involved in the study treated mice with certain molecules named Yamanaka factors, which are effectively reprogramming molecules that help rejuvenate cells or remove markers that are present as aging occurs. With the announcement of their research findings, Juan Carlos Izpisua Belmonte, a professor in Salk's Gene Expression Laboratory, shared that "this approach may provide the biomedical community with a new tool to restore tissue and organismal health by improving cell function and resilience in different disease situations, such as neurodegenerative diseases."[19]

Advancements on longevity proven in mice are an exciting step, but can these types of cellular rejuvenation or reprogramming approaches have similar outcomes in humans? Recently, several longevity-focused companies have launched and are being backed by significant investments from Silicon Valley leaders.

One of them is Altos Labs, which was founded in 2021 with a mission of understanding the biology underlying cellular rejuvenation. The team draws on leading academic and scientific researchers and is purportedly backed by the likes of Jeff Bezos. Altos's founding scientist is Juan Carlos Izpisua Belmonte whose Salk team findings I mentioned above. It is reported that the Altos team will be looking at the biomarkers on genes that may indicate aging or be able to measure the impact of any intervention that reverses aging.[20] This field, however, remains relatively nascent with many unknowns. For example, are there dangers with reprogramming as the process can change the cell's identity? Are these processes too early to test on humans? Should the approach be targeted more narrowly on specific diseases first?

From editing the individual building blocks of our genetic code, to potentially turning back our cellular clocks to extend life, the emerging technology built on our biology is humbling. I have been struck by just how many different types of approaches various teams are pursuing even with the narrow areas we have explored. The number of adjacent research areas and potential applications is truly vast and, given how quickly technologies are developing, it is not difficult to imagine new and potentially profound breakthroughs that may be on the horizon.

Feeding the Future

According to the Food and Agriculture Organization of the United Nations, roughly 38% of global land surface is used for agriculture with approximately one third of that land being used for crops and the remaining two thirds for livestock.[21] As the world's population increases, innovations that boost crop yields or create new or more efficient sources of protein production will be essential. Considering water availability and energy-related concerns, the challenge of feeding the world will not be a trivial one, as addressed in Part 1 citing Deere's significant innovations that help farmers with that plight.

Beyond Deere's impressive work, there is a wide range of other innovators developing technologies they hope will feed us into the future in sustainable and cost-effective ways. A Flagship Pioneering portfolio company, Indigo Ag (mentioned in Part 1), is focused on several potentially transformative activities at the intersection of agriculture and sustainability. One of the product lines that Indigo has developed stems from an observation that robust plants may have a microbial advantage in high stress environments. Indigo works to surface the bacteria or fungi that may provide these more robust plants an edge in the field. By isolating these microbes and coating seeds with them, the company touts that their "beneficial microbes [have] the capacity to protect crops from nearly every abiotic stress imaginable."[22]

Many other companies are pioneering cultured meat. This is where cell cultures are grown to create animal protein in a lab rather than raising livestock in fields. The allure is easy to understand – smaller carbon and water footprint, improved animal welfare, and the potential to scale to meet growing international demand. While the early proofs of concept have been delivered and early-stage investors from Breakthrough Energy to numerous others remain bullish on the technology, like with so many technologies we have explored, the path to commercial scale is yet to be proven.

One company pioneering in this space is Upside Foods. The company has an ambitious goal of creating chicken filets through cultured cells. The way the meat is presented – as a whole cut, for example, versus a nugget – creates production challenges that require considerable innovation in the lab. Upside approaches this by gathering cells, developing a high quality cell line, and then cultivating those cells to grow and multiply before molding the cells into a filet shape.[23] In June 2023, Upside was one of two US-based companies to receive approval from the US Department of Agriculture to start commercial sales of its cultured chicken product.[24] However, reports suggest that the process of creating Upside's signature cultured chicken filet remains a time-intensive and hands-on one, and there is uncertainty about whether the bioreactors (which are necessary to scale the process) will work.[25] This is a valuable reminder that there are few certainties when innovating in truly novel areas.

For all of the food we grow and animals we rear, fertilizer plays a critical role in making fields more productive. An essential component of fertilizer is ammonia, which helps ensure that soil has access to nitrogen to fuel plant growth. The main way we produce nitrogen today is through the Haber-Bosch process. However, this process is a major source of carbon emissions, contributing nearly 2% of global emissions due to the energy intensive nature of the production process.[26]

Recently, Stanford researchers demonstrated that it is possible to generate ammonia using water and nitrogen from the air. Richard Zare, a professor at Stanford, and his research team used nitrogen in gas form, water in liquid form, and a catalyst (magnetite) to create trace amounts of ammonia without needing to apply any electricity to the process.[27] This research remains in its early stages and the next steps are to explore whether the process demonstrated in the Stanford lab could scale. If so, this type of process could have a considerable impact on the amount of energy consumed and carbon produced in fertilizer production.

A Material Impact

We rely heavily on carbon-emitting sources for everything from creature comforts to must haves. From the plastic film protecting your chicken in the supermarket fridge, to the polyester in your running pants, fossil fuel-based products are deeply woven into our supply chains. Innovators believe there are opportunities to displace these unsustainable inputs with biologically-derived products.

The fashion industry has an enormous impact on the world around us. Statistics vary, but the industry is estimated to account for between 8-10% of global emissions and nearly 20% of the world's wastewater production.[28] Also astonishing is the amount of water required to produce a single kilogram of cotton – between 7,500–10,000 liters.[28] Considering the functional value and aesthetic pleasure fashion brings to just about everyone around the world, finding solutions to make the industry more sustainable is of tremendous value.

Modern Synthesis is a London-based start-up seeking to disrupt the underlying materials of the fashion industry. The company describes its approach as "merging biology with cutting edge textile processes, we are crafting an entirely new class of natural textiles that are circular by nature, and customisable by design."[29] Leveraging microbes, the company develops nanocellulose by feeding bacteria a type of agricultural sugar. The company believes this new type of textile will enable fashion companies to adapt and tailor their products more effectively and more sustainably.[30]

Category leaders are also focusing on how more sustainable, bio-based materials could transform their product offerings. Patagonia, a leading outdoor clothing retailer, uses polyester in some of its products. Polyester is a petroleum-based fiber that is durable and has insulating qualities useful for cold weather gear that Patagonia is known for. Since 2014, Patagonia has worked to include biobased sources of polyester.[31] In 2022, after years of research and experimentation, the company debuted its "SugarDown Hoody with a shell and liner made with the biobased polyester alternative."[31]

Packaging is all around us. Almost everything we buy, from fresh food to electronics, is enclosed in some form of packaging. It is typically made from petroleum-based products: plastic wraps and films, styrofoam blocks . . . the list is long. Unfortunately, these products are often used once and thrown away since they're difficult to recycle. As a consequence, the carbon footprint and waste associated with packaging is significant.

Due to the immense usage of packaging, a wide range of companies have chosen to innovate within this space. These companies have often leveraged nature-inspired solutions, including microbes, as we have seen in other sections of this chapter, and mushrooms, as I'll explore next.

US-based Ecovative designs a variety of products powered by mushrooms and their impressive root structures named mycelium. Ecovative uses mycelium due to its strength, ability to withstand pressure, and general durability and resistance to breaking down.[32] The company has developed a production platform that grows geometrical patterns of mycelia in vertical farms at industrial scales (see Figure 11.2).[32] In the case of packaging, Ecovative has developed Mushroom Packaging that is a combination of hemp hurd and mycelium. After the packaging has been used, it can be composted.[33] If products like Ecovative's Mushroom Packaging gain traction in the market, they could go a long way to reducing petroleum-based packaging and lowering emissions in the process.

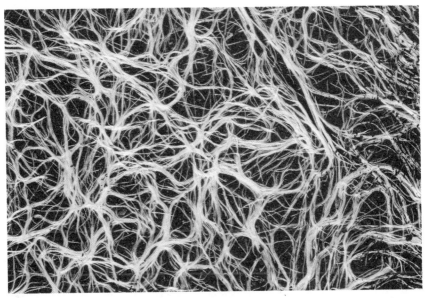

Figure 11.2 Mycelium is the root-like structure of a fungus or mushroom and is being used to create innovative and sustainable materials for a variety of applications.

In Chapter 10, I wrote about the impressive energy-focused developments that are likely to electrify our cars and homes, as well as potentially decarbonize industry. Where carbon capture technology can be used to take carbon from the air or an industrial smokestack and send that carbon deep into the earth, some companies are applying biological solutions to turn carbon into useful fuels and chemicals.

LanzaTech is one such example. Started in 2005, the company has been pioneering how microorganisms can convert flue gasses into products that would otherwise need to be developed using fossil fuels. The company genetically engineers microbes to feed on the carbon monoxide emitted from industrial sources. "It's basically eating a gas stream," according to Jennifer Holmgren, LanzaTech's CEO.[34] Within a proprietary LanzaTech bioreactor, microbes consume carbon in waste gasses and produce ethanol that can be "further upgraded and converted into high value sustainable materials and fuels."[35] The company's recycled carbon has been used in products from running shoes and party dresses to sustainable aviation fuel.[35] Today, LanzaTech's approach is operational at manufacturing facilities across the US, Europe, India, Asia, and Australia. The company is a valuable example of technology that has proven itself outside of the lab and has scaled to begin meeting the considerable demand for more sustainable sources of key chemicals and materials.

Accelerating Technological Development

Over the last few chapters, I have explored numerous research priorities and technologies that, in their own right, have been or are likely to transform our world. What has struck me as I have looked at these technologies is how much they can support adjacent innovations and have potential to accelerate developments across other disciplines. Enhanced computing capacity powered by new generations of silicon-based chips or through quantum computing may help scientists more rapidly unlock the secrets of our biological systems. AI will likely enable more creative testing of hypotheses on how proteins form – as we have seen with Google DeepMind's Alpha Fold – or how cells can be made young again. The imperative of making our supply chains and energy systems more sustainable will catalyze further innovation, likely drawing on fascinating and complex biological systems to solve those challenges.

Technological advancements in other domains may unlock new understanding of and opportunities within biological systems. We are likely to learn better how to code at the level of our DNA or how to further empower miniature but mighty microbes. Although it is clear that we are very early in our understanding of the technology that is biology, it certainly feels like we are on the brink of a sweeping change in how biological systems may positively shape our health and the wider world.

CHAPTER 12

Harnessing Technology's Potential

Across the five technology areas we have just explored, we have seen how today's impressive capabilities are the product of decades of hard work and evolution. There have been continuous refinements and advancements punctuated by unexpected breakthroughs. What strikes me as most exciting are the crossovers between technologies that have enabled some of these leaps within given industries. Given the rapid advancements we are experiencing today, potential breakthroughs within any of the technologies we have explored may spill over and aid the acceleration of advancements in adjacent or unrelated areas.

I will recap Part 2 very briefly to refresh our memories before sharing some reflections I believe are relevant for business leaders who are building during these exciting times.

- ◆ **AI/Robots:** Evolving since the 1950s, AI is having its breakout moment complete with seemingly endless possibilities and the weight of the world's expectations that the technology may address some of our most pressing issues. Robots are now being applied to a variety of tasks both menial and meaningful, from doing low level jobs at a supermarket to enhancing the capability of surgeons in the operating room.
- ◆ **Chips and Sensors:** Chips and sensors turbocharge almost every aspect of our technological lives, powering devices that enhance our health, saving us energy, and providing us with creature comforts.
- ◆ **Quantum:** Recent breakthroughs in quantum chips mean that a new paradigm of computing power may soon enable us to solve

141

phenomenally complex issues across numerous problem areas that today are unsolvable.

♦ **Energy:** With the world racing to achieve an energy transition, there are numerous technologies – from different types of batteries and solar power to fusion, DAC, and hydrogen – that may combine to power our future world.

♦ **Biological Systems:** From the food we eat, to the energy we consume, to health treatments that prolong or enhance our lives, biological systems play a foundational role in our lives and have tremendous potential to be explored and engineered further to meet some of our most complex challenges.

It is up to us to shape our collective future with purpose and intentionality, leveraging these technological innovations in ways that have a positive impact on the world. As I've reflected on many times, this is not to say we should move in this direction without focusing on key business fundamentals. This is about the union of purpose and profit, and I believe that businesses that successfully achieve this marriage will be rewarded – with talent, loyal customers, and enhanced brand reputation.

As we've explored the evolution and future promise of these technologies, I'd like to share a few key reflections. These are meant to provide business leaders with food for thought on how to consider the role technology can play to fuel better products and services.

♦ **Every company is a technology company:** I've been saying this for years, but these words have never been more relevant. No matter what industry you're in, you must view your organization as a technology company. I think back to when I worked with GM and the company was launching OnStar. At that moment, I said, "You are no longer a car company. You're now a technology company." And they agreed! OnStar was, at that time, an innovative technology offering that differentiated GM in the marketplace. Deere is another example: a traditional industrial company that transformed into a smart industrial company through its innovative use of technologies like AI, computer vision, cloud computing, and data analytics. Viewing technology as the enabler that can differentiate and empower your brand is a mindset I implore every CEO to embrace.

♦ **Tech is a way of life:** Once you embrace technology, you have to keep up with how technologies evolve and the implications for your business. This helps organizations evaluate more effectively and more quickly if a technology of particular value may be emerging.

We've seen so many companies get left behind because they didn't recognize the next wave as it was coming. Wang missed the PC wave, Intel missed the mobile phone wave, Kodak missed the digital photography era, Yahoo missed the search wave . . . the list goes on and on. The point here is that it's critical to closely follow new technologies and to understand how they are reshaping markets.

◆ **Explore to gain exposure:** As new innovations are under development (such as those in quantum computing), start experimenting and exploring capabilities. Gaining some exposure to emerging technologies can help you see where there may be the greatest impact and the biggest opportunities as the technology continues to evolve.

◆ **Embrace uncertainty:** As we have seen, it is not possible to determine what technologies will be adopted much less when technologies that are promising will reach maturity. Embrace the uncertainty, but do so in a structured way. Developing scenario planning capabilities can help businesses to see around corners – technological, business model, customer, geopolitical. These capabilities can enhance strategic and product planning capabilities, and enable organizations to determine where they want to place technological bets, even if they are relatively modest in relation to their priority focus areas at the time.

◆ **Vigilance is paramount:** Society has learned the hard way that new technologies (like most inventions) can be used for both good and nefarious actions. Facebook is the prime example of how a technology, when in the wrong hands, was used to undermine our very own democracy. What we must do now, particularly as generative AI becomes infused into almost every aspect of our lives, is to put up the right guardrails that work to minimize the damage technologies could potentially do, while also continuing to enable innovations to thrive so they can positively impact the world. Chapter 16 provides guidelines for how to infuse this approach in your organization.

◆ **Ethics are essential:** What's central to the point above is having ethical practices at the heart of your organization and its products and services. You should have someone focused on ensuring that your organization operates with ethics across every aspect of your business. These practices will ensure that your products and services are designed in line with those values, that your customer data is used in ways that are beneficial to them, that you have solid privacy practices in place, and that you're doing everything possible to eliminate biases or other potentially harmful outcomes. The list goes on, but your ethics provide a literal north star that guides your business when making key strategic decisions around using or developing technologies.

◆ **Demonstrate values through openness:** As you consider guardrails and establish ethics for your product offerings, you must also demonstrate that you're living those values openly and communicate that often with your stakeholders. It's critical that key audiences understand the choices you are making for your business's overall focus, as that explainability and transparency will help build trust. Deere did this in its transformation, and a company like OpenAI operates with openness around the technology models it is building. This type of open communication will help stakeholders understand and assess how your decisions around technologies are impacting them and our world, and demonstrate your efforts to make choices that benefit your stakeholders and humanity.

◆ **Ignite innovation and imagination:** I've said this in many ways throughout this book, but breakthroughs (whether in the development of technology or the application of it) most often come from imagining a better way to do something or finding a new solution to a problem, and then exploring how technology can play a role in delivering or accelerating that outcome. This has been the foundation for leap forward answers for centuries and was the essence of the world-changing inventions of the original Age of Reason. With so many amazing technologies at our fingertips today, we have arrived at another critical moment in time that holds the promise to deliver new discoveries ignited by our own imagination.

The Key Role of Communications

One of the exciting and challenging aspects of living through a period of such disruptive innovation is the potential for it to create large-scale, positive change. These developments typically surface a range of opinions, objectives, and priorities among various parties, from businesses to governments to citizens. Although these varying viewpoints are healthy, they require a process to bring parties together so all voices can be heard for the development of a balanced path forward.

Think about ChatGPT and the polarized views the world has about this technology and its potential impact on the world, from saving it to destroying it. Concerns and aspirations around this technology have spurred unprecedented dialogues across governments and industry. These discussions seek to explore the guardrails needed that could protect us from potential harms, while also enabling innovation to thrive in ways that positively impact our world.

Another complex area is the race to achieve net zero. This highly complex ambition involves multiple parties – from energy start-ups to government officials to policy makers to campaign groups – that must work together to identify and pursue credible paths forward for the energy transition.

As we navigate periods of significant change like this one, communications plays a central and critical role. The capacity to have difficult and productive conversations with key stakeholders, as well as those who hold potentially opposing viewpoints, is valuable in both of the scenarios described above and so many others.

I believe that most organizations struggle with how to approach these types of important conversations. For example, if you're a leading energy producer today and fossil fuels are your main focus, how do you consider conversations with campaign groups that view your business negatively? If you're a prominent campaign group that is seeking to accelerate the transition to low-carbon energy, how do you consider discussions with oil and gas firms due to reputational concerns associated with sharing a stage? Or, if you develop the foundation models that power generative AI systems, how do you communicate with government officials about how to enable your technology to thrive, while also engaging with customer groups about guardrails for transparent, explainable AI? As you are working in complex and uncertain territory with a wide range of stakeholders to establish the right guardrails that protect customers and society, what's the best way to communicate that effort in ways that are genuine and establish trust?

These challenges present opportunities to leverage the power of communications. I see three interlocking challenges that need to be addressed:

1. **Engage with perceived adversaries:** Rather than ignore adversaries or communicate indirectly with them via positioning/messaging, I recommend direct engagement. Bring those with differing viewpoints around a table for a direct and productive discussion. I am in no way implying this will be simple or straightforward, but to move the needle in some of these critical and complex arenas, it will require genuine, and at times potentially uncomfortable, dialogues. Hearing different perspectives on an issue can yield new productive paths forward. It goes back to my point about widening the problem-solving table – more experts and more voices can often yield new insights and new options.

2. **Create scaled platforms for dialogue across local, national, global arenas:** Establish a forum or venue for ongoing discussion/ exploration that unites business, investors, civil society, government, and others on a regular basis to explore complex topics. Together, these groups can share ideas, concerns, strategies, individual areas of expertise, etc. with the goal of getting to understand one another's positions and potentially break down real or perceived barriers between different stakeholder groups. Over time, regular dialogue provides an opportunity to develop initiatives that can accommodate a wider range of perspectives or solutions on challenging issues.

3. **Build trust through authenticity:** Today's complex technologies often create challenging situations for companies, particularly around making the right choices to mitigate any potential negative outcomes of those innovations. These decisions are often in uncharted territory and can be complex and uncertain (as we are seeing right now with generative AI). Therefore, it's critical that companies communicate authentically. This means being open and honest about the complexity of the challenges a technology presents, and demonstrating the earnest path the company is taking to address it. As these technologies evolve and additional steps are taken to address any new issues that surface, companies should communicate these updates with the same level of openness. This authenticity of voice will help to highlight a company's ethics and values, and demonstrate how decisions are grounded in those pillars. This approach will help establish one of the most essential elements with stakeholders: trust.

This chapter presents a few of the most essential efforts that can help us navigate this time of change and of promise. While aspects of this will certainly be complex, as much of it is unfamiliar and unchartered territory, we must embrace this responsibility and find the paths that enable today's innovations to deliver on their potential to ignite positive changes, whether that's the transition to cleaner energy or enabling AI to provide positive outcomes in areas like healthcare and education. This effort will require new organizational and leadership behavior, thinking, and skills. I address many of those in Part 3, and provide an actionable roadmap designed to help organizations find their place on this path of tech for good.

PART 3

Humanity and Technology:
The Path Forward

CHAPTER 13

Becoming a Tech for Good Organization

This chapter offers a guideline on how to get started on the journey of becoming a tech for good organization. As there is no "one size fits all," this chapter presents a general path to follow. This approach should be customized to fit an organization's specific goals and strategies around leveraging today's innovations to have a meaningful impact on humanity, while continuing to achieve commercial success.

As the stories in this book illustrate, there are many approaches to achieve this end.

♦ Deere exemplifies an organization that has transformed its entire business around this mission.

♦ Aquent leverages its roots as a pioneer and innovator in the recruitment arena to initiate key sustainability projects in multiple locations.

♦ Dell uses its core offering in its Solar Hubs projects to provide underserved communities with access to internet services.

♦ Unima was founded with the mission of offering a technology that brings diagnostic testing at a low cost to those living in remote areas.

As you've heard from so many CEOs, there is a palpable passion around their efforts, as they work to deliver a multitude of positive outcomes. First and foremost, this path enables a company to fulfill a higher objective of contributing good to the world by addressing a societal issue. This builds a meaningful, impact-driven corporate culture, which is critical to attract and retain today's talent, particularly Gen Zs and Millennials. Marketing is also elevated to its most authentic form by enabling constituents to experience the good a company is doing. These types of efforts help to build brands that are relevant, respected, and resilient. All of these elements combine to help fuel success and profitability.

What has emerged from the conversations I've had with executives implementing these efforts are a series of common threads that are essential to deliver on this mission. This chapter reviews the key takeaways that define a tech for good organization and how it operates from the inside out. As you read them, keep in mind this is a transformative journey that requires looking at traditional business operations through a new lens and replacing old behaviors with new ones to deliver new and better outcomes.

Embed Tech for Good in Your Company's DNA

Throughout this book, we've heard from many CEOs that embedding this effort into the core of their business is key to the success of their efforts. This approach makes a tech for good effort an unbreakable horizontal thread that is intricately woven into every business function, from strategy to IT to HR to marketing to finance. The effort starts at the very top of the organization, a key priority for the CEO and the C suite, who make it a core component of the company's mission and strategy. By contrast, this is not a siloed CSR initiative, which often sits to the side of an organization's primary business strategy and is often treated as such. This is not to say that CSR and other philanthropic efforts aren't important, but in most organizations they are not tightly woven into the company's objectives.

In Part 1, we looked at IBM's Sustainability Accelerator program, which brings this point to life. This program is tightly aligned with IBM's core business strategies, leverages its core competencies (technology and knowledge), and answers the needs of the communities and customers the company serves. This strategic approach ensures the effort is not siloed, but is a true reflection of what lives within the company's DNA. This impacts how executives and others throughout the organization view the program, ensuring it is treated as a critical component of the business. As such, programs like this will receive the attention and resources required to be successful.

Ignite a Passion for Problem Solving

Another common trait shared by the executives I spoke with is a genuine passion for problem solving. John May, CEO of Deere, transformed that venerable organization around the plight of helping to solve farmers' biggest issues, addressing many problems before they even happen. The company makes it its mission to fully understand the issues today's farmers face, asks the important questions about how to find the best solutions, and then partners with its customers to ensure the products they bring to market fully answer their needs. John and many other executives I spoke with emphasized they are not afraid early versions of new innovations might not be perfect and require further improvement. They understand that the process of developing something breakthrough often involves multiple iterations to get it right.

John Chuang, CEO of Aquent, has built a corporate culture around disruptive and creative solutions to problems, founding an organization with an innovative and technology-fueled approach to recruitment. Aquent applied that same pioneering spirit and drive to its sustainability effort. When the company hit roadblocks along the way, it was never deterred, but rather fueled in its quest to solve the problem.

Noubar Afeyan, CEO of Flagship Pioneering, has created an entire ecosystem of start-ups dedicated to making tremendous leaps in biotechnology innovation to solve some of humanity's greatest issues in healthcare, agtech (feeding the planet), and climate change. At the core of each is an unrelenting drive to discover a leap-forward solution that delivers breakthrough outcomes that better our health, our planet, or our ability to feed the world.

John Samuel, co-founder and CEO of Ablr, illustrated this same type of passion, with his personal experiences fueling his mission to remove barriers for people with disabilities, helping them to access critical aspects of life, including employment.

Embrace Curiosity and Imagination

When you look throughout history, including going back to the original Age of Reason, you'll notice that many of our world's most accomplished innovators share a common trait: immense curiosity. Their journeys of discovery quite often start with a simple question. For Sir Isaac Newton, his discovery of the law of gravity began when he asked why an apple fell straight to the ground vs. side to side or upward. Einstein is noted for his curiosity and passion for asking questions. He once said, "I have no special talents, I am only passionately curious." One of his questions, "What if I rode a beam of light across the universe?" started his quest that led to the development of the theory of relativity.[1]

I'll refer to Noubar Afeyan again here, like so many innovative start-ups, his company has helped launch start their journeys by asking an important "what if" question and then applying their imagination and scientific prowess to solve it. For example: "What if it was possible to understand how cells lose control of gene expression and how that causes disease?" That question was posed by a company called Foghorn Therapeutics, which is pioneering a new class of medicines that target genetic mutations in the chromatin regulatory system, also known as gene traffic control.[2] This is just one of many companies under the Flagship Pioneering umbrella that are founded with the mission to ask and answer critical "what if" questions with the hopes of delivering entirely new classes of solutions in important areas like healthcare.

Re-imagine the C Suite

Transforming an organization around tech for good requires viewing the roles of the CEO and C suite through a different lens. As we've heard from many CEOs, the effort will expand roles and responsibilities across every executive function. This not only involves behavioral and functional changes to ensure efforts are prioritized, but also infusing ethics and morality into decision making so that innovations are used for good and potential risks are mitigated. We reviewed much of this in Part 1, but I'll recap here.

◆ Starting at the top, the CEO will lead the charge to identify and shepherd the company's tech for good mission, supported by the executive team. This starts by asking those key questions outlined in Part 1, which we'll review in the next chapter on building a playbook. Today's CEO needs to expand his/her focus beyond company performance and market leadership to include the organization's larger impact on society and whether it is operating with the right values and ethics.

◆ The CTO will obviously play a critical role in a company's tech for good effort. One key responsibility is to identify those technologies that best fuel the company's goal to positively impact humanity. The CTO must also evaluate technologies from an ethical perspective, ensuring they are used in constructive ways and are not detrimental to people and the planet. For example, they must ensure AI tools aren't built with unconscious biases that could work against talent seeking employment or a promotion. The CTO must also assess technologies from an energy efficiency perspective with the goal of helping to reduce a company's carbon footprint. If the company develops technology, the CTO must ensure both positive and negative applications of new offerings are evaluated and tested so that appropriate guardrails and policies can be put in place.

♦ The CFO's focus will expand to make the right investments in people, processes, and products that enable the organization to deliver on its tech for good mission. This may involve investing in new hires (such as a chief ethics officer), new technologies that reduce a company's carbon footprint, or the resources required to implement a sustainability effort, for example.

♦ The CMO's focus is to find the most powerful way to bring to life the company's tech for good mission. This involves enabling customers and other constituents to experience it across paid, earned, owned, and shared channels. This powerful element will create deeper connections with key audiences who can experience firsthand the company's core values and how it is helping to better our world. More on marketing a tech for good effort can be found in Chapter 15.

♦ There should also be new members taking a seat at this table. Companies should consider appointing a chief ethics officer to oversee all internal governance efforts and ensure technologies are leveraged in a responsible manner that benefits mankind and mitigates risks that could have negative impacts on society (more on this in Chapter 16). Another consideration would be to appoint a chief humanitarian officer whose function would be to ensure all company efforts are focused on outcomes that benefit humanity, including both internal impacts on employees, as well as external outcomes.

Widen the Problem-Solving Table

As noted by Hala Hanna, executive director of MIT Solve, assembling a variety of experts around the problem-solving table unites a mix of knowledge, experience, and perspectives to ideate around answers to problems. This will enable a company to look at the situation through multiple lenses – science, engineering, marketing, finance, regulatory, HR, sustainability, etc. When working through this process, pull experts from inside and outside the organization to help identify both opportunities and potential roadblocks to ultimately find the right path and the right solution.

View Technology as the Great Enabler

Most companies in most industries have already been transformed by technology from an operations and process perspective. Organizations delivering on tech for good go far beyond that, viewing technology as an enabling and accelerating force to contribute something meaningful to humanity. In many organizations, particularly those mired in traditional frameworks and mindsets, this requires breaking away from conventional thinking. It involves a willingness to open the aperture wider when viewing technology with a drive to find existing or new innovations that hold the most promise to address some of today's most pressing problems, whether that's energy efficiency or finding a breakthrough solution to a problem. This is the antithesis of the mindset around tech for tech's sake. While this is the primary role of the CTO, it should be a mindset adopted throughout the entire organization.

Steep Values in Strong Ethics and Morality

As noted many times, strong ethics and morality are critical. Every executive I interviewed emphasized the importance of putting those values at the nucleus of their organization, as they are essential to help fuel the successful outcome of a tech for good effort. These foundational values must be deeply embedded into how an organization operates every day, ensuring it is using the right technology in the right way to maximize positive outcomes and minimize negative ones, be that bias against an employee or harming the planet. This includes how companies treat their customer data and the respect they pay to privacy and security. More on how to infuse these values into your organization can be found in Chapter 16.

Galvanize Your Culture Around Good

Building the type of corporate culture that attracts, motivates, and inspires today's talent is particularly challenging as the workforce has gone remote. Since so much of work happens on Zoom and other videoconferencing platforms, it requires working harder and smarter to ensure you are uniting your talent around common goals and values focused on societal impact.

This is paramount to many generations, but Gen Z and Millennials in particular. Those generations combined "account for 43% and 49% of the U.S. and global population, respectively. Not only are Millennials the largest workforce in U.S. history but together with Gen Z, they are poised to be on the receiving end of a wealth transfer as big as tens of trillions of dollars."[3] Both Gen Z and Millennials view societal impact as a "must have" when making both purchasing and employment choices, expecting more from companies in this realm than any other generation.[4]

Tech for good efforts can be a galvanizing force to accomplish these goals. The executives I interviewed spoke volumes about their efforts' impact on corporate culture and employee engagement. For example, Justina Nixon-Saintil, vice president and chief impact officer at IBM, noted that its sustainability efforts were key to higher levels of employee engagement. John Chuang, CEO of Aquent, also noted that its efforts have had a tremendous impact on building a strong culture centered around problem solving and contributing to sustainability.

The following are some of the basics on how to ignite a culture grounded in good inside the walls of your company:

- **Start at the top:** At the outset, the CEO should announce the effort internally and demonstrate a true passion for it. This will underscore leadership's commitment to the effort and help the entire company to rally around it. Obviously, this should not be a "one and done" effort. This kickoff must be the first of an ongoing communications effort that showcases how this effort is part of the company's DNA.

- **Build internal/external brand ambassadors:** In addition to company leadership communicating about the effort, work to create a base of internal and external ambassadors for it. This includes empowering employees to communicate about it on their social feeds as a means to share their excitement for and involvement in the effort. There may be external audiences who share in this type of outreach as well. For example, if your customers or partners are involved, encourage them to post photos or videos. You should also incorporate their voices in videos and outreach you create to illustrate the positive impact this effort is having on external audiences.

- **Celebrate milestones:** Tech for good efforts will be a critical element of your organization and its culture on an ongoing basis. As such, celebrate moments when your company hits key milestones, be that reaching a sustainability goal or achieving an objective around an external project. This not only highlights your company's progress, but also enables your entire organization to share in the excitement around the effort.

- **Reward involvement:** Your employees will play a key role in delivering on your tech for good effort. As such, build this effort into ongoing reviews to not only underscore its importance, but also provide an opportunity to reward exceptional contributions.

I hope you find these insights as inspiring as I did when they were shared with me by so many executives from companies large and small and across all types of industries. These key ingredients emerged time and again as defining principles of a tech for good organization. As mentioned, this is a process, a transformative journey requiring new thinking and new behavior. As such, fundamental changes like this will take time, but also position your organization for future success, as your brand will stand for something so much larger than profit. It will also incorporate a purpose that will have a lasting meaning and impact on the world.

CHAPTER 14

Key Questions to Find Your Pathway

A sking the right questions is often the first step in any transformative process, whether that's imagining a breakthrough solution to a problem or working to re-invent your company around a societal purpose. Part 1 outlined some key questions to ask when working to identify your path for a tech for good effort. Here, I'll recap and provide more detail. These questions are designed to help companies start the process at the highest level, providing the framework to ignite the effort.

What Do You Want Your Legacy to Be?

This question is the critical jumping-off point. Exploring the answer is ultimately about figuring out the higher purpose of your organization: what type of business you are *really* in. Throughout my career, I've asked this question of many CEOs. Typically, the answer is not the obvious one. It's not about being biggest or the best . . . chip, software, or tractor company. What the answer should capture is the larger purpose that sits far above your products or services. Ideally, it should be connected to those offerings, so it's relevant to what you bring to the world.

I thought it would be interesting to explore tech for good ideas around a powerful brand like Google. To better understand some of the company's initiatives in this realm of good, I spoke with Brian Cusack, principal at PartnerOcean LLC who worked at Google for 13 years, specializing in the healthcare advertising side of the business for much of his time there. Brian first spoke to the culture within Google and how he found it to be grounded in the right values and priorities.

"First let me say that I believe Google always defaulted to do the right thing for the right moral choice, the right end consumer choice. Before I left, there was so much conversation going on within the engineering groups around whether or not search was biased by definition because most of the code was written by white males or Asian/Indian males. So, if they're writing all the code, does that bias filter through into search results? And search results writ large, that could mean YouTube videos, as well as a number of different things. The question was, were we providing the best results for a single black woman in the city based on her experience if all the code was being written by someone who's never shared a life experience with her? Well, the answer is no, you're not. So that became part of a much larger initiative to figure out how you can involve a more diverse set of engineers, and then how do you find those engineers? And that's how Google began investing in Made with Code and other similar programs with the goal of starting to build a popula-tion of more diverse computer scientists and engineers who offer more diverse life experiences."

Brian also explained other early efforts at Google that had a societal benefit. One was when the Google Health Team and Deep Mind AI Team used machine learning to read x-rays.

"This was done not to replace radiologists, but to help them. For example, a radiologist might read 25 x-rays a day and the machines can read 10,000 a day, learn from that, and provide feedback to the radiologist ranging from your diagnosis is right on to hey, have you thought about this in addition to your diagnosis? This was simply an effort that's not about profit, but about helping radiologists do a bet-ter job for better clinical outcomes. Finding the commercial oppor-tunity could come later."

Another Google effort involved tracking the path of the sun around the globe and making that information available on micro regional levels so that people could determine the best placement of solar panels. This service, leveraging Google's data, was offered for free.

As I spoke with Brian, one idea that came to mind is the concept of Google owning the veracity of information. One of the biggest challenges we face with information today is determining what content to trust. As we all know, the outcomes of misinformation or fake news can have dire consequences and, with generative AI, this problem is at risk of becoming massively accelerated.

To help address that, what if Google worked to ensure information found through its search engine was truthful, and that misinformation and other questionable content were either labeled as such (perhaps via some type of AI-fueled software filter or other technology) or the validity of content was flagged in some way to alert the reader that it is either false or questionable? I recognize this is a lofty and complex goal, but there are steps the company could take to move in the direction of becoming the protectors and purveyors of truthful information. In November 2023, Google did take a step in this direction when it announced that YouTube (a brand Google owns) will soon require creators to disclose if their video includes AI-generated content. Those that don't disclose this will face penalties. Continuing along that path would deliver a massive service to society by addressing one of the biggest challenges we face today.

What Actions Can You Take That Reflect What's in Your Company's Soul?

Once you answer the first critical question, the next step is to imagine the paths your company could take to act on it and bring its legacy to life. For example, could you use your core offering in some way to help address a world issue that helps people and/or the planet? We've provided several examples thus far, but other ideas come to mind. For example, could Amazon use its fleet of drones to deliver supplies during times of emergency, like when a part of the world faces a natural disaster or is at war? Imagine there's an earthquake and vital medical supplies or food are needed. Could Amazon use its fleet to answer this need?

Another way to explore this answer is to find an initiative or series of initiatives to undertake that benefits society. For example, could your organization sponsor a series of sustainability efforts that would help in the fight against climate change? IBM and Aquent set great examples in this realm, and so many others have these types of efforts underway.

Are your customers facing an ongoing challenge that today's technology could help them solve? Clearly, Deere addresses this. To give just one example, its See & Spray™ technology "sees" the difference between a weed and a healthy plant, and therefore, only sprays the weed with herbicides. This reduces the use of herbicides by 2/3+, which has both a tremendous financial benefit to farmers and a huge environmental/sustainability impact – a win on multiple fronts.

How Can Technology Accelerate and Augment This Effort?

Once you've determined your higher purpose and identified efforts that bring it to life, the next step is to explore which technology or combination of technologies will enable, amplify, and/or accelerate these initiatives. This function should be spearheaded by your CTO or chief innovation officer. It should be an ongoing effort to ensure your company is in step with new innovations that deliver the best possible positive outcomes. In this book, we've provided stories of companies using a range of technologies, including machine learning, AI, solar panels, cloud computing, computer vision technology, robotics – all serving as the engines driving their tech for good missions. Dive into these types of tools to see which ones best augment or accelerate your effort.

Does Your Company Have the Ecosystem to Deliver on This?

Embedding a tech for good effort within the core of your organization requires having an ecosystem that supports it and fuels its success. This involves the essential three Ps: people, products, and partners.

PEOPLE

The book has covered the critical roles the CEO and the C suite will play in this effort. This involves expanded roles and responsibilities and appointing new players such as a chief ethics officer. Once this core team has established the overall direction for the effort, enlist input from a select group of employees who offer a variety of strengths and knowledge. Ask them for feedback and input to ensure your tech for good path will resonate with your talent. Ultimately, you'll want to give all employees opportunities to get involved so they can fulfill their personal goals of contributing to a societal cause. Think about what training and tools they'll need to be successful members of the team.

Consider appointing a tech for good advisory board, comprised of external constituents such as customers, technology innovators that are relevant to your effort, experts in academia, government representatives, and legal experts. Leverage their broad expertise as you develop and implement your effort. This will help widen the problem-solving table and ensure your effort is on track. Establish an ethics board to ensure all efforts within your organization reflect the principles and values you stand for.

PRODUCTS

Next, you need to look at what products/technologies are required to deliver on your effort. Think about the mindset around innovation we've addressed in the book. Ask the right "what if" questions to imagine a better way of doing something for a better outcome and think about the role technology can play in that process. If your company develops products, determine if there are new technologies (like AI) that could enhance existing offerings or if there's an opportunity to develop a completely new breakthrough. If you're using solutions from external providers to deliver on your effort, source those best to address the issue, assess costs and timeframes, and evaluate from an ethical perspective. Establish the appropriate guardrails so that the technology is safe and leveraged for the good of society and does not have unintended negative consequences.

PARTNERS

Many tech for good efforts require partnerships with external organizations in order to fully deliver on the mission. Think about the various types of partners who could drive the success of your effort. Are there innovative products or specialized services you'll need to accomplish your mission? Are there local or national government officials who could help accelerate the effort? Perhaps someone on your tech for good advisory board has a specific expertise that could be leveraged to move the initiative forward. Know what the requirements are for success and align yourself with the right resources to deliver on that.

Are You Choosing a Tech for Good Effort That Can Elevate Your Brand?

This type of effort is ultimately about reinventing your organization and its brand. It's about moving from a noun to a verb, meaning becoming a company that takes action and contributes good back into the world. In most cases, this requires a change in corporate behavior and a willingness to adopt new, unorthodox business practices.

As you move through this process, make sure you select an effort that will resonate with your customers. Also, be aware of what your competitors are doing. This effort should be unique to your organization and what's in its core – an authentic representation of your brand that differentiates you in the marketplace. John Chuang led with that when we spoke with him about Aquent. He chose a path for his company in sustainability that reflected Aquent's spirit of being a pioneer in its field and passionately innovating to solve problems. As we'll explore in the next chapter, when you choose the right tech for good path, marketing will become a powerful, organic force that will forge stronger and deeper connections with your constituents and elevate your brand to new heights.

Answering these fundamental questions is the critical jumping off point to start you on your journey. As we've addressed many times in this book, questions are often the best way to start any process involving change or innovation, whether that's transforming your company around a tech for good effort or working to develop a better solution to an existing problem. Make sure you have the right voices around the table as you start the journey of asking and answering these questions, as diverse perspectives often yield the best answers. And, as this is truly a journey, revisit these questions as you move forward to see if any of the answers change, as they may offer new ways to deliver better outcomes for your tech for good effort.

CHAPTER 15

Has Marketing Disappeared?

In the 1990s, I was working with one of the big advertising agencies and had an opportunity to pitch a PR program to one of its top clients. To help prepare our pitch, the ad agency gave me a massive 50-page creative deck. After an exhausting process of reviewing far too many pages of what I would call analysis paralysis, I finally arrived at the last page. It revealed that the logo had the ability to fly. Honestly, the preceding 49 pages had almost nothing to do with that final result. My gut reaction was that someone in creative thought it would be cool for the logo to fly, and the agency built an incredibly elaborate and expensive deck around that idea – the tail wagging the dog, so to speak.

My point here is that marketing is often a creative front, a very designed image for the brand to attract people and move them to a desired action. My last book, *Authentic Marketing: How to Capture Hearts & Minds Through the Power of Purpose,* provided an overview of the history of marketing, noting how marketing has been evolving from pure manipulation to (in many cases) a more authentic, substantive representation of a brand – one that showcases the company's soul, its values, and what it is doing to help humanity. To achieve this more authentic form of marketing, strategies and creativity should be now focused on how to most effectively bring this story and these values to life, enabling constituents to fully experience and become immersed in them.

A tech for good effort is central to this authentic form of marketing. With this approach, marketing as we have known it almost disappears. Audiences won't feel marketed to, but rather become engaged and immersed in stories and experiences that inspire them and ignite an affinity for the brand.

As someone who has dedicated my entire career to tech PR and helped to shape this segment of the marketing industry, I have always viewed PR's role as the discipline that builds a strong narrative or story around the "why" of a technology. This was particularly important in the early days of technology when engineers often wanted to push tech for tech's sake. Our focus was and remains to bring forth messages and storylines that articulate the benefits – why those tech advancements actually matter to people, to businesses, to markets, and to the world. As technology has finally evolved to impact humanity, tech PR is naturally evolving the "why it matters" narratives to showcase the amazing outcomes technology is delivering to help solve problems in areas like climate change, access to education, and better outcomes in medicine. It's a natural evolution of our own discipline and one we should all embrace.

More on the history of tech PR can be found through this link at the Museum of PR (https://www.commpro.biz/news/the-history-of-tech-pr-with-larry-weber).

These narratives can be brought to life through an integrated marketing program that leverages the many platforms we have at our fingertips today – particularly those that best enable customers to fully experience these stories. This type of experiential marketing will enable customers and other audiences to be moved by the effort, creating more of an emotional connection to the brand. In this chapter, I'll share a few of the most essential elements of this effort. And later, we'll explore how AI-based tools can help optimize and accelerate these activities.

Ignite the Power of Storydoing

The most powerful component of this effort is sharing your story with others. This involves the creative process of creating opportunities for your audiences to fully experience your tech for good efforts. I call this form of storytelling *storydoing*. This is the critical point in marketing in which brands evolve to become a dynamic verb as opposed to a static noun, as they showcase the actions they're taking to have a positive impact on the world.

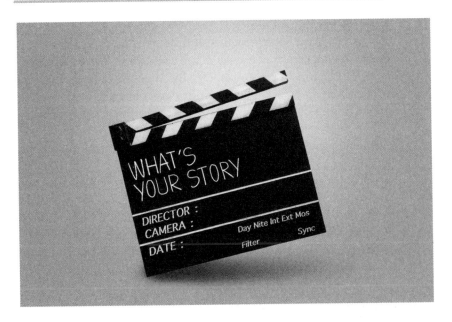

This storyline should be a thread woven into every effort across paid, earned, owned, and shared channels, from bylines to blogposts. Here are a few examples that use familiar tactics infused with inspiring stories to capture your audiences' hearts and minds:

- **Create compelling videos:** The world loves to learn and be entertained by videos. This powerful medium enables you to invite customers and other audiences into your tech for good efforts. These videos can include interviews with customers or other audiences positively impacted by your effort, as well as simply highlight work in progress on your projects. As we all know, videos today don't have to be professionally produced, as people prefer watching less polished videos simply created on a cell phone. These can be used across all of your owned media, including your website and social channels.

- **Blog about it:** Invite audiences along your journey by blogging about it on a regular basis. Let them know the progress you're making, the roadblocks you face and how you are overcoming them. Be open, candid, and real, as that will engage your readers and ignite more interest in continuing to read the next chapter of your story. Interview key players, particularly those directly impacted by your effort, to showcase the good it is delivering. Highlight milestones and accomplishments to show the progress you're making.

♦ **Capture earned media:** Tech for good efforts make for powerful stories that have all the right elements to attract the attention of media. With so much negativity in the world today, these stories provide an opportunity to infuse some much-needed positive, feel good content. Identify which media would be most interested in your story and then apply the familiar process of drafting and placing bylined articles. You can also invite media to write their own story. Offer them interviews with not only company execs, but more importantly, those most impacted by your effort. If possible, invite them to see the project in action to fully immerse them in it. Even press releases have a place in this effort and should be used to launch the effort or announce when your company reaches major milestones.

♦ **Engage through speaking:** Tech for good stories make excellent speaking platforms. Deere secured the keynote spot at CES through its impressive efforts. Find venues that align with your effort and pursue opportunities to share your story. Immerse your audience in multiple ways. Invite partners, customers, employees, and others involved in the effort to join you, as they'll bring different aspects of the effort to life. Leverage videos during presentations to showcase the work in action and the impact it's having.

♦ **Use webcasts and podcasts:** Today's audiences love a good webcast or podcast, so use these platforms to tell your story. This type of content inspires, entertains, and brings much needed positivity to your viewers and listeners.

♦ **Create brand ambassadors:** Often the most powerful and authentic communications come directly from your employees when they are empowered to share their involvement in and passion for a meaningful impact effort. To that end, consider appointing a group of employees best suited to be brand ambassadors for your tech for good effort. Encourage them to share their stories and enthusiasm on their social channels. They could also serve as guest bloggers on your website or be terrific interviewees in webcasts and podcasts. This will help spread positivity around your effort throughout your talent base and elevate your corporate culture.

♦ **Make it central to internal communications:** Since this type of effort lives within the heart of an organization, it should be a central theme in internal communications. Ensure company leadership communicates regularly about it, providing updates on progress, celebrating milestones, and rewarding individuals and teams that go above and beyond to help reach goals. These messages should be delivered with passion, underscoring management's enthusiasm and commitment to the effort.

AI Is Reshaping Marketing

As a disruptive technology that is reshaping everything it touches, generative AI is having a massive impact on marketing and will continue to do so as it gets increasingly infused into how we promote our brands. Many of the marketing elements described in this chapter will be enhanced and augmented by these new AI tools, which will accelerate outputs and maximize the impact of marketing tech for good efforts.

Here's a brief overview of some of the ways AI is poised to transform marketing:

◆ **Content creation:** Generative AI will enable marketers to more effortlessly create content customized to audiences' specific interests and preferences, particularly those around your tech for good effort. This content will be more personalized, which will be of stronger interest and more likely to be viewed or shared. AI tools can also enable marketers to create imagery and ads quickly and easily through automated processes that produce backgrounds that products can be easily dropped into. A number of big brands, from Amazon to Meta, have offerings in this space.

◆ **Creativity and ideation:** Marketers must often process vast amounts of market research to better understand trends and data on customers. AI expedites this process by delivering insights much faster. These "reveals" can be used to develop creative concepts and campaign ideas that are more targeted and better reflect key trends happening within their customer base. This could be used to gain insights into what types of societal impact effort best align with your customers' interests. These ideas should still be tested, with focus groups for example, to ensure outputs produced by AI resonate with customers and no biases have been baked in.

◆ **Next-gen search optimization:** AI will take search to new levels, as AI-fueled algorithms hold the promise to make search outcomes more personalized and accurate. All of this will impact keyword search and content optimization, which are core elements of SEO. New tools can help marketers automate these functions, helping to identify relationships between keywords, predicting user behavior, and identifying search trends.[1]

◆ **Fueling customer insights:** Understanding the impact of your tech for good effort, as well as tracking your progress, is essential. This is another area where AI will have a massive impact, heightening your ability to listen to customers and understand what they care about and how they're reacting to your efforts. Here are a few areas where AI is taking this effort to entirely new levels:

- **Social listening:** AI's social listening tools enable companies to hear what customers think on a massive scale and at warp speed. The ability to leverage unstructured data (or conversations) happening online holds the power to transform one of the biggest drivers of marketing today, customer experiences. And according to Gartner, 77% of board members view AI as one of the biggest game-changers for CX.[2] Use this process to understand what your customers care about and how they are reacting to your corporate purpose.

- **Sentiment analysis tools:** Also known as emotion AI, these tools leverage natural language processing systems to qualitatively measure your customers' "mood" about various dimensions of your business, including your purpose. By understanding how your customers feel in their posts, you can better analyze their reactions to determine what's resonating, what's not, and know what adjustments should be made to ensure your tech for good effort and other core dimensions of your organization are having a positive impact.

- **Data analytics tools:** As mentioned, today's AI tools will increase the speed and efficiency of using data to glean customer insights. Chatbots can be used for fact checking and validation, which is particularly helpful if the data produced delivers unexpected results. AI tools can also produce automated reports, which expedites the process of leveraging data to better understand and track audience behavior, such as retweets, mentions, likes, shares, click-through-rates, etc. All of this will help you assess the traction your efforts are gaining with stakeholders.

Other Ways to Measure and Track Your Progress

There are a variety of other ways to track your progress, ranging from newer methods to some very old-school means. Here's a quick overview:

- ◆ **Online customer communities:** Offered by companies such as C Space, this effort is like a next generation focus group that enables companies to test messages, programs, and products on a community of online consumers. Businesses can gain quantitative and qualitative insights to ensure everything from their products to their tech for good effort is in sync with what matters most to customers.

◆ **Surveys:** Although surveys have been used for decades, they continue to be a sound vehicle to discover customer perceptions and behaviors related to their purchasing decisions. Today, there are AI tools that can help create surveys and produce accurate insights quickly. Use surveys to find out what role your tech for good effort plays when customers buy a product. Learn how they feel about your effort and your ability to deliver on it. Is it meaningful to them? Does it make them feel good about buying your products? Would they recommend your products to someone else because of this?

Tools like Survey Monkey can also help companies better understand the impact of their tech for good effort on employees to see how it links to their job satisfaction, retention, and motivation. Find out whether it resonates with your employees and makes them feel proud. Ask them if they think it's authentic and if your company is delivering on its mission. Ask if they think aspects of the effort need to change and, if so, how. This not only provides critical feedback about how your tech for good effort is impacting your workforce, but also engages them in the process and enables their voices to be heard. In this way, it helps make it a community effort within the organization.

◆ **One-on-ones:** Never underestimate the old-school method of simply talking to your customers. Design a quick questionnaire that you can use to guide you through questions about their views of your company's tech for good effort and how it relates to purchases, brand perception and loyalty, making recommendations, giving reviews, etc. You'll gain important feedback, show customers you value their opinion, and help to ignite deeper engagement by making the connection.

Treatment of Data

Across any effort, customer data should always be used appropriately – in ways that protect their privacy and used only to customers' benefit. As mentioned, this data should be used as a powerful listening tool to better understand your customers, their values, priorities, aspirations, and pain points. This will not only help ensure that your product/service offerings are in step with their needs, but also shape the direction of your tech for good effort. Treat customer data with the utmost respect. Think about what John May shared about Deere's approach to data. The company treats it as a precious asset that belongs to their customers and is never used without their permission.

Embracing this more authentic form of marketing and leveraging AI in ways that can accelerate and augment the impact of your effort will help make your brand more relatable, more respected, and more resilient when and if things go wrong. In my experience, this more organic form of our craft makes the job of the marketer so much easier and far more gratifying. When you have powerful and meaningful stories to work with, you'll spend less time trying to find ways to make a brand stand out and more time simply applying the most creative and impactful ways of bringing a compelling tech for good story to life. As mentioned, this will be powerful content that has a strong place across all channels – paid, earned, owned, and shared. Once shared across these platforms, your stories will engage and inspire your constituents and influencers alike, giving them a true affinity with your brand and all of the good it stands for, as marketing almost disappears.

CHAPTER 16

Putting Innovations on the Path of Good

With so much potential at our fingertips from today's innovations, the pressing and highly topical questions are how do we as a society move forward to ensure we continue to unlock the full potential of technology to solve problems, while also mitigating risks and potential negative outcomes? And what roles should business vs. government play in balancing this delicate equation? The key word in that last sentence is balance. We hear so much from either side – the pros shouting tech will save the world, and the cons fearing tech will destroy us, particularly around generative AI. This is all about striking a balance, about responsible innovation that enables technology to better our world, while also putting guardrails in place that protect us.

My belief is that regulation and innovation don't have to represent opposing views. Regulation doesn't have to stifle innovation and advancing technology doesn't have to move forward recklessly. The two can constructively intersect with the collective goal of generating better outcomes all around.

What my research has revealed is that to achieve this balance, we need to look at 3 Es: ethics, engagement, and evolution. Also, we need to include stakeholders who are often on the sidelines of these discussions, namely consumers or citizens. Business and government won't be able to negotiate these fast-paced, uncertain, and high stakes judgments on their own.

Throughout my exploration of technology for good, I have spoken with a diverse range of people working on some hugely exciting challenges.

Some are technologists and executives, some have focused on regulation, others sit between business and government representing the views of consumers and citizens. As I think about the insights they shared with me, particularly in relation to how society navigates the complex change associated with rapidly developing technology, these three Es emerged time and again.

The Three Es: Ethics, Engagement, and Evolution

Here, I'm going to provide a quick overview of these three Es, highlighting the critical space they hold in ensuring technology is on a path of good.

- *Ethics* are paramount to responsible innovation, as they establish the very foundation upon how businesses should operate. Ethics provide a north star that guides businesses when making decisions around technologies and pursuing a path forward, ensuring they work within the right framework to accomplish their desired outcomes. For example, they can guide companies to make the right decisions around technologies like AI to ensure they are being used in ways that align with both laws/regulations, as well as with corporate values and ethics.

- *Engagement* is another essential element, as it involves bringing together the right parties – business, government, citizens – for productive discussions that can inform decision-making around the use of technology, necessary guardrails, and how to best move forward that takes diverse viewpoints into consideration. At the end of the day, this is about ensuring we are creating opportunities and spaces for productive discussions and debates that enable all critical voices and perspectives to be heard and factored into decisions.

- *Evolution* involves an understanding that technological development moves at warp speed today and we need to be ready for new innovations as they emerge, particularly with those that involve uncertainties about their use and potentially positive and negative impacts. The quote often attributed to John Maynard Keynes comes to mind, "when the facts change, I change my mind." Our ability to evolve with ever-evolving data and potentially shifting social priorities seems essential to me.

As I address a potential approach for enabling us to develop technology products that are on the path of good, I will be coming back to these 3 Es.

I will also touch on how key stakeholders such as business, government, and citizen-consumers can play pivotal roles.

Exploring the Three Es in the Context of Generative AI

As we dive into this subject, we will do so by looking at generative AI. The massive breakthroughs we have observed in this technology have brought the very issues of ethics, engagement, and evolution to the fore. We are in uncharted territory and working to develop a path forward. Although we'll explore AI, the principles and thinking would naturally apply to other technologies as well.

I'll start with how the current debate around AI regulation is developing. To open this story, I visited the United Kingdom, virtually. I had a fascinating and insightful discussion with Ollie Buckley, who is the founding executive director of the UK government's AI ethics advisory body, the Centre for Data Ethics & Innovation. Ollie serves as an advisor to companies, governments, and foundations on responsible AI, ethics in AI, and regulation of technology products.

Where Ollie started was counterintuitive to the discussion we often hear about regulation and innovation, which is that they are locked in battle. Ollie shared a very different perspective. "Regulation and innovation don't always have to be in tension. Good regulation can be pro-innovation," Ollie explained. "By demanding higher standards in areas like safety, fairness, or data protection, governments can create incentives for technologists to develop better products that are also better aligned with the best interests of both individuals and society."

Ollie emphasized that constructive government regulation can actually spur innovation from business. For example, regulations around transportation safety have helped to produce safer planes and cars. Think seat belts. Environmental standards set by the government have ignited innovation among manufacturers to produce more energy efficient refrigerators or cars, for example. The tremendous progress in the electric vehicle arena exemplifies this point. One of the largest vehicle markets in the world, California, mandated that any new cars sold in the state from 2035 must be electric or plug-in hybrids.[1]

This topic is front and center around generative AI, as the world grapples with how to effectively manage the potential uses and drive beneficial outcomes of this world-changing innovation. Many AI experts are emphasizing the need to find effective ways to contain this technology so that it doesn't slip beyond our control. Mustafa Suleyman, co-founder and CEO of Inflection

AI and DeepMind (now part of Google), argues that we must "divide power and decision-making authority between people and machines." In his recent book, *The Coming Wave*, Suleyman writes that this will require "an overarching lock uniting cutting-edge engineering, ethical values, and government regulation."[2] Note the emphasis that Suleyman places on ethical values.

There are other critical dimensions to this debate. Many prominent voices and leaders of AI companies, such as Suleyman, Sam Altman (CEO, OpenAI), and Dario Amodei (CEO/co-founder, Anthropic) believe that while this technology could do harm, it is also vital to address some of today's biggest challenges. One of the dividing lines in this complex issue is whether we should be focusing on the more immediate challenges of AI or more existential ones. For example, there is an important and growing discussion about how to reduce bias and discrimination in the datasets that train AI models, as well as in the models themselves. Concerns abound around the risk of this technology to disrupt election processes or flood our social networks with even more misinformation or disinformation. These are immediate challenges we're reckoning with as evidenced by near-daily news reports on these subjects.

However, others worry about longer term, existential threats that AI could pose. MIT physicist and AI researcher, Max Tegmark, is one of those concerned about our potential inability to control AI. Although he also believes in the ability for AI to solve numerous global challenges, he has shared that "ever since the term AI was coined in the 1950s, it was obvious to leaders in the field that if we ever succeeded in getting close to human-level AI, it was pretty likely we would face enormous risks, like extinction, but people kept thinking this was really far away."[3] Tegmark was one of the AI researchers, in March 2023, who proposed a pause in training powerful AI systems until safety standards could catch up. Researchers such as Tegmark highlight that AI systems may become so powerful, so quickly that our capacity to contain them – as Suleyman touches on in his book – may become impossible with potentially disastrous consequences.

Establish Ethics for Responsible Innovation

From product design to the use of data to how customers are engaged, responsible technology development starts with business and the ethics companies use to govern critical business decisions.

"The private sector must do so much more than simply comply with government regulations," said Ollie. "Companies must establish operating principles and procedures that reflect their core values and demonstrate that they operate against a clear set of ethics. These types of guidelines will enable businesses to answer complex questions around their development and use of technology in a manner that is aligned with their corporate values and culture."

IBM

In business, many organizations have established internal processes and procedures with technology ethics at the core. Among them is IBM, which is working diligently in many aspects to strike this delicate balance of responsible innovation. The company recognizes both the need to address risks created by technologies like generative AI, as well as enable the potential of this technology to positively impact our world. IBM has a history of striving to bring new technologies like AI to market responsibly, with trust and transparency front and center in its endeavors.

Like so many others we've spoken to, IBM views AI as a technology that can augment (vs. replace) what people do. The company was among the first to establish an AI Ethics Board and has been active in working with governments worldwide on regulatory approaches. I had the pleasure of speaking with Christina Montgomery, IBM's vice president and chief privacy and trust officer, who co-chairs the AI Ethics Board and also leads the company's industry and regulatory compliance work around privacy, data, and AI.

"At IBM, we see tremendous potential both to address societal risks posed by AI, as well as its ability to answer global challenges, along with everyday tasks like business productivity, improving supply chains, IT automation, cybersecurity, etc.," said Christina. "We are big proponents of AI and, as a business, have evolved into an AI and hybrid cloud company. We also just announced a new fund for venture company investment, investing in new companies in the generative AI space."

In addition to bringing AI-based innovations to market, IBM has played a leadership role in sharing its point of view with governments on how to responsibly regulate AI. As part of this effort, Christina presented testimony before the US Senate Judiciary Committee Subcommittee on Privacy, Technology, and the Law on May 16, 2023. This was part of a hearing on the "Oversight of AI: Rules for Artificial Intelligence." She presented along with Sam Altman and Gary Marcus, professor emeritus, New York University.

The presentation articulated IBM's recommendation on precision regulation of AI, offering an insightful and valuable path forward on risk-based regulation, which aims to find that balance between providing protection from potential harms, while also enabling innovation to thrive.

Here is a summary of IBM's testimony, which includes the company's four core elements of precision regulation. The first is Different Rules for Different Risks, which means that higher risk applications such as those that support decisions on credit or employment would require more stringent regulations than, for example, a chatbot offering up a restaurant recommendation. The second is Clearly Defined Risks, which offers clear guidance on AI uses or "categories of AI-supported activities that are inherently high risk." This will provide developers and deployers a "clear understanding of what regulatory requirements will apply to a tool they are building for a specific end use." Be Transparent, Don't Hide Your AI is the third element, which recommends that Congress make it a requirement for businesses to disclose when consumers will be interacting with AI and whether they can also engage with a person, if they desire. This also includes that AI developers should "disclose technical information about the development and performance of an AI model, as well as the data used to train it, to give society better visibility into how these models operate." The final element is Showing the Impact, which for higher-risk AI applications requires that businesses "conduct impact assessments showing how their systems perform against tests for bias and other ways that they could potentially impact the public, and attest that they have done so." Bias testing and mitigation for high-risks systems like law enforcement use cases should be done in a "robust and transparent" manner.[4]

Christina elaborated on the first point about how rules should be established based on the spectrum of risks of an AI-based solution, noting how AI decisions must be contextual in nature.

"There are some very low risk uses of AI and some very high risk uses of the technology. When you are using AI in a high-risk setting, for example, if you're going to use it to make credit decisions or benefits decisions or if law enforcement uses it, those have real world consequences on individual people that can impact their health, safety, fundamental rights, livelihood, etc. As such, those applications should have risk-based obligations falling on companies that are deploying the technology," said Christina.

PEGASYSTEMS

One company pursuing an ethical path around its offerings is Pegasystems, the leading enterprise AI decisioning and workflow automation platform provider. The company has put in place a variety of checks and guardrails in its use of AI to address any potential ethical issues. Pegasystems founder and CEO Alan Trefler shared the company's approach to delivering on this objective.

"We've worked hard with our application of AI to make sure we're considering the ethical ramifications because that's very important to us and also to our clients," he said. "We have an ethical check, compliance check, and ethical guardrails that we've actually built into the software to prevent people from accidentally violating an ethical quandary. For instance, if we're working with a financial institution to make decisions as it relates to what products are appropriate for somebody, what credit level should be granted, we need to make very sure that those decisions fall into an acceptable ethical framework and that involves both making sure that the math is correct, but also actively looking for situations in which there might be an ethical lapse," he added.

BIG TECH

Across the technology industry, many major brands are working to infuse ethical practices into their products and processes. These efforts focus on both AI and wider technologies. Having looked at four of the largest technology firms that are playing instrumental roles in the development or deployment of AI, it is clear that there are several common priorities though presently no silver bullet.

Microsoft, Google, YouTube, and Amazon are working to define their in-house approaches to the ethics of responsible AI technology development. Across each of these firms and noted on multiple positioning statements, I was struck by how people-centric their approach is. Safety, fairness, reliability, transparency, and trust are all part of the language these firms use. Microsoft, for example, is collaborating with partners and researchers to develop best practices around ethical AI design. On its website, Microsoft sums up the essence of responsible innovation.

> *"Responsible AI is really all about the how: how do we design, develop and deploy these systems that are fair, reliable, safe and trustworthy. And to do this, we need to think of Responsible AI as a set of socio-technical problems. We need to go beyond just improving the data and models. We also have to think about the people who are ultimately going to be interacting with these systems."[5]*
> —Dr. Saleema Amershi, principal researcher
> at Microsoft Research and co-chair of the Aether
> Human-AI Interaction & Collaboration Working Group

Similarly, Google emphasizes the importance of eliminating biases and elevating safety through an ethics review process and centering responsible design for its products. For example, a recent blog post on Google's website explores those ethical reviews and responsible design priorities.

"For our part, we've applied the AI Principles and an ethics review process to our own development of AI in our products – generative AI is no exception. What we've found in the past six months is that there are clear ways to promote safer, socially beneficial practices to generative AI concerns like unfair bias and factuality. We proactively integrate ethical considerations early in the design and development process and have significantly expanded our reviews of early-stage AI efforts, with a focus on guidance around generative AI projects."[6]

YouTube and Amazon have placed transparency and open communication at the heart of their responsible AI efforts. YouTube (a Google owned brand) announced that it will soon mandate that creators disclose if their video includes AI-generated content or face penalties. Amazon emphasizes the following: 1) the importance of fairness among various subpopulations; 2) explainability to understand and evaluate the outputs of an AI system; and 3) transparency around communicating information about an AI system so stakeholders can make informed decisions.[7]

Ethics and Brand Reputation

While the most important aspect of responsible and ethical use of technology is the impact on society, these efforts also shape how the world views a company's brand and reputation. When a company decides its legacy is to leverage tech for good in some capacity, operating with the right ethics and principles go hand-in-hand with that mission. This path of good will be visible to your constituents, speak to their values, and have a lasting impact on how they view your brand and what it stands for in the world.

Christina Montgomery spoke to this issue. "We recognize that society grants our license to operate and that our customers vote with their wallets. As such, we know our efforts around ethical development of and use of technology has a profound impact on our brand and reputation. We had to answer key questions, such as what is our brand going to stand for in the AI space and what technologies are we going to use and not use? All of these elements have a critical impact on our brand."

Government AI Regulatory Efforts

Governments around the world have moved quickly in an effort to mitigate potential risks associated with the rise of AI. As part of their efforts to spur responsible innovation, governments are introducing rafts of new legislation while launching new consultative or regulatory bodies focused on AI. For example, the US government established the White House Executive Order on the Safe, Secure and Trustworthy Development and Use of Artificial Intelligence, which is coming into effect. This executive order "establishes a government-wide effort to guide responsible artificial intelligence (AI) development and deployment through federal agency leadership, regulation of industry, and engagement with international partners." It directs more than 50 federal entities to execute more than 100 actions in areas like safety and security, bias and civil rights, privacy, consumer protection, among many others.[8]

There is also a flurry of other bills proposed by the US Congress that attempt to regulate the technology. The bills cover a broad range of aspects of AI, from security and accountability, to information sharing between technology companies and the government, to licensing models for high-risk applications and transparency measures. According to technology lobbying firm, The Information Technology Industry Council (ITI), it is tracking 50+ federal bills (introduced and those in draft form), as well as 50+ initiatives including executive orders and regulatory efforts around this technology.[9]

The UK and Europe are pursuing different approaches to the AI regulatory challenge though with no less legal or regulatory vigor. In the UK, the country is approaching AI regulation on a use case or industry basis. For example, what may be relevant to consider in order to regulate AI for financial services may look very different from how AI should be regulated in healthcare. This is a vertical approach to AI regulation. The UK's Department for Science, Innovation, and Technology launched a white paper in March 2023 entitled "A pro-innovation approach to AI regulation" seeking consultation with a wide range of stakeholders. Additionally, the UK has launched the AI Safety Institute, touting the entity as the "first state-backed organization focused on advanced AI safety for the public interest."[10]

In contrast, Europe has taken a horizontal approach, attempting to regulate AI as a technology itself. The European Union has taken this more aggressive approach through its AI Act, the world's first AI law designed to regulate the technology based on its capacity to cause risk. The EU first drafted the law in April 2021 and has updated it recently to include more stringent regulations, given the risks posed by generative AI. In general, the riskier the application (such as medical applications, for example), the more strict the rules – and some uses of AI would be banned altogether if they are deemed too high of a risk. This includes "social scoring systems that govern how people behave, some types of predictive policing, and emotion recognition systems in school and workplaces."[11]

Engage for Better Outcomes

So far, I have focused quite a bit on regulation and ethics, looking at the roles that governments and business have played to date on shaping AI. However, they are only two of the three key stakeholder sets that need to be involved in developing guardrails and guidance on new technologies. The third key stakeholder set is consumers and citizens. Both governments and business have valuable roles to play in consulting with, educating, and engaging productively with us, with society.

Governments and businesses have incredible powers to convene. Market research budgets range from hundreds of millions to billions per year around the globe. What consumers and citizens think and care about is often of great interest, shaping product design opportunities and policies or laws. What we have experienced with technological innovation over the last 20 years is that the pace of innovation is accelerating. New technologies can break through from academic or corporate R&D labs into full public view seemingly overnight, creating an urgent need to quickly assess and understand the implications these innovations can have on our world. Engaging and convening to understand what we want technology to achieve for us – and what use cases we would like to avert – is more important than ever.

eVTOL Engaging Government, Business, and Consumers

There are exciting examples of where engagement between government, business, and consumers/citizens on frontier technologies have yielded valuable results. One technology that we will be hearing more about in the coming years is eVTOL: electric vertical takeoff and landing aircraft. Technological advancements mean that flying cars are soon going to be on our actual horizons. However, in 2017 in the UK, as aircraft manufacturers advanced their research and testing for eVTOL, the UK's innovation foundation – Nesta – saw a critical gap: the need to engage with the public on what, if anything, it saw as productive use cases for this new technology and for their smaller cousins, drones.

I spoke with Tris Dyson, managing director and founder of Challenge Works, a social enterprise within Nesta. Challenge Works develops challenge prizes – an innovation method that tries to overcome market failures by spurring new business models and products through competitions with financial rewards. He talked to me about a public engagement program named Flying High that Challenge Works developed to spur collaboration between cities, technology developers, regulators, and citizens on the desired role that drones and eVTOL might play in the UK.

"It was clear that the technology for eVTOL and drones was advancing rapidly," Tris said. "However, what was missing was guidance from consumers and citizens about how the technology could be best put to use, what people would see as helpful given the way the technology might impact their cities and neighborhoods."

One of the most interesting aspects of the Flying High program was that the engagement played a creative, educative, and consultative role across the cities where the program was delivered. "We developed a way for the information and perspectives we were gathering to feed directly into regulatory guidance for the government and regulators, and market intelligence for the technology developers," Tris noted.

These types of platforms are exciting ways to share information across stakeholder groups, but they also serve a broader purpose of feeding into product, regulatory, and legislative design processes. They can support us in being more intentional about our exploration of these technologies, about what we want the technology to do for us, and how we make that happen. Moreover, they shouldn't be just one-off projects. The discussions we need to have around new technologies and their place in our society can only happen if we are determined to have them, and we should create the mechanisms to engage in ongoing, rich, evolving discussions. Given the existing engagement and communications platforms that both governments and, importantly, businesses have, the capacity to engage more proactively and consistently is possible and, I would argue, essential.

Prepare for Rapid Evolution

I used the word *evolving* earlier and did so intentionally. The third E that is critical for navigating rapidly developing technologies that may have profound social impacts is evolution. The speed at which technologies are developing, particularly within the AI space, means that what we thought was impossible three months ago may be possible today. And what may be possible or even desirable in the future may evolve. Without an ability to evolve as technology advances, as we gather data, as we engage, may mean that the preferences or regulatory priorities we set may not adapt effectively.

As we have seen with the exploration of the ethics and safety tools that companies are deploying, there is a considerable push on businesses to put these considerations at the heart of their product, corporate, and communications strategies. Similarly, we have engagement tools on hand that can create purposeful and meaningful discussions between government, business, and citizen/consumer stakeholders. If we can build in a concept of evolving as we go, it should mean we are more resilient as technology advances.

Practically what does that mean? As an example, for both governments and business, it means more rapid and varied data collection on what is possible technologically and potentially preferred by consumers and citizens. This data collection should be open to anyone who wishes to analyze it in the hopes that insights can inform product, regulatory, and legislative decisions. As part of the evolving nature of these technologies, we should also be engaging in a multidisciplinary way. As I mentioned earlier, technological advancement will continue to be enhanced by the arts and humanities. Consider how much time technology firms are spending on ethics.

I believe that emphasizing this mindset, particularly within government and business, could have beneficial effects. Many of the leaders with whom I've spoken implement these types of principles in their businesses on a daily basis. We now need to redouble our efforts across government, business, and the public with nuanced, meaningful conversations on topics like AI. We don't have all the answers today; that is an impossibility. As we gather new data, we should actively evaluate if our preferences or priorities should evolve. In order to do so, we need to have the mindset that evolution will be both essential and beneficial.

The Pathway for Businesses

Just as companies have had to evolve and respond to protect customer data and privacy, they will have to find their path to demonstrate that their technology products are developed responsibly. In doing so, they will be able to delight customers while also protecting stakeholders from the potential negative outcomes of technologies like generative AI. Companies that operate with the effective guardrails and ethics around this and other technologies will have an advantage. Over time, these practices will be the new table stakes demanded from both customers and partner organizations.

Whether your company develops technology or is empowered by it in daily business operations, it's critical to consider how ethics, engagement, and evolution can deliver against the goal of responsible development and use of today's innovations.

The following is a framework for how organizations can put the 3Es – ethics, engagement, and evolution – at the heart of their businesses. I encourage you to adopt and modify as appropriate, based on your company's size and industry. This framework cuts across key functions within the organization – from leadership teams to strategy, product to communications. I expect that the tools in the 3E framework will evolve as new technological innovations and challenges come to market, and I encourage you to develop and share your adaptations.

Leadership and Governance

◆ **Appoint a chief ethics officer:** This person will lead the function to create a framework for the company to operate around the right ethics and morals across all efforts. This function will work to establish internal policies and procedures that ensure technologies like AI, as well as customer data and privacy, are being used in ways that align with both the law and with the company's corporate values and ethics. If the company is large, the officer may establish a team to execute ethics efforts.

◆ **Form an ethics board:** This group will oversee and guide the entire effort. It should include experts from several areas (technology, marketing, legal, governance, external/independent representatives, etc.) who can effectively steer the company's path to ensure it has the right policies in place for ethical considerations, and help guide the company when it has to make decisions that have ethical implications.

◆ **Establish governance and guardrails:** Once the pillars and principles are established, the ethics officer and board will establish internal governance processes and define appropriate guardrails that deliver on them. These must be clearly articulated and understood across the organization so the entire company can operate around them in every function. As mentioned above, some of those guardrails include testing technologies to identify and mitigate risks on issues like biases, safety, and security. Transparency around the use of technologies like generative AI should also be established, as well as the outcomes of any testing on risks, etc. For those companies that develop technologies, they must start with datasets that have strong integrity and put appropriate filters in place to help minimize some of the potential harms like biases. What's critical is to leverage these practices at the outset of any technology-based effort, ensuring ethics are a priority from the very beginning vs. an after-thought "add on."

Strategy

♦ **Develop ethics principles and pillars:** The ethics officer and board will determine the principles the company will operate by every day across every aspect of the organization, including its use of technology. These principles will serve to guide their practices around AI and must be deeply embedded across the entire organization. This involves core tenets like transparency, fairness to minimize biases, testing to identify and mitigate harmful outcomes, as well as safety and reliability. All employees should be educated on these pillars and all company actions must reinforce adherence to these principles.

♦ **Embed into DNA:** As mentioned, operating with the right ethics and morality are critical table stakes today. As such, these core values must be communicated and understood across the entire organization. They should be reinforced continually and brought to life in the actions and decisions made by company leadership.

Product

♦ **Ensure ongoing vigilance:** As technologies evolve and new innovations come to market, they must all be put through this ethical filter. For example, one of the features of machine learning is that AI models can change over time, which means they must be monitored to ensure they operate as intended. This requires ongoing testing to ensure risks are mitigated. This effort must be a priority across the leadership team, particularly the CTO who must look at innovations through this risk/reward lens.

Communications

♦ **Engage constituents:** While most of the focus is on the roles of public and private sector organizations, the voice of constituents and consumers could aid in developing appropriate outcomes. Their perspectives could help both governments and businesses determine where boundaries should be drawn. Businesses should proactively engage their customers to secure their perspective, concerns, and aspirations. This third-party voice could be instrumental as businesses, governments, and the public work to develop desirable paths forward.

Applying the three Es – ethics, engagement, and evolution – within your organization will help put it on a path of responsible innovation and help ensure you are using and/or developing technology in ways that maximize their potential for positive outcomes and minimize any potential damage. Again, this is all about striking the balance of enabling innovation to thrive, while putting up appropriate guardrails to avert negative outcomes like bias. As with so many initiatives we've addressed in this book, as technologies evolve and regulations are established, it will require a continual revisiting of these three Es to ensure you are putting your company on the right path to deliver on the concept of responsible innovation.

CHAPTER 17

A Time for Reason

Although my previous six books focused on marketing, I felt passionately about writing this one because there's a takeaway I believe is a business imperative that defines this era. We are standing at one of those critical junctures where if we do the right things, we can change the trajectory of our world. As you've heard from so many experts, technology has reached yet another tipping point, one that gives us the capability to address major issues across so many areas, from healthcare to access to education. This will only come to fruition if we decide to embrace this opportunity, take this challenge on, and make it our mission and our passion to use the technology we have now to positively impact humanity.

As someone who has spent my entire career helping technology companies shape new markets or disrupt existing ones and build leadership positions within those, I see a huge opportunity for organizations today to do something so much bigger that has a much higher purpose. This is not to say in any way that profit should be pushed aside. The world doesn't work like that. What this is about is marrying profit with purpose. The means to that end is using the advanced technologies we have today – responsibly and with morals at the center – to make a difference.

My vision is that the leaders of today's economy contribute to this ecosystem of good we are starting to build across the globe. Every company must find their own individual path on this journey, and there are many to choose from. Some organizations have transformed their entire company around tech for good, while others integrate it into the technologies they develop or the projects they undertake. Whatever path you choose, it's important that it be aligned with your core and infused into your business strategy and operations.

This chapter contains a few thought starters that present potential paths around a tech for good effort. These represent a mere sampling of some of the societal issues we face that companies can help to tackle with technology. I encourage companies to find the path that best aligns with the vision they have around their legacy and the mark they want to leave on the world.

Big Data for Social Good

As our world becomes increasingly digital, virtually all organizations are now data companies possessing massive stores of data, which can be applied to benefit society. This concept of data for good is being embraced by many companies around the world. For example, SAS is using data and analytics to help address humanitarian issues around poverty, health, human rights, education, and the environment. One example is when SAS helped the International Organization for Migration access and analyze decades of global trade data in a matter of minutes so that it could quickly source homebuilding materials to provide shelter for 45,000 displaced families following an earthquake in Nepal.[1]

A company called DataKind helps nonprofits connect with data scientists to collaborate on projects that help organizations enhance their data literacy and develop evidence-based decision making.[2] MedAware is another company using data for good. Leveraging machine learning, the company aims to help prevent problems (including deaths) that can result from errors in prescription medication by alerting prescribers to inaccurate information.[3]

An idea that comes to mind is what if the big financial institutions like JP Morgan democratized data when granting housing loans? Rather than using zip codes to generalize whether people living in certain underprivileged communities can afford a housing loan, they should move to individual data to get a true view of each person's capability of taking on a loan.

Closing the Digital Divide

While technology can be the great enabler, it can also be the source of leaving the less fortunate behind. One example of this is when people don't have access to the internet. Often those without connectivity are in lower income brackets, and this exacerbates inequalities, as it creates additional barriers to education and economic opportunities needed to break out of the poverty cycle.

Many companies are working to close this divide. As mentioned earlier in the book, Dell's Solar Community Hubs provide technology stations that bring internet access to under-served communities, connecting them to the digital world and providing access to critical things like education, work, and healthcare. Another company we referenced, Ablr, is working to remove barriers for people with disabilities and creating employment opportunities.

My thinking is that other digital-first companies should work to ensure that everyone has access to the internet at a low price point or have free access. For example, what if Facebook leveraged its satellite technology to provide no cost connectivity anywhere in the world? Now that would do wonders to help address the digital divide.

Veracity of Information

Misinformation, disinformation, or fake news is a chronic issue plaguing our society, often with dire outcomes. Digital media, particularly social media platforms, are often leveraged in this realm because they are easy to access/ use, provide a quick distribution channel, and are difficult to correct once false information is out there. The ramifications of this problem became exceedingly apparent during the 2016 presidential election, when misinformation is believed to have influenced election results.

The concern right now is that generative AI will be leveraged to turbocharge the problem of misinformation and fake news. To help address this, digital media companies can take actions that help people sort out truth from misinformation, and many are moving along this path. As mentioned earlier, YouTube will soon require creators to disclose if their video includes AI-generated content. Facebook is also taking a number of actions by working to identify and limit the spread of false news through its community and third-party fact checkers. It also works to make it a challenge for those posting fake news to buy ads on the site, and applies machine learning to detect fraud, etc. We need to continue along this path and amplify our efforts to help combat this massive and potentially destructive issue.

Equal Access to Healthcare

Although most of us take for granted access to healthcare, nearly 80% of rural America is medically under-served, and almost 8% of the US population lacks healthcare insurance. These two issues are among the reasons people lack access to healthcare, which is an essential human right.

As you read earlier in this book, scores of companies are taking this on. Unima, for example, created a technology that enables people to achieve rapid diagnostics at the lowest possible cost and outside of the laboratory setting. The company is working to address equity in healthcare by bringing this valuable service to people living in even the most remote places in the world. In addition, Johnson & Johnson has made extensive efforts in this realm, working to ensure people in under-served communities have access to medicines that address diseases like HIV, Ebola, and tuberculosis.[4] With today's innovations delivering so many new breakthroughs in this realm, there is a plethora of opportunities to create more equitable access to medicine.

Doing Your Part to Fight Climate Change

Every company must do their part to fight the raging battle against climate change, working to minimize their GHG emissions and achieve a net zero carbon footprint. Part 1 of this book featured several examples of companies with efforts underway on this path. Many companies are going beyond that. The examples we provided in Part 1 (Aquent's solar projects and IBM's Sustainability Accelerator Program) illustrate how organizations can make a larger contribution to the fight against this pressing issue.

Once you choose your path, the next critical step is determining the "how" of this process. I've spoken with many executives who have shared their insights into this effort. Retooling an organization around good often requires fundamental changes to many aspects of business, from expanding and reshaping the role the C suite plays, to the types of investments companies make, to how technology is viewed, including the role it can play in our world. Breakthrough outcomes often require breaking away from the constraints of conventional business thinking. We can't be afraid to take that on.

This effort will be transformative. It can help your company leave behind a legacy that will have meaning. It will help attract, retain, and motivate today's talent. It will engage your constituents and customers at a deeper level, enabling them to experience the work your company is doing to better the world. It will help your brand become more relevant, respected, and resilient. It will take your company to new places. Think about the fact that a business once thought of as a tractor company ended up being the keynote speaker at CES. Deere's work in agtech is inspiring and motivating, and exemplifies how today's technology can solve real problems that have a profound impact on not just those using it, but also on the whole planet. This is about solving problems that seem unsolvable. Those words bring me back to Flagship Pioneering and the tremendous work underway across so many organizations in that ecosystem working to deliver remarkable leap forward solutions across health and sustainability.

Delivering on a New Age of Reason

One of the amazing outcomes of writing this book is encountering the shared enthusiasm for today's technology to positively impact humanity. In a world filled with so much negativity, it has been truly inspiring and uplifting to speak with so many experts who are genuinely excited about the potential for today's innovations – and those on the horizon – to make a difference. Several people I spoke with agreed that this type of positivity is just what the world needs right now, as we all struggle to process the deluge of negative events that seem to dominate our world and our news feeds.

What also came through so clearly through my conversations with executives is the passion they share to do good, to tackle problems head on with such determination, and to make their contribution to help change the world. I believe this starts with being a techno-optimist – of seeing the true potential today's innovations hold to impact humanity, whether that's fighting climate change, improving our health, or helping to feed the world. This optimism helps people "see" the full potential of today's technology and fuels their drive to leverage it across a variety of applications.

As noted multiple times in this book, we can't blindly use technology and ignore the need for responsible innovation and guardrails that protect us from potential harms. That requires infusing the three Es (ethics, engagement, and evolution) and other practices cited in Chapter 16. While this is an incredibly complex paradigm, it's the one we must navigate. Every day that I write this book another article comes out about the perils and promise of generative AI, and the conundrum of moving forward in the right way to address that complex equation. While we must find the best path to mitigate negative outcomes, we must also allow innovations to flourish so we can find new solutions to societal issues.

We also can't be afraid to fail as we're working to develop leap forward solutions. So many executives admit that getting it right the first time is not the expectation. Finding new solutions that catapult us forward is typically an iterative and, at times, messy process – one of trial and error. This is a journey of learning with the end goal of eventually getting it right. When we do, we'll find new and novel solutions to perplexing or vexing problems.

Just as in the original Age of Reason, many breakthroughs began by asking the right "what if" questions. Then, it's critical to apply reason and the spark of imagination to answer them. This is where the unique creative and reasoning abilities of humans come into play. No technology can match those capabilities. However, technology can be the force that augments our strengths, empowering us to deliver capabilities beyond our realm. Think about how the robotics surgical system extends the eyes and hands of a surgeon, and how AI can process massive datasets and make sense of complex patterns humans might not have the ability to see. It's the powerful combination of people leading an effort and using technology as the engine that enables the magic to happen.

Although our problems today are certainly complex, our technologies are so advanced they are ready to tackle those issues. Just as the global challenges we face are complex and interrelated (e.g., climate change impacts farmland and our ability to grow enough crops to feed the world, as well as causing many health issues), there's an interrelationship with today's technologies that are being integrated to solve those very issues.

I started writing this book with a strong belief that we are on the cusp of a new era where technology has finally evolved to deliver amazing benefits to the world. After speaking with so many innovators across multiple industries and conducting significant research, I am even more convinced that we are standing at this amazing point in time. While nothing is written in the stars that this will magically happen, if we embrace this moment, proceed with the right mindset and values, and take the right actions, we can solve problems that seem unsolvable and deliver on the promise of this new Age of Reason.

Acknowledgments

Writing books evokes profound gratitude. I am very grateful to the many professionals who shared their time and thoughts with me, further developing my premise that technology and humanity can solve many of the world's problems. First and foremost, I want to thank Laura Feng, a long-time business and writing partner who is extraordinary. I also want to thank a new colleague, Deran Garabedian, for his important contributions and writing around many of the technologies featured in Part 2. Thank you very much, Deran. A big thank-you to the venerable David Kirkpatrick for his insightful foreword and his career of excellence in technology journalism.

I would also like to thank all of those professionals who so generously gave their time and insights: John May (Deere), Esther Dyson (Wellville), Catherine Mohr (Intuitive Foundation), Justina Nixon-Saintil (IBM), John Chuang (Aquent), Peter Durlach (Microsoft), Noubar Afeyan (Flagship Pioneering), John Samuel (Ablr), Hala Hanna (MIT Solve), Keith Figlioli (LRVHealth), Patrick Wheeler (Tuck Dartmouth), Swale Nunez (Enoem), Helen Greiner (iRobot), Christina Montgomery (IBM), Alan Trefler (Pegasystems), Brian Cusack (PartnerOcean), Olivia Lanes (IBM), Calista Redmond (RISC-V International), Marc Mustard (ABB), Kelly Vigier (Robotic Software), Tamara Askew (Deloitte), Cole Clark (Deloitte), Roy Mathew (Deloitte), Ollie Buckley (Centre for Data Ethics & Innovation), Tris Dyson (ChallengeWorks), Andrew Beebe (Obvious Ventures), Alex Schindelar (Energy Intelligence), Brian McGee (Anocca), Zachary Schisgal (Wiley), Sangeetha Suresh (Wiley), Amanda Keane (Racepoint Global), Andrei Antonescu (Racepoint Global), and Michael Rose (Racepoint Global).

I'm grateful to my clients, colleagues, and friends who have inspired my writing projects throughout the years. Thank you for being part of my journey.

About the Author

Larry Weber, chairman and CEO of Racepoint Global, is a renowned expert on marketing who has founded multiple global technology public relations and interactive marketing agencies and cofounded the largest interactive advocacy organization in the world. He is widely regarded as a thought leader on trends and dynamics reshaping business, marketing communications, and customer engagement, including the seismic shifts from digital technologies, such as the internet, social media, and, most recently, generative AI.

Larry has provided global companies with effective strategies to lead through the many waves of technology that have shaped our world. Today, as a new wave of technology has evolved to benefit humanity, Larry is offering a strategic blueprint for organizations to transform their brand around "tech for good." This business imperative is not only an opportunity, but also a responsibility of every corporation to leverage today's breakthroughs and address world problems such as climate change. This transformative effort will create brands that are highly relevant, respected, and resilient and, as such, appeal to all stakeholders.

Larry has authored six business/marketing books, including *The Provocateur: How a New Generation of Leaders Are Building Communities, Not Just Companies* (Random House/Crown Business, 2002), business bestseller *Marketing to the Social Web: How Digital Customer Communities Build Your Business*, second edition (Wiley & Sons, 2009), *Sticks & Stones: How Digital Business Reputations Are Created Over Time. . .and Lost in a Click* (Wiley & Sons, 2009), *Everywhere: Comprehensive Digital Business Strategy for the Social Media Era* (Wiley & Sons, 2001), *The Digital Marketer* (Wiley & Sons, 2014), and *Authentic Marketing: How to Capture Hearts and Minds Through the Power of Purpose* (Wiley & Sons, 2019).

Notes

Chapter 2

1. UNCTAD website, Now 8 Billion and Counting: Where the World's Population Has Grown Most and Why That Matters, November 15, 2022, https://unctad.org/data-visualization/now-8-billion-and-counting-where-worlds-population-has-grown-most-and-why
2. USDA website, Economic Research Service U.S. Department of Agriculture, https://www.ers.usda.gov/data-products/ag-and-food-statistics-charting-the-essentials/farming-and-farm-income/#:~:text=Similarly%2C%20the%20acres%20of%20land,recorded%20in%20the%20early%201970s
3. YouTube Video, CES 2023 Keynote, https://www.youtube.com/watch?v=1kjZMHZl538
4. Deere website, Quick Facts, https://ces2023.deere.com/facts
5. Deere website, https://www.deere.com/en/our-company/history/
6. Successful Farming, Laurie Bedord, January 9, 2023, https://www.agriculture.com/news/technology/john-deere-is-working-to-transform-consumers-perception-of-agriculture
7. Deere website, https://about.deere.com/en-us/our-company-and-purpose/technology-and-innovation/
8. Deere website, https://www.deere.com/en/news/all-news/john-deere-receives-sbti-validation-of-greenhouse-gas-emission-reduction-targets/#:~:text=Through%20its%20SBTi%20targets%2C%20Deere,30%25%20within%20the%20same%20timeframe.
9. Deere website, https://www.deere.com/en/our-company/sustainability/emissions/#:~:text=As%20the%20company%20closes%20out,of%20the%20end%20of%202022
10. Fierce Wireless, John Deere Cultivates Data Business with 500,000 Connected Machines, April 6, 2023, https://www.fiercewireless.com/wireless/john-deere-cultivates-data-business
11. Deere website, News Releases, https://www.deere.com/en/news/all-news/fy23-fourth-quarter-earnings/
12. Deere website, https://about.deere.com/en-us/explore-john-deere
13. Deere website, https://www.deere.com/en/our-company/sustainability/

Chapter 3

1. United Nations, https://www.un.org/sites/un2.un.org/files/2021/08/fastfacts-health.pdf

2. United Nations, UN News, A Liveable Future for All Is Possible, If We Take Urgent Climate Action: flagship UN report, March 20, 2023, https://news.un.org/en/story/2023/03/1134777

3. *MIT Tech Review*, The UN Just Handed Out an Urgent Climate To-Do List. Here's What It Says, Casey Crownhart, March 20, 2023, https://www.technologyreview.com/2023/03/20/1070070/urgent-climate-to-do-list-ipcc/

4. Business Insider, VCs Are Investing in These Hot Areas of Climate Tech, Catherine Boudreau, January 15, 2023, https://www.businessinsider.com/vc-venture-capital-funding-investing-climate-tech-startups-companies-hot-2023-1

5. Tech Crunch, Farmers Are Key to Lithos Carbons Quest to Remove Gigatons of Carbon, Tim De Chant, Oct. 20, 2022, https://techcrunch.com/2022/10/20/farmers-are-key-to-lithos-carbons-quest-to-remove-gigatons-of-carbon/

6. Green Biz, Inside Frontier, the Fund Pioneering New Model Carbon Removal Investments, Leah Garden, July 13, 2022, https://www.greenbiz.com/article/inside-frontier-fund-pioneering-new-model-carbon-removal-investments

7. Elko Daily, The Inflation Reduction Act's Rollout Is Bringing Green Jobs Across the US—See the Projects Happening Near You, Lauren Liebhaber, April 27, 2023, https://elkodaily.com/news/the-inflation-reduction-acts-rollout-is-bringing-green-jobs-across-the-us-see-the-projects/collection_f5542073-8846-52b8-bb7e-2644243e10f0.html#1

8. World Economic Forum website, Tackling the Climate Crisis with Innovative Green Technologies, https://www.weforum.org/impact/first-movers-coalition-is-tackling-the-climate-crisis/

9. Andreessen Horowitz Website, It's Time to Build for America: Announcing Our $500m+ Commitment to Companies Building in American Dynamism, https://A16z.Com/Its-Time-To-Build-For-America-Announcing-Our-500m-Commitment-To-Companies-Building-In-American-Dynamism/

10. Microsoft, Blogs, Microsoft Will Be Carbon Negative by 2030, Brad Smith, Jan. 16, 2020, https://blogs.microsoft.com/blog/2020/01/16/microsoft-will-be-carbon-negative-by-2030/

11. United States Steel website, https://www.ussteel.com/sustainability/overview

12. Environmental + Energy Leader, US Steel Commits to Carbon Capture, Jessica Hunt, March 6, 2023, https://www.environmentenergyleader .com/2023/03/u-s-steel-commits-to-carbon-capture/
13. Leafscore, Lydia Noyes, Blog Post, The Top 10 Publicly Traded Companies Fighting Climate Change in 2023, January 5, 2023, https:// www.leafscore.com/blog/top-10-publicly-traded-companies-fighting-climate-change-in-2021/
14. IBM Website, Blog Post, August 7, 2023, https://www.ibm.com/blog/ transforming-sustainable-agriculture-the-nature-conservancy-centre-and-ibm-unite-to-reduce-crop-residue-burning-in-north-india/
15. Aquent website, https://aquent.com/about-us/sustainability

Chapter 4

1. *The New York Times Magazine*, Suddenly, it Looks Like We're in a Golden Age for Medicine, David Wallace-Wells, June 23, 2023, https:// www.nytimes.com/2023/06/23/magazine/golden-age-medicine-biomedical-innovation.html
2. *Newsweek*, Magic Mushrooms, $1 Hearing Aids: Medical Marvels Disrupting Healthcare, Meghan Gunn, Ned Potter, Kerri Anne Renzulli, June 14, 2023, https://www.newsweek.com/2023/06/30/magic-mushrooms-1-hearing-aids-medical-marvels-disrupting-healthcare-1805918.html
3. Whoop website, https://www.whoop.com
4. Stratascale, Artificial Intelligence for Healthcare Administration: A Powerful Tool for Alleviating Administrative Burdens, Michael Sable, February 9, 2023, https://www.stratascale.com/artificial-intelligence-for-healthcare-administration-a-powerful-tool-for-alleviating-administrative-burdens
5. Harvard Medical School, AI Predicts Future Pancreatic Cancer, Ekaterina Pesheva May 8, 2023. https://hms.harvard.edu/news/ai-predicts-future-pancreatic-cancer?utm_source=newsletter&utm_medium=email&utm_campaign=newsletter_axiosam&stream=top
6. Intuitive website, press resources, https://www.intuitive.com/en-us/ about-us/newsroom/press-resources
7. Websitevoice blog, 10 Assistive Technology Tools to Help People with Disabilities in 2023 and Beyond, November 24, 2021, https:// websitevoice.com/blog/assistive-technology-tools/
8. WeWalk website, https://wewalk.io/en/
9. Access Afaya website, https://www.accessafya.com
10. MIT Solve website, https://solve.mit.edu/challenges/2021-health-security-pandemics/solutions/46796

Chapter 5

1. Merriam-Webster website, https://www.merriam-webster.com/dictionary/ Kairos.
2. Dell.com, Connecting Underserved Communities to Digital Education, Work, and Healthcare, https://www.dell.com/en-us/dt/corporate/social-impact/transforming-lives/education/solar-community-hubs.htm# tab0=0
3. Unima website, https://www.unimadx.com
4. Oracle.com, blog, The World Bee Project Works to Sustain Buzz with Oracle Cloud and AI, https://www.oracle.com/corporate/blog/oracle-cloud-ai-world-bee-111319.html
5. World Economic Forum website, Tech for Good: Here are 6 Tech Firms Improving the World, Gabi Thesing, January 25, 2023, https://www .weforum.org/agenda/2023/01/tech-for-good-innovations/
6. Uplink website, https://uplink.weforum.org/uplink/s/top-innovators
7. GatesNotes, The blog of Bill Gates, *The Age of AI has begun*, March 21, 2023, https://www.gatesnotes.com/The-Age-of-AI-Has-Begun
8. Axiom AM e-newsletter, Mike Allen, *1 Big Thing, AI Explosion*, March 26, 2023
9. *Wired Magazine*, In Sudden Alarm, Tech Doyens Call for a Pause on ChatGPT, March 29, 2023, https://www.wired.com/story/chatgpt-pause-ai-experiments-open-letter/
10. Associated Press, AI Warning: Human Extinction Threat Should be a Global Priority, says Experts, Matt O'Brien, May 30, 2023, https:// apnews.com/article/artificial-intelligence-risk-of-extinction-ai-54ea8aad c60d1503e5a65878219aad43
11. Axios, 1 Big Thing: The Global Elite Is Excited and Terrified by AI, Ina Fried, April 19, 2023, https://www.axios.com/newsletters/axios-login-11b9ffc2-0589-43d0-97bc-7399983d0c0a.html?utm_source=newsletter &utm_medium=email&utm_campaign=newsletter_axioslogin&stream =top
12. Techonomy, Caitlin Hamilton, Climate Tech, Compassion, and the Innovation Crucible: Highlights of TE22, November 23, 2022, https:// techonomy.com/climate-tech-compassion-and-the-innovation-crucible-highlights-of-te22/
13. *Harvard Business Review*, Reid Hoffman on Building AI and Other Tech More Responsibly, HBR IdeaCast Episode 907, April 25, 2023, https:// hbr.org/podcast/2023/04/reid-hoffman-on-building-ai-and-other-tech-more-responsibly
14. Marc Andreessen Substack, Why AI Will Save the World, June 6, 2023, https://pmarca.substack.com/p/why-ai-will-save-the-world

Chapter 6

1. Rosieriveters, Admiral Grace Hopper, Pioneering Computer Programmer, https://www.rosieriveters.com/admiral_grace_hopper_pioneering_computer_programmer#:~:text=Programming%20the%20First%20Computers,-Perseverance%20was%20on&text=Admiral%20Hopper%20became%20the%20third,II%2C%20and%20Mark%20III%20computers

2. Britannica, Minicompters, https://www.britannica.com/technology/minicomputer

3. The Observation Deck, Reflecting on the Soul of a New Machine, February 10, 2019, http://dtrace.org/blogs/bmc/2019/02/10/reflecting-on-the-soul-of-a-new-machine/

4. Wikipedia, Enterprise Software, https://en.wikipedia.org/wiki/Enterprise_software

5. Statista, Number of Daily Active Facebook Users Worldwide as of 3rd Quarter 2023, https://www.statista.com/statistics/346167/facebook-global-dau/#:~:text=Facebook%3A%20number%20of%20daily%20active%20users%20worldwide%202011%2D2023&text=During%20the%20second%20quarter%20of,increase%20on%20the%20previous%20quarter

6. Search Engine Journal, The History of Social Media, September 2, 2022, https://www.searchenginejournal.com/social-media-history/462643/#close

7. Flagship Pioneering website, https://www.flagshippioneering.com/stories/ai-and-biology-are-the-principal-and-mutually-enabling-innovation-engines-of-our-generation

Chapter 7

1. Wikipedia, Prometheus, https://en.wikipedia.org/wiki/Prometheus

2. *New York Times*, Are Fears of AI and Nuclear Apocalypse Keeping You Up?, October 1, 2023, https://www.nytimes.com/2023/10/21/books/review/robert-oppenheimer-john-von-neumann-prometheus.html

3. *Stanford News*, Stanford Researcher Examines Earliest Concepts of Artificial Intelligence, Robots in Ancient Myths, February 28, 2019, https://news.stanford.edu/2019/02/28/ancient-myths-reveal-early-fantasies-artificial-life/

4. Free Code Camp, The History of Artificial Intelligence from the 1950s to Today, April 10, 2023, https://www.freecodecamp.org/news/the-history-of-ai/

5. *Forbes*, History of AI in 33 Breakthroughs: The First Expert System, October 29, 2022, https://www.forbes.com/sites/gilpress/2022/10/29/history-of-ai-in-33-breakthroughs-the-first-expert-system/?sh=792831274f86

6. Free Code Camp, The History of Artificial Intelligence from the 1950s to Today, April 10, 2023, https://www.freecodecamp.org/news/the-history-of-ai/

7. Tech Target, The History of Artificial Intelligence: Complete AI Timeline, August 16, 2023, https://www.techtarget.com/searchEnterpriseAI/tip/The-history-of-artificial-intelligence-Complete-AI-timeline

8. *MIT Technology Review*, The Inside Story of How ChatGPT was Built from the People Who Made It, March 3, 2023, https://www.technologyreview.com/2023/03/03/1069311/inside-story-oral-history-how-chatgpt-built-openai/

9. CNBC Make It, On ChatGPT's One-Year Anniversary, It Has More Than 1.7 Billion Users—Here's What It May Do Next, November 30, 2023, https://www.cnbc.com/2023/11/30/chatgpts-one-year-anniversary-how-the-viral-ai-chatbot-has-changed.html

10. Deloitte, Ensuring a Human-Centered Approach to AI, July 12, 2023, https://www.deloittedigital.com/us/en/blog-list/2023/human-centered-ai.html

11. LinkedIn, How AI Can Help Close the Education Gap, August 13, 2023, https://www.linkedin.com/pulse/how-ai-can-help-close-education-gap-bill-gates/?trackingId=

12. LinkedIn, This Is How AI Will Transform the Way Science Gets Done, July 25, 2023, https://www.linkedin.com/pulse/how-ai-transform-way-science-gets-done-eric-schmidt/?trackingId=

13. Flagship Pioneering website, https://www.flagshippioneering.com/stories/ai-and-biology-are-the-principal-and-mutually-enabling-innovation-engines-of-our-generation\

14. Possible podcast, Siddhartha Mukherjee on the Future of Disease and Diagnostics, https://www.possible.fm/podcasts/sid/

15. Healthcare IT News, When Physicians and Health IT Leaders Embrace an "AI as an Ally" Mindset, July 24, 2023, https://www.healthcareitnews.com/news/when-physicians-and-health-it-leaders-embrace-ai-ally-mindset

16. Forrester Research, Generative AI Will Supercharge The Green Market Revolution, July 16, 2023, https://www.forrester.com/blogs/generative-ai-will-supercharge-the-green-market-revolution/

17. AI Business, Robotics and Artificial Intelligence: The Role of AI in Robots, November 26, 2021, https://aibusiness.com/verticals/robotics-and-artificial-intelligence-the-role-of-ai-in-robots#close-modal

18. Robotnik, History of Robots and Robotics, https://robotnik.eu/history-of-robots-and-robotics/
19. Reason and Meaning, Aristotle, Robots, and a New Economic System, April 5, 2014, https://reasonandmeaning.com/2014/04/05/more-on-needing-a-new-economic-system/#google_vignette
20. Wikipedia, History of Robots, https://en.wikipedia.org/wiki/History_of_robots#:~:text=Unimate%2C%20the%20first%20digitally%20operated,of%20the%20modern%20robotics%20industry.%22
21. TechTarget, The History of Artificial Intelligence: Complete AI Timeline, August 16, 2023, https://www.techtarget.com/searchEnterpriseAI/tip/The-history-of-artificial-intelligence-Complete-AI-timeline
22. Wikipedia, History of Robots, https://en.wikipedia.org/wiki/History_of_robots#:~:text=Unimate%2C%20the%20first%20digitally%20operated,of%20the%20modern%20robotics%20industry.%22
23. BBVA, Applications and Advances in Robotics Today, May 11, 2021, https://www.bbva.ch/en/news/applications-and-advances-in-robotics-today/
24. ABB, World's Most Remote Robot Automates Amazon Reforestation Project, June 13, 2023, https://new.abb.com/news/detail/104065/worlds-most-remote-robot-automates-amazon-reforestation-project
25. NCBI, Robotics in Medicine, August 2019, https://www.ncbi.nlm.nih.gov/pmc/articles/PMC6625162/
26. Knowledgehut, The Future of Robotics, September 21, 2023, https://www.knowledgehut.com/blog/data-science/future-of-robotics

Chapter 8

1. BBC, The Humble Mineral That Transformed the World, https://www.bbc.com/future/bespoke/made-on-earth/how-the-chip-changed-everything/
2. Contrary, The Evolution of Chips, December 15, 2022, https://contrary.com/foundations-and-frontiers/evolution-of-chips
3. Charterworks, Chip War by Chris Miller, December 9, 2022, https://www.charterworks.com/chip-war-chris-miller/
4. Stastica, Semiconductor Foundries Revenue Share Worldwide from 2019 to 2023, by Quarter, https://www.statista.com/statistics/867223/worldwide-semiconductor-foundries-by-market-share/#:~:text=In%20the%20second%20quarter%20of,11.7%20percent%20of%20the%20market.
5. The Verge, How ARM Conquered the Chip Market Without Making a Single Chip, with CEO Rene Haas, https://www.theverge.com/23373371/arm-chips-chip-shortage-ceo-rene-haas-tech-intel-apple-decoder
6. ASML website, https://www.asml.com/en

7. Charterworks, Chip War by Chris Miller, https://www.charterworks
.com/chip-war-chris-miller/

8. Nvidia website, https://www.nvidia.com/content/dam/en-zz/Solutions/
about-nvidia/corporate-nvidia-in-brief.pdf

9. Contrary, The Evolution of Chips, December 15, 2022, https://contrary
.com/foundations-and-frontiers/evolution-of-chips

10. Charterworks, Chip War by Chris Miller, December 9, 2022, https://
www.charterworks.com/chip-war-chris-miller

11. Modor Intelligence, Semiconductor Industry Size & Share Analysis -
Growth Trends & Forecasts (2023–2028), https://www.mordorintelligence
.com/industry-reports/semiconductor-industry-landscape#

12. Electronics 360, Balancing Semiconductor Innovation vs Sustainability,
https://electronics360.globalspec.com/article/20060/balancing-
semiconductor-innovation-vs-sustainability#:~:text=Semiconductor
%20manufacturing%20contributes%20up%20to,of%20carbon%20
dioxide%20by%202030.

13. Today's Medical Developments, Semiconductors and Their Role in
Advancing Medical Device Technology, https://www.todaysmedical
developments.com/news/semiconductors-role-advancing-medical-
device-technology/#:~:text=Diagnostic%20devices%20–%20Diagnostic
%20devices%20are,vital%20signs%20and%20health%20indicators

14. Today's Medical Developments, Wireless Drug Patch for Chronic Disease
Treatment Delivery System, January 20, 2024, https://www.todays
medicaldevelopments.com/news/wireless-drug-patch-chronic-disease-
treatment-delivery-system/

Chapter 9

1. Vox, Quantum Computing: To Boldly Go Where Einstein Feared to
Tread, June 21, 2016, https://www.vox.com/2016/6/21/11982514/quantum-
theory-cloud-computing-ibm-albert-einstein

2. Wikipedia, Solvay Conference, https://en.wikipedia.org/wiki/Solvay_
Conference

3. Business Insider, The World's Brightest Scientific Minds Posed for This
1927 Photo After Historic Debates About Quantum Mechanics, April 22,
2016, https://www.businessinsider.com/solvay-conference-1927-2015-4?r=
US&IR=T

4. American Institute of Physics, *Physics Today*, Richard Feynman and The
Connection Machine, 42(2), 78, 1989

5. Wikipedia, Deutsch-Jozsa algorithm, https://en.wikipedia.org/wiki/
Deutsch%E2%80%93Jozsa_algorithm

6. McKinsey, Quantum Technology Sees Record Investments, Progress on Talent Gap, April 24, 2023, https://www.mckinsey.com/capabilities/mckinsey-digital/our-insights/quantum-technology-sees-record-investments-progress-on-talent-gap

7. Imperial College London, Towards Using Quantum Computing to Speed Up Drug Development, October 20, 2023, https://www.imperial.ac.uk/news/248638/towards-using-quantum-computing-speed-drug/

8. D-Wave, Quantum in Life Sciences: The Future Is Now, 2021, https://www.dwavesys.com/media/knedq0pb/dwave_life-sci_overview_v2.pdf

9. Deloitte, Quantum Computing for Climate Action, September 2023, https://www2.deloitte.com/content/dam/Deloitte/us/Documents/quantum-computing-climate-change-2023.pdf

10. McKinsey Digital, How Quantum Computing Can Help Tackle Global Warming, May 27, 2022, https://www.mckinsey.com/capabilities/mckinsey-digital/our-insights/how-quantum-computing-can-help-tackle-global-warming

11. ParityQC, Quantum Computing for Electric Mobility: A Case Study, https://parityqc.com/quantum-computing-for-electric-mobility-a-case-study

12. IBM, Boeing Seeks New Ways to Engineer Strong, Lightweight Materials, https://www.ibm.com/case-studies/boeing

13. NVIDIA, Rolls-Royce and Classiq Announce Quantum Computing Breakthrough for Computational Fluid Dynamics in Jet Engines, May 21, 2023, https://nvidianews.nvidia.com/news/nvidia-rolls-royce-and-classiq-announce-quantum-computing-breakthrough-for-computational-fluid-dynamics-in-jet-engines

14. Rigetti.com, Rigetti Computing Awarded Innovate UK Grant to Develop Quantum Machine Learning Techniques for Financial Data Streams, January 11, 2024, https://investors.rigetti.com/news-releases/news-release-details/rigetti-computing-awarded-innovate-uk-grant-develop-quantum

15. Nature.com, The AI-quantum Computing Mash-up: Will it Revolutionize Science?, January 2, 2024, https://www.nature.com/articles/d41586-023-04007-0

Chapter 10

1. IEA Research, Solar PV, https://www.iea.org/energy-system/renewables/solar-pv

2. *Financial Times*, Renewable Energy Surge of 50% Driven by China, IEA says, January 11, 2024, https://www.ft.com/content/2233f1de-221d-40f3-b2ae-4e07da500f44

3. US Department of Energy, The War of the Current: AC vs. DC Power, November 18, 2014, https://www.energy.gov/articles/war-currents-ac-vs-dc-power

4. BBC Science Focus, Welcome to Devil's Valley: The World's Oldest Geothermal Power Plant, July 4, 2022, https://www.sciencefocus.com/planet-earth/first-geothermal-power-plant

5. BBC Future, The Forgotten 20th Century 'Sun Engine', April 21, 2023, https://www.bbc.com/future/article/20230420-the-forgotten-20th-century-sun-engine

6. Gulf News, The LNG Story is Fascinating, December 30, 2012, https://gulfnews.com/business/analysis/the-lng-story-is-fascinating-1.1125471

7. US Department of Energy, The History of Nuclear Energy, https://www.energy.gov/ne/articles/history-nuclear-energy

8. IEEE Spectrum, Who Really Invented the Rechargeable Lithium-Ion Battery?, July 30, 2023, https://spectrum.ieee.org/lithium-ion-battery-2662487214

9. IEA, Trends in Electric Light-Duty Vehicles, https://www.iea.org/reports/global-ev-outlook-2023/trends-in-electric-light-duty-vehicles

10. United Kingdom Department of Transport, Lifecycle Analysis of UK Road Vehicles, November 25, 2021, https://assets.publishing.service.gov.uk/government/uploads/system/uploads/attachment_data/file/1062603/lifecycle-analysis-of-UK-road-vehicles.pdf

11. *New York Times*, E.V.s Start With a Bigger Carbon Footprint. But That Doesn't Last, October 19, 2022, https://www.nytimes.com/2022/10/19/business/electric-vehicles-carbon-footprint-batteries.html

12. IEA, Trends in Electric Light-Duty Vehicles, https://www.iea.org/reports/global-ev-outlook-2023/trends-in-electric-light-duty-vehicles

13. *Financial Times*, Wang Chuanfu, The Driving Force Behind BYD's rise, January 4, 2024, https://www.ft.com/content/22527628-733e-4188-9678-ab3210fdb1ba

14. *Guardian*, 'Revolutionary' Solar Power Cell Innovations Break Key Energy Threshold, July 6, 2023, https://www.theguardian.com/environment/2023/jul/06/revolutionary-solar-power-cell-innovations-break-key-energy-threshold

15. *Wall Street Journal*, What If You Never Had to Charge Your Gadgets Again?, January 12, 2024, https://www.wsj.com/tech/personal-tech/what-if-you-never-had-to-charge-your-gadgets-again-955ea960

16. EuroNews, The Race for Renewable Batteries: What's the Future of Solar and Wind Storage?, July 21, 2022, https://www.euronews.com/green/2022/07/21/the-race-for-renewable-batteries-whats-the-future-of-solar-and-wind-storage

17. Oxford City Council, Energy Superhub Oxford, https://www.oxford
.gov.uk/building-projects/energy-superhub-oxford

18. Invinity, Case Study: Energy Superhub Oxford (ESO), https://invinity
.com/energy-superhub-oxford/

19. *MIT Technology Review*, We're Going to Need A Lot More Grid Storage.
New Iron Batteries Could Help, February 23, 2022, https://www
.technologyreview.com/2022/02/23/1046365/grid-storage-iron-
batteries-technology/

20. Recharge News, Ten Energy Storage Technologies That Want to Change
the World, November 30, 2024, https://www.rechargenews.com/energy-
transition/ten-energy-storage-technologies-that-want-to-change-the-
world/2-1-1556351

21. *Financial Times*, Can 'Water Batteries' Solve the Energy Storage
Conundrum?, January 9, 2024, https://www.ft.com/content/5f0c2623-
dfd4-4542-8d94-8bf1dfefcec7

22. *Guardian*, Octopus Energy Raises $800mn and Aims to Create 3,000
Green Jobs in UK, December 18, 2023, https://www.theguardian.com/
business/2023/dec/18/octopus-energy-raises-800m-aims-create-
3000-green-jobs-uk

23. McKinsey, Using Digital and AI to Meet the Energy Sector's Net-zero
Challenge, July 18, 2023, https://www.mckinsey.com/capabilities/
quantumblack/our-insights/using-digital-and-ai-to-meet-the-energy-
sectors-net-zero-challenge

24. *Financial Times*, Governments Join Race for Commercial Fusion Power,
September 6, 2023, https://www.ft.com/content/77320fbd-5f87-4d1f-
b29b-a661672fd222

25. Global Corporate Venturing, Investors Bet on Fusion Payoff Within a
Decade, December 15, 2023, https://globalventuring.com/corporate/
energy-and-natural-resources/investors-nuclear-fusion/

26. CFS website, https://cfs.energy/technology/#arc-commercialization

27. US Department of Energy, DOE Explains. . .Tokamaks, https://www
.energy.gov/science/doe-explainstokamaks

28. *NEI Magazine*, Commonwealth Fusion Systems and Eni Agree on Fusion
Collaboration, March 17, 2023, https://www.neimagazine.com/news/
newscommonwealth-fusion-systems-and-eni-agree-on-fusion-
commercialisation-10682640

29. *Financial Times*, Nuclear Fusion: From Science Fiction to 'When Not If',
December 17, 2022, https://www.ft.com/content/65e8f125-5985-4aa8-
a027-0c9769e764ad

30. *Science*, U.S. Unveils Plans for Large Facilities to Capture Carbon Directly from Air, August 11, 2023, https://www.science.org/content/article/us-unveils-plans-for-large-facilities-to-capture-carbon-directly-from-air

31. Climeworks website, Orca: The First Large-Scale Plant, https://climeworks.com/plant-orca

32. TechCrunch, A Step Forward for CO_2 Capture, December 3, 2021, https://techcrunch.com/2021/12/03/co2-capture-iceland-climeworks-orca/?guce_referrer=aHR0cHM6Ly93d3cuZ29vZ2xlLmNvbS8&guce_referrer_sig=AQAAABv4FGLRvdAJ7Q6JQpM98FKajoqOzcShz0wdUPMR m2wCiSy15cBOe3aSBeOACjO4A8TmFnfLL8H-lDy6ubZSQQDyxG1t tryG4FAwYKqh_ZoiJnuOudl-9W9CE8n2MNYchZP9z8PMnUgndsT4yH0 aFxMkwOtHUBdbH8neK8ld9IaL&guccounter=2

33. Reuters, World's Largest Plant Capturing Carbon from Air Starts in Iceland, September, 13, 2021, https://www.reuters.com/business/environment/worlds-largest-plant-capturing-carbon-air-starts-iceland-2021-09-08/

34. Oxy.com, Occidental Enters into Agreement to Acquire Direct Air Capture Technology Innovator Carbon Engineering, August 15, 2023, https://www.oxy.com/news/news-releases/occidental-enters-into-agreement-to-acquire-direct-air-capture-technology-innovator-carbon-engineering/

35. Oxy.com, Occidental and Blackrock Form Joint Venture to Develop STRATOS, the World's Largest Direct Air Capture Plant, November 7, 2023, https://www.oxy.com/news/news-releases/occidental-and-blackrock-form-joint-venture-to-develop-stratos-the-worlds-largest-direct-air-capture-plant/

36. Energy Intelligence, Our Take: Capturing Hearts and Minds, November 28, 2023, https://www.energyintel.com/0000018c-15c2-dba8-adbe-bfff4be60000

37. *Power Magazine*, Pioneering Hydrogen-Powered Gas Peaking: Inside Duke Energy's DeBary Project, November 16, 2023, https://www.powermag.com/pioneering-hydrogen-powered-gas-peaking-inside-duke-energys-debary-project/

Chapter 11

1. Youtube, In Conversation With Noubar Afeyan, The Original Information Technology Industry Is Biology, April 28, 2023, https://www.youtube.com/watch?v=oqK1M9Bt9gY

2. PBS, The Discovery of DNA's Structure, https://www.pbs.org/wgbh/evolution/library/06/3/l_063_01.html

3. *Journal of Biological Chemistry*, Arthur Kornberg's Discovery of DNA Polymerase, December 2005, https://www.jbc.org/article/S0021-9258(20)59088-1/fulltext

4. Nature Reviews Genetics, The Dawn of Recombinant DNA, October 15, 2007, https://www.nature.com/articles/miledna02

5. Smithsonian, National Museum of American History, Monoclonal Antibodies, https://americanhistory.si.edu/collections/object-groups/antibody-initiative/monoclonal

6. NIH, National Library of Medicine, National Center for Biotechnology Information; Research Techniques Made Simple: Polymerase Chain Reaction, March 2013, https://www.ncbi.nlm.nih.gov/pmc/articles/PMC4102308/

7. *The New York Times*, Girl, 4, Becomes First Human to Receive Engineered Genes, September 15, 1990, https://www.nytimes.com/1990/09/15/us/girl-4-becomes-first-human-to-receive-engineered-genes.html

8. *The New York Times*, F.D.A. Approves Altered Tomato That Will Remain Fresh Longer, May 19, 1994, https://www.nytimes.com/1994/05/19/us/fda-approves-altered-tomato-that-will-remain-fresh-longer.html

9. *The New York Times*, Scientist Reports First Cloning Ever of Adult Mammal, February 23, 1997, https://www.nytimes.com/1997/02/23/us/scientist-reports-first-cloning-ever-of-adult-mammal.html

10. National Human Genome Research Institute, The Human Genome Project Fact Sheet, https://www.genome.gov/about-genomics/educational-resources/fact-sheets/human-genome-project

11. *Guardian*, Craig Venter Creates Synthetic Life Form, May 20, 2010, https://www.theguardian.com/science/2010/may/20/craig-venter-synthetic-life-form

12. Broad Institute, Questions and Answers About CRISPR, https://www.broadinstitute.org/what-broad/areas-focus/project-spotlight/questions-and-answers-about-crispr

13. IQVIA, Global Medical Spending to Reach $2.3 Trillion by 2028, https://www.iqvia.com/newsroom/2024/01/global-medicine-spending

14. Breakthrough Energy, Fellows Project - Novel Farms, https://breakthroughenergy.org/fellows-project/novel-farms/

15. Global Cancer Observatory, World Health Organization, 2020, https://gco.iarc.fr/today/online-analysis-table?v=2020&mode=cancer&mode_population=continents&population=900&populations=900&key=asr&sex=0&cancer=39&type=0&statistic=5&prevalence=0&population_group=0&ages_group%5B%5D=0&ages_group%5B%5D=17&group_cancer=1&include_nmsc=0&include_nmsc_other=1

16. *Wall Street Journal*, Cancer Is Striking More Young People, and Doctors Are Alarmed and Baffled, January 11, 2024, https://www.wsj.com/health/healthcare/cancer-young-people-doctors-baffled-49c766ed

17. Immatics.com, Immatics Corporate Presentation, January 22, 2024, https://investors.immatics.com/static-files/4eb058de-2c8c-4384-8b6e-2569e1379dab

18. Beamtx.com, Base Editing Applications, https://beamtx.com/science/base-editing-applications/

19. Salk.edu, Cellular Rejuvenation Therapy Safely Reverses Signs of Aging in Mice, https://www.salk.edu/news-release/cellular-rejuvenation-therapy-safely-reverses-signs-of-aging-in-mice/

20. *MIT Technology Review*, Meet Altos Labs, Silicon Valley's Latest Wild Bet on Living Forever, September 4, 2021, https://www.technologyreview.com/2021/09/04/1034364/altos-labs-silicon-valleys-jeff-bezos-milner-bet-living-forever/

21. FAO, Land Use in Agriculture by the Numbers, May 7, 2020, https://www.fao.org/sustainability/news/detail/en/c/1274219/

22. Indigoag.com, Indigo Biological Science, https://www.indigoag.com/biologicals/science

23. Upside Foods, Innovation, https://upsidefoods.com/innovation

24. *MIT Technology Review*, Two Companies Can Now Sell Lab-Grown Chicken in the US, June 21, 2023, https://www.technologyreview.com/2023/06/21/1075342/two-companies-can-now-sell-lab-grown-chicken-in-the-us/?utm_source=the_spark&utm_medium=email&utm_campaign=the_spark.unpaid.engagement&utm_content=*%7Cdate: m-d-y%7C*

25. *Wired*, Insiders Reveal Major Problems at Lab-Grown-Meat Startup Upside Foods, September 15, 2023, https://www.wired.com/story/upside-foods-lab-grown-chicken/

26. The Royal Society, Ammonia: Zero-Carbon Fertiliser, Fuel and Energy Store, February 2020, https://royalsociety.org/-/media/policy/projects/green-ammonia/green-ammonia-policy-briefing.pdf

27. Stanford.edu, New Method for Making Ammonia Could Take Bite Out of Global Energy Use, April 24, 2023, https://news.stanford.edu/2023/04/24/ecofriendly-ammonia-just-add-water/

28. BBC, Can Fashion Ever be Sustainable, March 11, 2020, https://www.bbc.com/future/article/20200310-sustainable-fashion-how-to-buy-clothes-good-for-the-climate

29. LinkedIn, Modern Synthesis, https://www.linkedin.com/company/mod-synth

30. Modern Synthesis, https://www.modernsynthesis.com/#tech

31. Patagonia, Biobased Polyester, https://www.patagonia.com/our-footprint/biobased-polyester.html

32. Ecovative, Why Mycelium, https://www.ecovative.com/pages/why-mycelium

33. Ecovative, Packaging, https://www.ecovative.com/pages/packaging

34. *MIT Technology Review*, Turning Exhaust Gas into Fuel, September, 15, 2010, https://www.technologyreview.com/2010/09/15/261850/turning-exhaust-gas-into-fuel/

35. LanzaTech, Corporate Presentation May 2023, https://ir.lanzatech.com/static-files/c4c130ac-3d57-4693-9ef4-95008a211ec5

Chapter 13

1. A More Beautiful Question Blog, Einstein and Questioning, https://amorebeautifulquestion.com/einstein-questioning/#:~:text=One%20more%20bit%20of%20Einstein,then%20set%20out%20to%20answer

2. Flagship Pioneering website, https://www.flagshippioneering.com/companies/foghorn-therapeutics

3. NASDAQ, How Millennials and Gen Z are Driving Growth Behind ESG, September 23, 2022, https://www.nasdaq.com/articles/how-millennials-and-gen-z-are-driving-growth-behind-esg

4. United Way, Why CSR Is the Key to Companies to Connect with Gen Z, September 28, 2022, https://uwsd.org/blog/why-csr-is-the-key-for-companies-to-connect-with-gen-z/

Chapter 15

1. *Forbes*, How AI Will Revolutionize the Future of SEO, April 29, 2023, https://www.forbes.com/sites/forbesagencycouncil/2023/04/19/how-ai-will-revolutionize-the-future-of-seo/?sh=5d026932138a

2. Determ, Five Ways AI Social Listening Supercharges Business Insights, August 11, 2023, https://www.determ.com/blog/5-ways-ai-social-listening-supercharges-business-insights/

Chapter 16

1. California Air Resources Board, California Moves to Accelerate to 100% New Zero-Emission Vehicle Sales by 2035, August 25, 2022, https://ww2.arb.ca.gov/news/california-moves-accelerate-100-new-zero-emission-vehicle-sales-2035

2. Axios, AI pioneer Mustafa Suleyman: AI Needs a "Containment" Plan, September 6, 2023, https://www.axios.com/2023/09/06/mustafa-suleyman-ai-containment-plan

3. *Wall Street Journal*, AI Expert Max Tegmark Warns That Humanity Is Failing the New Technology's Challenge, August 18, 2023, https://www.wsj.com/tech/ai/ai-expert-max-tegmark-warns-that-humanity-is-failing-the-new-technologys-challenge-4d423bee

4. Testimony of Christina Montgomery, Chief Privacy and Trust Officer, IBM, May 16, 2023, https://www.ibm.com/policy/wp-content/uploads/2023/05/Christina-Montgomery-Senate-Judiciary-Testimony-5-16-23.pdf

5. Microsoft website, Research Collection: Research Supporting Responsible AI, April 13, 2020, https://www.microsoft.com/en-us/research/blog/research-collection-research-supporting-responsible-ai/

6. Google website, 3 Emerging Practices for Responsible Generative AI Practices, July 27, 2023, https://blog.google/technology/ai/google-responsible-generative-ai-best-practices/

7. Amazon.com, Transform Responsible AI from Theory into Practice, https://aws.amazon.com/machine-learning/responsible-ai/

8. CRS Reports, Highlights of the 2023 Executive Order on Artificial Intelligence for Congress, November 17, 2023, https://crsreports.congress.gov/product/pdf/R/R47843#:~:text=14110%20on%20Safe%2C%20Secure%2C%20and,The%20E.O

9. Fast Company, Everything You Need to Know About the Government's Efforts to Regulate AI, September 25, 2023, https://www.fastcompany.com/90955937/everything-you-need-to-know-about-the-governments-efforts-to-regulate-ai

10. UK Department of Science, Innovation and Technology, Introducing the AI Safety Institute, November 2023, https://www.gov.uk/government/publications/ai-safety-institute-overview/introducing-the-ai-safety-institute

11. AP News, Europe Agreed on World-Leading AI Rules. How Do They Work and Will They Affect People Everywhere?, December 11, 2023, https://apnews.com/article/eu-ai-act-artificial-intelligence-regulation-0283a10a891a24703068edcae3d60deb

Chapter 17

1. SAS website, Analytics Helping Humanity, https://www.sas.com/en_us/data-for-good.html.

2. Cando, Four Companies that Use Data Science for Social Impact, April 28, 2021, https://candor.co/articles/career-paths/4-companies-that-use-data-science-for-social-impact#

3. General Assembly Blog, 5 Companies Using Data for Social Impact, https://generalassemb.ly/blog/5-companies-using-data-social-impact/

4. Johnson & Johnson website, 4 Ways Johnson & Johnson Has Worked to Make Access to Medicines Around the World More Equitable, https://www.jnj.com/latest-news/how-johnson-johnson-helps-improve-global-access-to-medicines

Index

215